BEING CHILDREN OF GOD

Volume 1

A BOOK OF SECRETS

Being Children of God

Volume 1

A BOOK OF SECRETS

Shaliah
FOUNDATIONALIST PRESS
MMXXV

Published by Foundationalist Press
in consultation with the **Judeo Christian Church**™.
Use of the Yodh emblem and denominational marks appears with the permission of the Judeo Christian Church, JudeoChristians.org.

Trademarks
"Judeo Christian Church," "Judeo Christians," and the stylized **Yodh** emblem are trademarks and service marks of the Judeo Christian Church.
"Foundationalist Press" and the Foundationalist Press emblem are trademarks of Foundationalist Press.

ISBN: 979-8-9989281-2-3

Colophon
This work is set in Merriweather, a serif typeface designed for readability in both print and digital formats. Its balance of traditional clarity and modern accessibility reflects the intent of *Being Children of God*: to recover what is ancient, clarify what has been obscured, and invite readers into covenant through words that endure.

Table of Contents

Preface — A Call to Return to Foundation

Christianity today stands trembling at a crossroads, awaiting its fifth great awakening.

For nearly two millennia, theological interpretations have drifted inexorably further from the foundation laid by Jesus and His direct disciples. The result is a faith unrecognizable from its origins—one built on doctrinal invention, institutional tradition, and inherited distortions.

This work invites you to journey back to that foundation—not as an act of rebellion, but as an act of rediscovery. At its core, this series seeks to answer one question: What would a true primitive Judeo Christianity— rooted in Jesus's actual teachings—look like?

To answer this, we must strip away centuries of interpretation, not only examining the texts themselves but the **lens through which they were first understood**. By doing so, we uncover the clarity and depth of the faith that Jesus called "the will of the Father"—obedience to our God and Heavenly Father YHWH, Creator of heaven and earth.

Beyond Reformation—Restoration

For Protestantism—defined by its protest against Catholic tradition — this carries profound implications.

To truly reform Christianity is not merely to **fix** Catholicism but to **transcend** it, returning to the unaltered faith that existed **before** any distortions took root.

This restoration cannot be accomplished without addressing the central theological figure who shaped modern Christianity most outside of Jesus himself: Saul of Tarsus, aka the apostle Paul.

To go beyond Catholicism while leaving Paul's influence unchallenged is to **stop short of Jesus's explicit warning**:

"See that no one deceives you." (Matthew 24:4).

Jesus declared what his expectations were regarding continued obedience and observance of the Law & Prophets, what modern Christians know as the Old Testament, in Matthew 5:17-19.

> *"Do not think that I have come to abolish the Law or the Prophets; I have not come to abolish them but to fulfill them. For truly, I say to you, until heaven and earth pass away, not an iota, not a dot, will pass from the Law until all is accomplished. Therefore, whoever relaxes one of the least of these commandments and teaches others to do the same will be called least in the kingdom of heaven, but whoever does them and teaches them will be called great in the kingdom of heaven."*

Matthew 5 clearly articulates how intently Jesus upheld the Law & Prophets, and expected his followers to do the same, so long as Heaven and Earth exist.

What does this say to the later theological developments of Paul that sought to put faith in Jesus over the Lawful Will of our Heavenly Father?

Jesus himself gave a **dire warning** on the dangers of this exact mindset just two chapters later in Matthew 7:21-23.

> *"Not everyone who says to me, 'Lord, Lord,' will enter the kingdom of heaven, but the one who does the will of my Father who is in heaven. On that day many will say to me, 'Lord, Lord, did we not prophesy in your name, and cast out demons in your name, and do many mighty works in your name?' And then will I declare to them, 'I never knew you; depart from me, you workers of lawlessness.'"*

Once we fully understand how intently Jesus upheld the Law & Prophets, and that he expected others to do the same, we have to reconcile that with modern traditions that claim otherwise, contrary to scripture.

These two verses leave no room for reinterpretations that **dilute or "relax"** Old Testament Law. Any theology that claims to follow Christ must uphold the same reverence for the Law and the Prophets that He did.

Yet, for nearly 2,000 years, the dominant interpretation of Christianity has centered not on Jesus's words & God's Law — but on Paul's commentary, leading to **a complete theological inversion**.

An Inquiry That Cannot Be Ignored

Through **12 seemingly simple Inquiries spread across four volumes**, the *Being Children of God* series uses the lenses of **scripture and history** to uncover hidden knowledge that the Institutional Churches either **cannot**—or **will not**—reveal. This is not a work of apologetics, nor a mere critique of Christian traditions. It is a forensic investigation, tracing back distortions to their origins and exposing how theological sleight-of-hand reshaped an ancient Hebraic faith into something unrecognizable.

This series does not ask for blind faith. It does not demand adherence to inherited assumptions. Instead, it follows a simple methodology: **every doctrine must be tested against the unbroken standard of YHWH's Law and the words of Jesus Himself.**

Christianity today stands at a crossroads. One road leads to recovering the foundational YHWH-centered Judeo-Christian faith practiced by Jesus and his direct disciples, the other road loops around to wander the wilderness of inherited lawlessness for another two millennia.

Prologue: How did we get here?

The crossroads faced by modern Christianity is nothing new. Going back for thousands of years Christians have been faced with, and have chosen, differing paths.

Each denominational divergence not only pushed Christians farther and farther from each other, but farther from the core foundational Hebrew Bible laws that the teachings of Christ said to uphold, to the last pen stroke, so long as heaven and earth exist. These divergences between Christian sects are called schisms.

A Crash Course on Schisms

Christianity's history is marked by a series of schisms—breaks within the faith caused by theological, political, and cultural disagreements.

Each division created ripple effects that shaped the modern landscape of Christianity.

---

1. The First East/West Schism (451 AD)

- **What Happened:** The *Council of Chalcedon* (451 AD) attempted to clarify Christ's dual nature (fully divine, fully human). The council declared Christ was *"in two natures, without confusion, without change, without division, without separation."*
- **The Split:** The decision was rejected by the Oriental Orthodox Churches (like the Coptic, Ethiopian, and Armenian churches). They viewed the council's conclusions as a deviation from earlier church traditions.
- **The Result:** A permanent fracture occurred, with the Oriental Orthodox, Coptic, and Ethiopian Churches separating from would later split into the Roman Catholic and Eastern Orthodox branches.

Key Takeaway: Even early on, theological nuance became a dividing line, emphasizing the danger of over-intellectualizing faith without anchoring it in the covenantal foundation.

2. The Great East/West Schism (1054 AD)

- **What Happened:** A series of political, theological, and cultural disputes boiled over into open division between the *Eastern Orthodox Church* (centered in Constantinople) and the *Roman Catholic Church* (centered in Rome).
- **Theological Disputes:**
    - *Filioque Clause:* The Western church added *"and the Son"* to the Nicene Creed without a council agreement, altering the understanding of the Holy Spirit's procession.
    - *Papal Supremacy:* The Eastern Church rejected the Pope's claim to universal authority.
- **The Result:** In 1054, Pope Leo IX and Patriarch Michael Cerularius excommunicated each other. Christianity split into the *Roman Catholic Church* and the *Eastern Orthodox Church.*

Key Takeaway: The tension between centralized authority (Papal supremacy) and decentralized tradition highlights the ongoing struggle between institutional power and foundational faithfulness.

---

3. The Reformations (1517 & 1534 AD)

- **What Happened:** Martin Luther (1517) nailed his *95 Theses* to the church door in Wittenberg, criticizing corruption, indulgences, and the Catholic Church's deviation from scripture.
- **Key Issues Raised by the Reformers:**
    - *Sola Scriptura:* Scripture alone as the ultimate authority.
    - *Sola Fide:* Salvation through faith alone.
    - *Corruption in Clergy:* Selling of indulgences and abuses of power.
- **The English Reformation (1534):** King Henry VIII declared himself head of the *Church of England* after the Pope refused to annul his marriage.

The Result: The *Protestant Reformation* created multiple new distinct branches of Christianity.

- *Lutheranism*

- *Calvinism*
- *Anglican Church*

Key Takeaway: The Reformers sought to return to scripture, yet their movement inadvertently created new theological splinters, all still rooted in Pauline distortions.

---

4. The Counter-Reformation (1545–1563 AD)

- **What Happened:** In response to the Reformers, the Catholic Church launched the *Counter-Reformation,* primarily through the *Council of Trent.*
- **Key Actions Taken:**
  - Reaffirmation of Catholic doctrines.
  - Elimination of some church abuses (e.g., selling indulgences).
  - Establishment of the *Jesuit Order* to combat Protestant teachings through education and missionary work.
- **The Result:** The Catholic Church solidified its doctrines and strengthened its institutional authority, but the theological chasm with Protestantism became permanent.

Key Takeaway: The Counter-Reformation sought reform without addressing deeper theological inconsistencies. It was more reactive than transformative.

What This Means for Us Today
Every schism, every reformation, every counter-reformation has been an attempt—sometimes sincere, sometimes self-serving—to define what it means to follow God faithfully. Yet, with each split, the core foundation—the covenantal relationship with YHWH and the eternal Law—was pushed further into the background.

- The **First Schism** highlighted the danger of theological overreach.
- The **Great Schism** revealed the cost of centralized power.

- The **Reformations** championed scripture but opened doors to further fragmentation.
- The **Counter-Reformation** emphasized institutional loyalty over foundational truth.

Each step brought Christianity further from its Hebraic roots and farther into distortion. By the time of the **Great Awakenings**, Christianity was already a fractured faith desperately searching for revival.

Looking Ahead: With this historical context in mind, we can now briefly examine the *Great Awakenings*—moments when humanity seemed to wake up and ask, *"Where did we go wrong, and how do we return to God?"*

The Great Awakenings: Revivals punctuated by further schism.

These were transformative periods marked by widespread revival, characterized by passionate preaching, renewed personal devotion, and a return to foundational principles when the Church had fallen into stagnation or drifted from its core mission.

1. The First Great Awakening (1730's–1740's):

This movement swept through Europe and later the American colonies, emphasizing personal conversion, heartfelt faith, and repentance. Preachers like Jonathan Edwards and George Whitefield ignited fervor with messages that challenged complacent Christianity, calling believers to experience a direct and personal relationship with God.

Denominations from this Great Awakening:

- **Methodism** *(John Wesley, George Whitefield)*
- **Baptists** *(Expansion and Revival Movement)*

2. The Second Great Awakening (1790's–1850's):

Spanning the young American Republic, this revival inspired societal reforms and a focus on communal worship. Preachers like Charles

Finney led tent meetings that brought thousands to repentance and catalyzed movements for abolition, temperance, and education.

Denominations from this Great Awakening:

- **Church of Christ** *(Restoration Movement, Barton Stone, Alexander Campbell)*
- **Seventh-day Adventists** *(William Miller, Ellen G. White)*

3. The Third Great Awakening (1850's–1900):

Marked by global missionary efforts, this awakening reflected a response to industrialization and urbanization. It sought to align Christian values with modern challenges, emphasizing service and practical applications of faith.

Denominations from this Great Awakening:

- **Holiness Movement** *(Roots of Pentecostalism, Wesleyan influence)*
- **Christian Science** *(Mary Baker Eddy)*

4. The Fourth Great Awakening (late 1950's–1980's):

A response to the cultural upheavals of the 20th century, this awakening revived evangelicalism, focusing on personal piety, charismatic worship, and the spread of the gospel through media.

Denominations from this Great Awakening:

- **Calvary Chapel** *(Chuck Smith)*
- **Vineyard Movement** *(John Wimber)*

These awakenings highlight a consistent pattern:

When Christianity loses its direction, messengers arise to call believers closer to the foundation of faith.

Christianity stands on the cusp of a Fifth Great Awakening— a return to the covenantal truth and practice modeled by Jesus and His earliest disciples.

The Schism History Forgot

- What if there was a schism that was more consequential than all of the others?
- What if this schism is conspicuously not recognized by history?
- What if this schism happened within the disciple's lifetimes?
- What if Jesus warned them it would, and how?

A Blind Church

Today, many modern churches seem to find themselves blindly wandering farther and farther into the wilderness of confusion and lawlessness, far removed from the clarity of faithful obedience practiced and taught by Jesus.

At the heart of this impairment are profound distortions introduced through Pauline theology and Greco-Roman influences.

These influences have reshaped Jesus's foundational teachings of God's eternal covenant.

The simplicity of Jesus's faithful obedience has been traded for terms added to and taken away from God's Law, and as a result, the vibrant unity of the early faith has given way to fragmentation, confusion and lawlessness.

To uncover what was lost, we must peel back the stratified layers of systematic distortion and expose the Hidden Knowledge concealed at the intersection of scripture and history.

This delicate task requires lines of inquiry—asking the right questions, allowing history and scripture to speak for themselves, and remaining loyal to seeking God's truth.

Not to our own preconditioned notions. Not to the self-serving doctrinal decrees of institutional Pauline Churches.

If humanity is ever to truly follow Christ's teachings into the embrace of God, we must first ask: How did Jesus understand and teach scripture? We must learn how to look at the Word of God through His eyes—free from the distortions we've inherited.

We must fully realize how Christ's vision differs from what is seen in Pauline churches today, and track the accumulative distortions over time.

As we retrain our eyes to see God's Word as Christ did, and realign as He intended, we will be able to progressively see more and more secrets that our Bible has been hiding in plain sight for over 2,000 years

Inquiry 1: How Did Jesus Understand & Teach Scripture?

To fully grasp how modern Pauline Christian churches have deviated from the covenant between humanity and God—the very covenant that Jesus sacrificed Himself to reconcile—we must first understand scripture as messiah did: through a late "Second Temple" understanding of Hebrew Biblical structure and hierarchy.

1. Introduction: The Bible as a Unified Testimony

Key Insight:

To Jesus and his earliest disciples, the scriptures were not fragmented doctrines—**they were a living, breathing testimony of God's covenant with His people.** They were meant to always be understood in the context of the whole Hebrew Bible.

When Jesus walked the earth:
The scriptures weren't standardized, bound in leather covers or split into neat chapters and verses. They existed in scrolls, carefully preserved and reverently read aloud in the Temple and synagogues, they existed in Greek translations that were the most widely available versions at the time, and they existed in other variations found by archeologists. These are understood today as the proto-Masoretic Texts, the Greek Septuagint, and the Qumrān Texts - of which the Dead Sea Scrolls are a part.

Despite the slight variations of Hebrew Scripture known to be in use in Judea at the time, to Jesus, Peter, James, John, and the other disciples, the scriptures weren't isolated moral anecdotes or abstract philosophical musings—they were a single, continuous narrative of God's covenant, love, justice, and restoration.

The Hebrew Bible is not simply to be understood as being a Christian Old Testament written in Hebrew. There are structural and hierarchical differences in understanding that, over twenty centuries, drifted farther into distortion and farther away from the understanding and teachings of Jesus.

To Jesus, every word, every commandment, every prophecy points toward a larger story - a **divine symphony that reveals our Heavenly Father's character and purpose for humanity.**

Most Jewish and Catholic academics agree that during Jesus' time, the Greek Septuagint (with books arranged like our Old Testament) was the variation most referenced by everyday Judeans, but, it is also known that Jews including Jesus understood the arc of scripture hierarchically, in terms of the Law (Torah), the Prophets (Nevi'im), and the Writings (Ketuvim), which is how modern Jews order the Hebrew Bible.

Ordering and potential apocrypha aside- the books of modern Christian Old Testaments and Modern Hebrew Bibles are nearly 100% identical.

We will examine the historical ordering and hierarchies of the books comprising Hebrew scripture in greater detail later in this inquiry. For now we will be focusing on how Jews of the time, including Jesus & his direct disciples, prioritized & classified the books within it.

To Jesus and his disciples, and most Jews at the time, the Torah Law wasn't just a rulebook; the Nevi'im Prophets weren't just fortune tellers or warnings; the Ketuvim Writings weren't just poetic reflections. They were threads in a tapestry woven by the hands of the Eternal God, each thread connected and essential to the overall design.

This inquiry aims to reclaim that perspective—not by adding new interpretations, but by returning to the way Jesus and His closest disciples approached, taught, and lived out scripture.

We'll explore how they treated the Hebrew Scripture as a unified testimony, how they avoided the trap of proof-texting, and how their teachings call us back to a relational understanding of God's Word— one rooted in love, alignment, and covenant obedience.

Takeaway:
Scripture was never meant to be reduced to isolated verses or fragmented teachings. It's a woven story, a covenantal conversation, and a divine invitation to know our God in Heaven, YHWH, intimately.

1.1 A Unified Story, Not Disjointed Verses

To Jesus and His earliest followers, the Hebrew Bible, called **"Miqra"**: מִקְרָא in Hebrew —was not a fragmented collection of doctrines or isolated moral lessons. They were a singular, living testimony of God's covenant with His people. Every scroll, every story, every commandment, and every prophecy contributed to a unified narrative of divine justice, mercy, and redemption.

In the modern era, much of this cohesion has been lost due to proof-texting—the practice of isolating individual verses to support preconceived ideas or doctrines. This approach treats scripture like a string of pearls, each valuable on its own but disconnected from the others. However, the Hebrew Bible is more accurately understood as a tapestry, with each thread intentionally woven into the larger design.

Jesus's Example: Teaching from a Unified Story

When Jesus taught, He didn't rely on isolated verses to make His points; He wove together multiple strands of the Hebrew Bible to reveal deeper truths. For example:
- In the *Sermon on the Mount* (Matthew 5–7), Jesus references multiple commandments from the Law of Torah while drawing ethical conclusions that align with YHWH's intent, not just surface obedience.
- This wasn't a random assortment of proof-texts—it was a cohesive narrative from Genesis to Malachi, illustrating a divine plan.

The Dangers of Proof-Texting

Proof-texting leads to dangerous distortions of scripture. For example:
- Jeremiah 29:11 ("For I know the plans I have for you, declares the LORD...") is frequently quoted as a personal promise of prosperity. In context, it was a specific assurance given to the Israelites exiled

in Babylon, not a universal financial prosperity promise for all people at all times.

- Leviticus 19:28 ("Do not cut your bodies for the dead or put tattoo marks on yourselves.") is often quoted as a blanket prohibition against tattoos. However, in context, this was addressing ritualistic mourning practices associated with Canaanite pagan worship—not modern artistic expressions.

Understanding the Tapestry

The Hebrew Bible is not merely a moral instruction manual or a book of rules—it's a relational covenant, a historical record, and a prophetic vision for humanity's alignment with God. When viewed in its entirety, it paints a picture of YHWH's steadfast love, His expectations for justice and holiness, and His vision for restored harmony between Himself, humanity, and creation.

Takeaway:

Jesus did not cherry-pick scripture to suit His message—He illuminated the unified story of YHWH's covenant and intent. To follow in His footsteps, we must approach scripture with the same reverence, seeing it not as isolated pearls but as an intricate tapestry where every thread holds meaning in relation to the whole.

1.2 Jesus's Use of Scripture

Key Insight: Jesus didn't invent new doctrines—He illuminated existing ones. His every word, parable, and confrontation pointed back to the Law, the Prophets, and the Writings.

When Jesus was tempted in the wilderness, He didn't respond with philosophical musings or personal reflections. He didn't appeal to His divine authority to banish Satan outright.

Instead, He responded with the written Word of God: three times, three verses, all from Deuteronomy (*Matthew 4:1–11*). This was not an accident; it was a deliberate display of the authority, reliability, and sufficiency of scripture.

But Jesus's use of scripture wasn't confined to moments of spiritual combat. It permeated His teaching, His rebukes, His compassion, and His calls to repentance.

The Wilderness Temptation (Deuteronomy in Action)

- **When Satan tempted Jesus to turn stones into bread, Jesus replied:** *"Man shall not live on bread alone, but on every word that comes from the mouth of God." (Deuteronomy 8:3).*

- **When Satan tempted Jesus to throw Himself down from the temple, Jesus answered:** "Do not put the Lord your God to the test." (Deuteronomy 6:16).

- **When Satan offered Him all the kingdoms of the world, Jesus declared:** *"Worship the Lord your God, and serve Him only." (Deuteronomy 6:13).*

Each answer was not just a rebuttal—it was a declaration of alignment with God's will and a demonstration of scripture's power to guide and guard against temptation.

The Emmaus Road (A Guided Tour Through the Hebrew Bible)

After His resurrection, Jesus appeared to two disciples on the road to Emmaus. Their eyes were downcast; their hearts were heavy with confusion and loss. But Jesus didn't simply comfort them with empty words or vague encouragements. Instead:

> *"And beginning with Moses and all the Prophets, He explained to them what was said in all the Scriptures concerning Himself." (Luke 24:27).*

In this moment, Jesus gave a masterclass in biblical interpretation— showing how every scroll, every prophecy, and every Psalm pointed to his role in God's plan.

Imagine the scene: the Law, the Prophets, and the Writings unfolding like a tapestry before their eyes, every thread pointing to the fulfillment of God's promises.

Parables Rooted in Torah Law Principles

Jesus's parables were not arbitrary stories—they were deeply rooted in the Law's ethical and moral framework.

- The Parable of the Good Samaritan (*Luke 10:25–37*) reflects the heart of Leviticus 19:18: *"Love your neighbor as yourself."*

- The Parable of the Lost Sheep (*Luke 15:1–7*) echoes the compassion of Ezekiel 34:11–12: *"I myself will search for my sheep and look after them."*

- The Parable of the Wicked Tenants (*Matthew 21:33–46*) draws heavily from Isaiah 5:1–7, where Israel is described as God's vineyard.

Each parable wasn't just a lesson—it was a bridge back to scripture, calling listeners to see the Law and Prophets with fresh eyes.

Jesus and the Prophets: Confronting Legalism with Isaiah

Jesus often confronted the religious leaders of His day using the words of the Prophets:

- *"These people honor me with their lips, but their hearts are far from me."* (Isaiah 29:13; quoted in Matthew 15:8–9).

- In the Cleansing of the Temple, *Jesus quoted Jeremiah 7:11: "My house will be called a house of prayer for all nations. But you have made it a den of robbers."* (Mark 11:17).

Jesus didn't invent these rebukes—He resurrected them. He brought the prophetic voice back into focus, reminding Israel of her calling and her covenant.

The Sermon on the Mount: Scripture Elevated, Not Erased

In His most famous teaching, Jesus declared:

> *"Do not think that I have come to abolish the Law or the Prophets; I have not come to abolish them but to fulfill them." (Matthew 5:17).*

Jesus then unpacked key commandments:

- *"You have heard that it was said to those of old, 'You shall not murder; and whoever murders will be liable to judgment.' But I say to you that everyone who is angry with his brother will be liable to judgment; whoever insults his brother will be liable to the council; and whoever says, 'You fool!' will be liable to the hell of fire." (Matthew 5:21–22).*
- *"You have heard that it was said, 'You shall not commit adultery.' But I say to you that everyone who looks at a woman with lustful intent has already committed adultery with her in his heart" (Matthew 5:27–28).*

At every turn, Jesus didn't diminish the Torah Law—He intensified it. He brought it from external physical obedience to internal mental alignment.

The Pattern: Jesus Didn't Invent—He Illuminated

- Jesus didn't add to scripture. He clarified it.
- Jesus didn't twist scripture. He restored it to its proper context.
- Jesus didn't see scripture as fragmented verses. He treated it as a cohesive, unified revelation of God's heart and will.

When He said, *"It is written..."* it wasn't an empty appeal to authority— it was an invitation to alignment. Jesus's use of scripture reveals something profound: The Bible isn't a collection of proof-texts—it's a living, breathing testimony. Every word points back to YHWH's covenantal love and forward to humanity's opportunity to align with it.

Scripture wasn't a tool Jesus wielded; it was the foundation He stood upon.

1.3 A Communal Understanding of Scripture

Key Insight: Scripture wasn't interpreted in isolation—it was read, taught, and lived out in community. The synagogue was not just a place of worship; it was a center for education, discussion, and alignment with YHWH's commands.

Scripture in the Synagogue: A Community Experience

In first-century Judaism, the synagogue wasn't simply a place for weekly religious gatherings—it was the beating heart of Jewish community life. Synagogues functioned as:

- **Centers of Worship:** Regular prayers, hymns, and blessings created a rhythm of worship around scripture.
- **Educational Hubs:** Boys were taught to read and recite Torah Law, and adults engaged in active discussion and reflection on its meaning.
- **Spaces of Community Accountability:** Scripture wasn't just read—it was wrestled with, interpreted, and applied as a community.

The Torah scroll was publicly unrolled, carefully read, and handled with reverence.

This public reading wasn't a passive experience—it was interactive. After the reading, discussions and commentary followed, often led by rabbis or respected elders.

In contrast to modern individualistic approaches to Bible study—where scripture is often read in private and interpreted through personal biases—the synagogue was a space where scripture was collectively understood, challenged, and applied.

Jesus in the Synagogue: A Community Example

Jesus Himself was deeply embedded in this community tradition. He didn't reject synagogue life—He participated fully in it.

Luke 4:16–21 – Jesus Reads from Isaiah:
- Jesus entered the synagogue in Nazareth, His hometown.
- He stood up to read from the scroll of Isaiah, specifically Isaiah 61:1–2.
- After reading, He declared: "Today this scripture is fulfilled in your hearing." (Luke 4:21).

This moment wasn't just a reading—it was an interpretation. Jesus was participating in the community rhythm of synagogue worship, but He was also demonstrating His authority as the fulfillment of the prophecy He read aloud.

But notice the context:

- Jesus didn't pull Isaiah out of context for personal application.
- He read it aloud before the gathered community.
- His interpretation became a moment of public teaching and revelation.

This scene illustrates the deep community nature of scripture. The word of God wasn't something to be hoarded in isolation—it was meant to be shared, discussed, and responded to together.

The Role of Discussion and Commentary

After the public reading of Torah Law or the Prophets, there was time for Midrash—a community discussion and exploration of the text. This wasn't abstract theology—it was applied wisdom.

Questions would be asked:
- What does this commandment mean for our community?
- How do we live this out in our homes, our fields, and our markets?
- Where are we falling short, and how can we return to YHWH's intent?

This community approach ensured:

- Alignment: The community would remain tethered to YHWH's intent, not personal or cultural whims.
- Accountability: Misinterpretations could be challenged and corrected collectively.
- Practical Application: Scripture wasn't just read—it was embodied in shared action.

Contrast with Modern Individualism

Today, many approach scripture as a personal devotional tool. Quiet time with the Bible has become a cornerstone of modern spirituality. While private reflection is valuable, it carries risks when divorced from community accountability:

- **Confirmation Bias:** We may gravitate towards verses that affirm our pre-existing beliefs.
- **Isolation from Context:** Scripture may be misapplied without a broader understanding of cultural, historical, and literary context.
- **Lack of Correction:** Without a community to challenge us, errors in interpretation can harden into false doctrine.

Jesus's model—reading aloud, teaching publicly, and interpreting in community—reminds us that scripture thrives when it's shared, not siloed.

Community Obedience: Shared Covenant, Shared Responsibility

Understanding scripture community goes beyond intellectual debate—it's about shared obedience. In synagogue worship, the end goal of reading and discussing scripture was not academic mastery but community alignment with God's will.

- The Sabbath was kept together.
- Festivals were celebrated together.
- Sacrifices were offered together.

When scripture was misinterpreted or ignored, it wasn't just an individual failing—it affected the whole community.

This collective responsibility carries a profound message for today:
- We are accountable not just for how we understand scripture, but for how we live it out together.
- Scripture calls us not just to private devotion, but to public justice, mercy, and alignment.

Takeaway:

Scripture was never meant to be a private possession—it was always a shared inheritance. In the synagogue, scripture wasn't just read—it was wrestled with, discussed, and applied as a community.

- Jesus demonstrated the community power of scripture in synagogues throughout His ministry.
- Discussions and interpretations weren't distractions from the Word—they were essential to understanding and applying it.
- Modern believers must remember that scripture isn't just a personal love letter—it's a community covenant.

Key Reflection: Are we reading scripture with the same community humility and shared responsibility as Jesus and His earliest followers?

1.4 The Authority of the Hebrew Bible

Jesus didn't diminish the authority of the Hebrew Bible—He elevated it.

The Law, the Prophets, and the Writings were not antiquated texts to be dismissed but foundational pillars of His ministry, teachings, and mission.

Jesus's Affirmation of the Law

In Matthew 5:17–19, Jesus made His stance on the Law unmistakably clear:

"Do not think that I have come to abolish the Law or the Prophets; I have not come to abolish them but to fulfill them. For truly I tell you, until heaven and earth disappear, not the smallest letter, not the least stroke of a pen, will by any means disappear from the Law until everything is accomplished."

This declaration carries several key implications:

- **Affirmation, Not Abolition:** Jesus was not erasing the Torah Law or rendering it obsolete—He was faithfully upholding its purpose and spirit.
- **Endurance of God's Word:** The Law and Prophets remain valid until their intended purpose is fully realized – which Jesus told his followers to uphold so long as heaven and earth exist.
- **Every Detail Matters:** Even the smallest details of the Torah Law are significant, and binding, according to Jesus.

This wasn't just lip service. Jesus consistently demonstrated this principle through His teachings, interactions, and rebukes.

Jesus's Corrective Teachings: Tradition vs. Scripture

Jesus often confronted the religious authorities of His time—not because they followed the Law of Moses too strictly, but because they misinterpreted and misapplied it.

Example: Confronting Pharisaic Legalism (Mark 7:1–13)

- In this confrontation, the Pharisees criticized Jesus's disciples for eating with unwashed hands, a violation of *traditions of men* rather than Torah Law commandments.
- Jesus's response was sharp: *"You have let go of the commands of God and are holding on to human traditions."*(Mark 7:8)

- He pointed out how their traditions had actually nullified the intent of God's commandments, particularly regarding honoring one's father and mother.

Key Lesson: Jesus wasn't dismissing the Law—He was exposing how human additions had obscured its intent.

Example: The Greatest Commandments (Matthew 22:36–40)

When asked to identify the greatest commandment, Jesus quoted directly from the Torah Law:

"Love the Lord your God with all your heart, soul, and mind." (Deuteronomy 6:5)
"Love your neighbor as yourself." (Leviticus 19:18)

He then declared: *"All the Law and the Prophets hang on these two commandments."*

These verses show Jesus teaching his followers the proper spirit needed to better uphold God's Law and Prophets – these verses do not show Jesus teaching His followers to stop upholding God's other Laws in the Hebrew Bible.

Key Lesson: Jesus didn't replace the Law; He upheld it, expecting us to do the same, both in letter and spirit.

The Law as a Living Covenant

For Jesus, the Law wasn't a set of arbitrary rules—it was a living covenant between YHWH and His people.

- The commandments were designed to foster a relationship of love, trust, and alignment with God.
- Obedience to the Law wasn't about ritualistic performance; it was about living in harmony with God, others, and creation.

In John 14:15, Jesus emphasized this relational aspect:

> *"If you love me, keep my commandments."*

This wasn't a new commandment—it was an echo of the covenantal love expressed throughout the Law.

Comparing Jesus with First-Century Jewish Groups

Understanding Jesus's approach to the Hebrew Bible becomes even clearer when contrasted with the prevailing religious movements of His time:

1. **The Pharisees:**
   - Known for their emphasis on oral tradition and building a "hedge" around the Law.
   - Jesus rebuked them for elevating tradition above scripture (e.g., Mark 7).
   - However, He also commended their commitment to righteousness (e.g., Matthew 23:3).
2. **The Sadducees:**
   - Focused only on the Law (first five books) and rejected oral traditions and prophetic texts.
   - Denied the resurrection, angels, and spirits.
   - Jesus corrected them using scripture: *"You are mistaken because you do not know the Scriptures or the power of God."* (Matthew 22:29)
3. **The Essenes:**
   - A separatist group focused on ritual purity and apocalyptic expectations.
   - While Jesus shared some similarities (e.g., emphasis on holiness and repentance), He did not withdraw from society as they did.

Key Lesson: Jesus's approach to scripture was balanced, deeply rooted in the Torah Law, and free from legalistic distortions or selective omissions.

The Law in Jesus's Ministry

Jesus embodied the Law's principles in every aspect of His life:

- Justice: Defending the marginalized and confronting hypocrisy.
- Mercy: Healing the sick, feeding the hungry, and forgiving sins.
- Faithfulness: Living in complete obedience to God's will, even unto death.

His actions were not separate from the Law—they upheld it, pointed God's people back to it, affirmed its sufficiency and binding authority so long as heaven and earth exist.

The Relevance for Modern Believers

In many modern Christian contexts, the Hebrew Bible is often treated as a prequel to the New Testament—useful for moral lessons but overshadowed by the Gospels and Epistles.

This reductionist view misses the richness of the Law, Prophets, and writings as Jesus understood and taught, insisting his followers upheld them as reverently and totally as he did:

- The Law, Prophets, and Writings are not Obsolete: Its principles of justice, mercy, and holiness remain eternally relevant.
- It's not a checklist: The Law was never meant to be legalistic—it was always about relational alignment with God.
- Jesus is the lens, not the eraser: He illuminates the Law's true meaning but doesn't erase it.

When we view scripture through Jesus's lens, we see a continuous, unified covenantal story—one that invites us into alignment with God's will.

Section Takeaway:

To Jesus and His disciples, scripture wasn't fragmented theology or cultural relics—it was a living, cohesive testimony of YHWH's covenant.

- Jesus didn't diminish the Law; He explicitly upheld it, declaring not one stroke of a pen of it should be relaxed.
- His rebukes of Pharisaic legalism were about preserving the Law's intent, not dismissing it.
- Scripture is not a burden—it's a guide to relational alignment with God, others, and creation.

Key Reflection: Are we reading the Law, Prophets and Writings as Jesus did—with reverence, clarity, and a focus on alignment rather than legalism?

2. Structure of Scripture

Key Insight: The hierarchical Hebrew understanding of scripture in Jesus's time reflects a nuanced understanding most modern Christians have never been taught. The 3-tier understanding of the Law, the Prophets, and the Writings—was not arbitrary. It was the clearly understood structure of God's covenantal story maximizing clarity, purpose, and covenantal alignment. To Jews of the time, including Jesus and his disciples, this structured way of understanding the entire Hebrew Bible was important, not the sequence individual books were published.

2.1 The Impact of Structure on Understanding

The Hebrew Bible Jesus and His disciples most likely referenced and taught from—the Greek Septuagint—had the individual books sequenced in a chronological ordering. But, as stated above, the structural understanding was not based on printed sequence, but on the over-arching theological narrative arc.

This structural understanding isn't about order; it's about emphasis, context, and clearly seeing the layers of God's covenant.

Hebrew Biblical Structure

As stated above, the understood Judaic scriptural hierarchy has three levels:

1. **Torah (Law):** The foundation—God's instructions for righteous living and covenantal alignment.
2. **Nevi'im (Prophets):** The enforcement—prophets called Israel back to obedience when they strayed from the Law.
3. **Ketuvim (Writings):** The reflection—writings of wisdom, poetry, and contemplation of God's covenant through the lived experiences of His people.

Key Insight: This cohesive structure has led many modern Jews to use the acronym of the first letters of each component, T–N–K (pronounced "Tanakh"), to describe their modern Hebrew Bibles, in which the sequence of individual books follows the hierarchical structure understood by Jesus during his ministry.

The Christian Understanding: A Shift in Emphasis

When Christianity adopted the Hebrew Scriptures, they adopted the Septuagint – a version arranged mostly chronologically by its Jewish compilers to aid in teaching the history of their people during Hellenistic diaspora, or exile, from Judea.

Largely, from what we now know, the earliest *Old Testaments* used were this translation as well: which we will explore in furthering depth ahead.

In this translation, over 300 years old by the time of Jesus, the sequence did not follow a Torah → Prophets → Writings progression, instead, it was broken down as follows:

Historical Books: Genesis → Esther
Wisdom Literature: Job → Song of Solomon
Prophets: Isaiah → Malachi

While the content remains functionally identical, the hierarchical understanding held by Jesus, his direct disciples, and their "Late Second Temple" Jewish contemporaries, is not an understanding most modern Christian believers have been taught.

Theological Distortions of this Lost Knowledge:

- **Prophets as Fortune-Tellers, not Covenant-Enforcers:** In the Christian understanding the prophets conclude the Old Testament, often giving the impression that their primary purpose was to predict the coming of the Messiah. In the Hebrew understanding, the Prophets are situated between the Law and the Writings, serving as covenantal enforcers calling Israel back to obedience.
- **Loss of Reflective Space:** The Writings, intended to offer reflection and wisdom *after* prophetic correction, are instead understood as preempting the prophets, disrupting the structural understanding of repentance → reflection → restoration.
- **Disconnected Covenant Narrative:** The Christian understanding diminishes the sense of an ongoing covenantal story as Jesus understood it. With no deeper understanding of understood hierarchical structure, the Septuagint sequence presents the illusion of a hard stop before the New Testament, rather than one continuous arc from Genesis to Revelation.

Key Takeaway: When the sequencing of scripture is prioritized over perceived theological hierarchy, the *emphasis* shifts. The theological narrative fragments, and the overarching relationship between the books making-up scripture lose their intended covenantal context.

Scriptural Cohesion in Jesus's Teachings

Jesus always taught scripture within the hierarchical structure of Torah Law – Prophets – Writings, despite the sequence of books in the Septuagint.

- In Luke 24:44, He references all three divisions: *"Everything must be fulfilled that is written about me in the Law of Moses, the Prophets, and the Psalms."*

- The Psalms, included in the Writings, are highlighted as part of this cohesive testimony.

This reference wasn't accidental. It demonstrated Jesus's recognition of the divine intentionality in how scripture was understood.

Example: The Sermon on the Mount (Matthew 5–7)

- The Law serves as the foundation for Jesus's ethical teachings.
- The Prophets reinforce those teachings by calling for justice, mercy, and humility.
- The Writings are echoed in Jesus's wisdom and reflections (e.g., the Psalms and Proverbs).

Key Insight: Jesus didn't view scripture as a chronological anthology; He saw it as a theological symphony, with each division playing its part in a grand theological composition.

Why Structure Matters Today. The modern Christian approach to scripture, especially Old Testament scripture, often treats it as a buffet: selecting verses, ignoring context, and extracting personal meaning without regard for the larger covenantal narrative. That Jesus's structural understanding of scripture did not survive into the modern Christian era is a regrettable, but correctable, occurrence.

Without Jesus's understanding we risk:

1. **Misapplication of Prophecy:** Viewing prophets as mere predictors of future events instead of covenant enforcers.
2. **Neglect of Torah Law:** Dismissing God's instructions as obsolete, instead of seeing them as foundational principles for righteousness.
3. **Isolation of Writings:** Treating Psalms and Proverbs as devotional soundbites rather than reflective responses to covenantal living.

Following this structure doesn't just change how we *read* scripture—it changes how we *live* it.

Restoring the Narrative Flow as Jesus understood it.

1. **Torah (Law):** Understand as The Foundation when reading. They are God's instructions for righteous living.
2. **Nevi'im (Prophets):** Read the prophets as God's covenant auditors, calling His people back to alignment.
3. **Ketuvim (Writings):** Read as reflections on the lived experience of those living in covenantal alignment—and those desperately seeking to re-align.

When we approach scripture with this structure, we see the same narrative arc Jesus taught from:

- **Covenant Given (Torah)**
- **Covenant Broken (Prophets)**
- **Covenant Reflected Upon (Writings)**

Reflection:

Do we approach scripture as Jesus did—with reverence for both its content and its structure?

Or do we treat it as a fragmented anthology, shaped more by tradition than by divine intention?

2.2 Torah (Law): The Foundation

Key Insight: The Torah Law isn't merely a historical document or a list of religious rules—it's the bedrock of God's covenantal relationship with humanity.

Every commandment, story, and law serves a purpose in revealing God's character, His expectations, and His vision for human flourishing.

Understanding the Law as Jesus did

The Torah Law—comprising the books of Genesis, Exodus, Leviticus, Numbers, and Deuteronomy—is not simply an ancient legal code. It is a divine blueprint for life, worship, justice, and community harmony.

- **Genesis (The Origins):** Establishes the foundations of creation, humanity's purpose, and the earliest covenantal promises.
- **Exodus (Deliverance and Covenant):** Chronicles God's deliverance of Israel from Egypt and the giving of the Ten Commandments at Mount Sinai.
- **Leviticus (Holiness and Worship):** Provides detailed instructions on holiness, sacrificial rituals, and the priesthood.
- **Numbers (Wilderness and Faithfulness):** Documents Israel's journey through the wilderness, highlighting obedience, rebellion, and God's guidance.
- **Deuteronomy (Covenant Renewal):** Reiterates and summarizes the covenant for a new generation before entering the Promised Land.

The Torah Law isn't just a book of rules—it's a divine narrative revealing God's heart, wisdom, and desire for His people to live in alignment with His will.

The Law as a Covenantal Blueprint

At its core, the Law is about covenant—a sacred, binding agreement between God and His people.

- **A Covenant of Identity:** Israel is set apart as God's chosen people, called to embody His holiness in their conduct and worship.
- **A Covenant of Justice:** The Law provides principles for ethical living, social justice, and protection for the vulnerable.
- **A Covenant of Worship:** It establishes the proper way to approach and honor God through sacrifices, feasts, and holy days.

Without the Law, the rest of scripture loses its foundation. The Prophets become warnings without context, and the Writings lose their reflective significance.

Key Takeaway: The Law isn't just a legal code—it's a divine charter for a just, compassionate, and God-centered society.

Jesus and the Law

Jesus repeatedly affirmed the authority and centrality of the Law in His teachings:

- **Temptation in the Wilderness** (Matthew 4:1-11): When confronted by Satan, Jesus didn't rely on personal arguments or philosophical reasoning—He quoted Deuteronomy three times. Each response was rooted in the Law, underscoring its enduring authority.

- **The Greatest Commandments (Matthew 22:36-40): Jesus distilled the entire Law into two commands:**
  - *"Love the Lord your God with all your heart, soul, and mind."*
  - *"Love your neighbor as yourself."*

  These principles are drawn from Deuteronomy 6:5 and Leviticus 19:18, showing Jesus's deep reliance on the Law's core message.

- **The Sermon on the Mount** (Matthew 5–7): Jesus didn't abolish the Torah—He clarified and upheld it. He elevated the understanding of commandments like "Do not murder" and "Do not commit adultery" to address the heart and intent behind actions.

Key Insight: Jesus didn't view the Law as outdated or burdensome. He treated it as the foundation for righteous living, justice, and worship.

The Misunderstood Nature of the Law

Modern Christianity often misrepresents the Law as a list of oppressive, outdated rules. This distortion stems from:

- **Selective Reading:** Focusing on laws that seem culturally strange while ignoring their historical context and purpose.
- **Legalistic Misinterpretations:** Viewing the Law as a rigid code of impossible demands rather than a covenantal guide to love and justice.
- **Pauline Confusion:** Misunderstanding the role of Law in light of the writings attributed to Saul of Tarsus.

Example:
- The dietary law prohibiting pork (Leviticus 11:7-8) wasn't arbitrary—it was rooted in health, environmental stewardship, and cultural separation from pagan practices.

When read through a covenantal lens, the Torah's Law reveal divine wisdom, not arbitrary burdens.

Why the Law Still Matters Today

The Law isn't obsolete—it's foundational. Its principles remain relevant because they are anchored in eternal truths:

- **Justice:** Laws protecting the poor, the orphan, and the foreigner reflect God's heart for equity.
- **Holiness:** Instructions about purity and worship teach us about setting apart space, time, and actions for God.
- **Community:** The Law emphasizes community responsibility and mutual care, countering modern hyper-individualism.

The Law's principles guide not just individuals but entire societies. Its call to justice, love, and holiness resonates through every era and culture.

Modern Application of the Law

- **Ethics and Morality:** Principles like honesty, integrity, and compassion are timeless.
- **Justice Systems:** Many modern legal systems borrow principles from Torah Law, such as fair trials and protections against false accusations.

- **Spiritual Practices:** The Law's focus on rest (Sabbath), reflection, and worship remain vital for spiritual health.

Example:
The Sabbath law isn't just about not working—it's about trust. It's a command to step back, let go, and trust that God will sustain us even when we cease striving.

The Law as a Living Document

The Law isn't a relic—it's alive. Its principles breathe life into communities, guide individuals toward righteousness, and reveal God's unchanging character.

Key Takeaway: Without the Law, nothing in scripture makes sense—it is the foundation upon which everything else is built.

- It sets the stage for the Prophets' calls to repentance.
- It provides the context for the Writings' reflections on life, suffering, and hope.
- It forms the backbone of Jesus's teachings and ministry.

When we ignore or dismiss the Law, we sever ourselves from the root of God's revelation.

Reflection: Do we see the Law as Jesus saw it—not as a list of burdens, but as a divine blueprint for love, justice, and holiness? Have we allowed modern misunderstandings to obscure its beauty and purpose?

2.3 The Pentateuch: Teaches "Five Lessons," Not "Divine Law"

Key Insight: The Greek term *Pentateuch*—meaning "five scrolls"—is not inherently inaccurate, but it reflects a subtle shift in emphasis. While the Law was viewed by Jesus and His disciples as the divine constitution given directly by YHWH, the Pentateuch often becomes a historical or literary artifact in Christian theology.

In Judaism:
- The Law is seen as the **eternal constitution** of God's covenant with Israel.
- Every commandment, law, and narrative holds **binding authority** and remains **spiritually active**.

In Christianity:
- The Pentateuch is often treated as a **historical backdrop** leading to the New Testament.
- The moral teachings are emphasized, while the legal and ritual components frequently mistranslate **"fulfilled"** as **"obsolete"** rather than **"satisfied"** or **"upheld"**

Theological Consequences:
- When viewed merely as a prelude to the New Testament, the Law loses its weight as a living covenant for alignment with God's will.
- This shift fractures the continuity of scripture, turning divine commands into distant moral lessons rather than eternally binding instructions.

Takeaway: The Law isn't just a storybook—it's the blueprint for a covenantal society under YHWH. When reduced to a historical curiosity, its eternal wisdom is obscured.

2.4 The Torah as Law vs. The Pentateuch as Narrative

Key Insight: Language shapes perception. "Torah" conveys the weight of divine authority; "Pentateuch" sounds academic and distant.

In Judaism:
- The Torah Law is not merely a text—it is a **constitution** given directly by God.
- It's both **legal (binding)** and **narrative (revealing God's character and plan)**.

In Christianity:
- The Pentateuch is often treated as **"prelude theology"**—stories leading up to the arrival of Jesus.

- Its **legal elements are de-emphasized**, while moral and allegorical lessons are highlighted.

Key Differences in Approach:

Covenantal Obedience vs. Moral Symbolism:
- Judaism views commandments as living obligations.
- Christianity often treats commandments as moral suggestions.

Eternal Binding vs. Temporary Guidelines:
- In Judaism, the Torah Law remains authoritative.
- In modern Christianity, it's often seen as obsolete.

Example:

- The Sabbath law is often viewed as legalistic in Christianity but as a profound covenantal rhythm in Judaism.
- Kosher dietary laws are dismissed as cultural relics rather than seen as divine instructions for mindfulness and holiness.

Takeaway: The Torah is not just "law"—it's the foundation for understanding God's relationship with humanity.

Reducing it to mere narrative distorts its purpose and limits its transformative power.

2.5 Jesus's Relationship with the Torah Law

Key Insight: Jesus's relationship with the Torah Law wasn't adversarial—it was deeply affirmational.

In **Matthew 5:17-19**, Jesus stated:
"Do not think that I have come to abolish the Law or the Prophets; I have not come to abolish them but to fulfill them. For truly I tell you, until heaven and earth disappear, not the smallest letter, not the least stroke of a pen, will by any means disappear from the Law until everything is accomplished."

Misunderstood Fulfillment:

- *"Fulfill"* doesn't mean *"replace"* or *"abolish."*. It means *"uphold"* or *"satisfy"*.
- Jesus *lived out* the Law perfectly and restored its true intent where human legalism had distorted it.

Examples of Jesus Upholding the Torah:

- **Healing on the Sabbath:** Jesus clarified that the Sabbath was made for humanity, not humanity for the Sabbath (Mark 2:27).
- **Greatest Commandments:** When asked to summarize the Torah, Jesus drew directly from Deuteronomy and Leviticus (Matthew 22:36–40).
- **Confronting Hypocrisy:** In Mark 7, Jesus rebuked religious leaders for prioritizing human traditions over divine commandments.

Takeaway: Jesus didn't come to override the Torah—He came to *fulfill it by example*, to restore its true intent, and to demonstrate how it leads to love, justice, and alignment with God.

2.6 Cultural Perception of the Pentateuch

Key Insight: Words carry cultural weight. The shift from *Torah Law* to *Pentateuch* wasn't accidental—it was the result of cultural and linguistic evolution, primarily through Greek influence.

The Septuagint Shift:

The Septuagint, the Greek translation of the Hebrew scriptures, was a monumental work but also introduced subtle shifts in perception.

- "Torah" became "Nomos" (Law), and later "Pentateuch" (Five Scrolls).

Why This Matters:

- *Law* conveys authority, permanence, and divine command.

- *Pentateuch* suggests literature, history, and academic study.

The Hellenistic Filter:

- Greek philosophy prioritized abstract reasoning over covenantal obedience.
- This cultural lens began to *reframe the Law* from an active constitution into an academic study of ancient religious practices.

Example:

- The Law's commandments about ritual purity and dietary laws were reinterpreted as symbolic rather than practical and covenantal.
- Greek-influenced Christianity began to see the Law as "preparatory material" rather than an ongoing guide for living.

The Consequence:

- Modern Christians often view the Law as irrelevant to their daily lives, rather than as a foundation for faith and ethics.
- This creates a fracture between the Hebrew roots of scripture and its Greco-Roman reinterpretation.

Takeaway: The Law was never meant to be a dusty historical relic—it's a living covenant. The shift from *Law* to *Pentateuch* represents more than semantics; it reflects a theological drift with profound consequences.

Thematic Takeaway for Section 2

The Torah is not just ancient literature—it's the foundational constitution of God's covenant. Every story, commandment, and principle carries weight and purpose. When we shift our perspective back to seeing it as Jesus and his direct disciples did—not as a burden, but as a blessing—we find scriptural clarity, covenantal alignment, and God's purpose.

To Jesus, the yoke of God's Law was light, and easy to bear.

In Matthew 11:28-30, Jesus says,

> *"Come to me, all who labor and are heavy laden, and I will give you rest. Take my yoke upon you and learn from me, for I am gentle and lowly in heart, and you will find rest for your souls. For my yoke is easy, and my burden is light.".*

The same applied to Jesus's direct disciples. James, brother of Jesus, described the Law as being the source of liberty, and prosperity.

> *But those who look into the perfect law, the law of liberty, and persevere, being not hearers who forget but doers who act—they will be blessed in their doing. (James 1:25-27)*

> *So speak and so do as those who will be judged by the law of liberty. (James 2:12)*

---

3. Prophets (Nevi'im): Amplify and Enforce the Torah

The Torah laid the foundation, but it wasn't the end of the story. The Prophets arose not to replace the Torah, but to *amplify it, enforce it,* and *call people back to it.*

- How did the Prophets use the Torah as their foundation?
- How did they call out misalignment and guide Israel back to obedience?
- What can we learn from their warnings, promises, and calls to repentance?

In the next section, we'll explore how the Prophets acted as the covenant's guardians, calling Israel—and us—back to the foundation of God's will.

3.1 The Prophets—Amplify and Enforce the Torah

Key Insight: The Prophets were not inventors of new doctrines or spiritual innovators—they were guardians and enforcers of the Torah, calling Israel back to covenantal alignment when they strayed.

The Prophets as Covenant Guardians

The prophetic books—**Joshua, Judges, Samuel, Kings, Isaiah, Jeremiah, Ezekiel, and the Twelve Minor Prophets**—were not separate from the Torah. They were **extensions of it**, voices crying out to remind Israel of their covenantal obligations.

- **Joshua and Judges:** Show the consequences of obedience and disobedience to the Torah as Israel transitioned from wandering to settlement.
- **Samuel and Kings:** Detail the moral and spiritual failures of leaders who neglected the Torah.
- **Isaiah, Jeremiah, Ezekiel:** Serve as grand, poetic warnings of impending judgment and hopeful promises of restoration—all rooted in Torah principles.
- **The Twelve Minor Prophets:** Each echo a specific aspect of Torah ethics, justice, and covenant fidelity.

The Prophets didn't introduce new commandments; they held up a mirror and said, *"Look how far you've drifted from God's instructions!"*

Example: Elijah on Mount Carmel (1 Kings 18)
When Elijah stood against the prophets of Baal, he didn't innovate a new spiritual system.

- He called Israel back to the **Shema** (*Deuteronomy 6:4–5*: *"Hear, O Israel: The Lord our God, the Lord is one."*)
- and to the foundational commandment against idolatry (*Exodus 20:3*: *"You shall have no other gods before me."*).

Elijah's confrontation wasn't about spectacle—it was about clarity: *"How long will you waver between two opinions? If the Lord is God, follow him; but if Baal is God, follow him."* (1 Kings 18:21)

The Prophetic Function: Three Key Roles

1. **Watchmen on the Walls:**
   - Prophets warned Israel of the consequences of breaking covenant law.
   - Example: Ezekiel as a "watchman" (Ezekiel 33:7).
2. **Covenantal Prosecutors:**
   - Prophets often spoke in legal terms, as though in a courtroom, prosecuting Israel for violating their covenant with YHWH.
   - Example: Isaiah 1:18, *"Come now, let us reason together, says the Lord: though your sins are like scarlet, they shall be as white as snow."*
3. **Voices of Hope and Restoration:**
   - Even in judgment, the prophets pointed to hope, renewal, and restoration.
   - Example: Jeremiah 31:33, *"I will put my law within them, and I will write it on their hearts. And I will be their God, and they shall be my people."*

They acted as **spiritual shepherds**, guiding Israel back onto the straight and narrow path.

Each role reinforced—not replaced—the Torah.

Prophets as Interpreters, Not Innovators

The Prophets didn't invent moral or ethical principles—they **applied Torah principles to real-world crises.**

- **Micah 6:8:** *"He has shown you, O man, what is good; And what does the Lord require of you but to do justly, to love mercy, and to walk humbly with your God?"*
- This wasn't a new commandment—it was a summation of Torah principles.

When the Prophets spoke against oppression, idolatry, and injustice, they were interpreting Torah through the lens of their specific time and situation.

Example: Amos and Social Justice (Amos 5:24)

- Amos railed against Israel's wealth-driven corruption and exploitation of the poor.
- His iconic cry, *"But let justice roll on like a river, righteousness like a never-failing stream!"* was not a new revelation—it was an application of Torah laws about fair wages, honest trade, and protection of the vulnerable (e.g., Deuteronomy 24:14–15).

The **essence of the prophets' message was simple:** *Return to YHWH. Return to the covenant. Return to the Torah.*

Prophetic Warnings in Modern Context

The prophetic role isn't confined to ancient Israel—it's a timeless pattern.

- **Religious Legalism vs. True Obedience:** Prophets warned against hollow ritualism without true repentance (Isaiah 1:13–17).
- **Economic Injustice:** They spoke out against systems that exploited the poor (Micah 2:1–2).
- **Idolatry of Wealth and Power:** They called leaders to account for abusing their authority (Jeremiah 22:13–17).

Today, the same warnings resonate:

- Are we using religion as a veneer for corruption?
- Are we turning a blind eye to injustice while maintaining outward piety?
- Are we bowing to modern idols—materialism, nationalism, or celebrity culture—while neglecting God's commandments?

The prophetic voice still calls us back to **Torah alignment**.

Prophets and Jesus: The Ultimate Fulfillment

Jesus didn't dismiss the prophets—He upheld their message.

- In His teachings, He echoed Isaiah's call for justice.
- In His actions, He lived out Jeremiah's heart for repentance and renewal.
- In His mission, He embodied Ezekiel's vision of restoration.

Luke 4:16–21 illustrates this vividly. Jesus stands in the synagogue, reads from **Isaiah 61**, and declares:

> *"Today this scripture is fulfilled in your hearing."*

He wasn't overturning the prophets' message—He was **bringing it to life.**

Takeaway for 3.1

Key Takeaway: The Prophets didn't replace the Torah—they amplified it, enforced it, and called Israel back to it. They acted as watchmen, covenant enforcers, and voices of hope.

The prophetic message isn't distant history—it's a timeless call: *"Return to YHWH. Return to the covenant. Return to the Torah."*

If the Torah is the foundation and the Prophets are the enforcers, the Writings are the **heartbeats of reflection and worship.**

- How do Psalms, Proverbs, and Job reinforce Torah principles?
- How do the wisdom writings teach us to live in alignment with God's commandments?
- What can the poetic beauty of the Writings teach us about reverence, humility, and gratitude?

In the next section, we'll explore the **Ketuvim (Writings)** as reflections of Torah wisdom, teaching us how to align our hearts and minds with God's eternal truths.

3.2 Writings (Ketuvim): Reflect Wisdom and Worship Grounded in the Torah

Key Insight: The Writings are not disconnected reflections or mere poetic musings—they are spiritual responses to life under the covenant of the Torah, offering worship, wisdom, and practical guidance for daily living.

The Role of the Writings in the Tanakh:
The **Writings** include a diverse collection of texts:

- **Psalms:** Songs of praise, lament, and worship.
- **Proverbs:** Practical wisdom for righteous living.
- **Job:** Exploration of suffering, faith, and divine justice.
- **Ecclesiastes:** Philosophical reflections on life's meaning and purpose.
- **Song of Solomon:** Celebration of love and covenantal intimacy.
- **Ruth:** A story of loyalty, kindness, and covenant faithfulness.
- **Lamentations:** Mourning over the destruction of Jerusalem, but with threads of hope.
- **Daniel:** Faithfulness in exile and God's sovereignty over empires.
- **Ezra-Nehemiah:** Restoration of community and worship after exile.
- **Chronicles:** A retelling of Israel's history with an emphasis on faithfulness and worship.

The **Writings act as a bridge** between **covenantal instruction (Torah)** and **prophetic correction (Nevi'im)**. They offer the *emotional and spiritual soundtrack* of a people navigating the tension between God's promises and their lived reality.

The Psalms: Worship Rooted in Obedience

The **Psalms** are not random poetic verses—they are deeply theological reflections rooted in **Torah principles**.

- **Psalm 1:** Describes the blessed man as one who *"meditates on the law of the Lord day and night."*

- **Psalm 19:** Declares that *"The law of the Lord is perfect, refreshing the soul."*
- **Psalm 119:** The longest psalm in the Bible, dedicated entirely to the beauty, wisdom, and necessity of Torah obedience.

In the Psalms, worship and obedience are inseparable. Singing to YHWH is not just emotional—it's deeply covenantal.

Example: David and the Psalms

David, who authored many Psalms, wasn't just a king—he was a shepherd, a warrior, and a worshipper. His Psalms show the full range of human experience:

- **Joy** (*Psalm 23: "The Lord is my shepherd; I shall not want."*)
- **Desperation** (*Psalm 22: "My God, my God, why have you forsaken me?"*)
- **Repentance** (*Psalm 51: "Create in me a clean heart, O God."*)

Each psalm ties back to **Torah principles**—obedience, repentance, trust, and faithfulness.

Takeaway: The Psalms teach us that worship isn't separate from obedience—it is the *natural outflow* of a heart aligned with God's commandments.

Proverbs: Wisdom Grounded in Torah

The **Proverbs** offer distilled wisdom for daily living, echoing the principles of the Torah.

- **Proverbs 3:5–6:** *"Trust in the Lord with all your heart and lean not on your own understanding; in all your ways submit to Him, and He will make your paths straight."*
- **Proverbs 11:1:** *"The Lord detests dishonest scales, but accurate weights find favor with Him."*

These are not abstract moral lessons—they are **practical applications of Torah principles** in relationships, business, and community.

Example: The Fear of YHWH

- Proverbs frequently emphasize *"The fear of the Lord is the beginning of wisdom."* (Proverbs 1:7)
- This isn't about fear in the sense of terror—it's about reverence, alignment, and obedience.

Takeaway: Proverbs remind us that **Torah obedience isn't just about rituals—it's about living wisely in every aspect of life.**

Job, Ecclesiastes, and the Deep Questions of Faith

- **Job:** Wrestles with the question of suffering in the context of a covenant relationship with God.
- **Ecclesiastes:** Explores the fleeting nature of life and the importance of living in alignment with God's commandments despite life's mysteries.
- **Song of Solomon:** Celebrates love, intimacy, and covenant fidelity in a deeply poetic and metaphorical form.

These books remind us that **faith isn't just about certainty—it's about trust, even in uncertainty.**

Example: Job's Integrity

- Despite losing everything, Job declares: *"Though He slay me, yet will I hope in Him."* (Job 13:15)
- Job's story isn't about easy answers—it's about steadfast faith in the face of unexplainable suffering.

Takeaway: The Writings teach us that faithfulness to Torah isn't just about external actions—it's about internal alignment with God's will, even in hardship.

The Narrative Books: Ruth, Ezra-Nehemiah, Chronicles

- **Ruth:** Demonstrates loyalty and faithfulness, showing that obedience to God often involves acts of kindness and selflessness.
- **Ezra-Nehemiah:** Chronicles the return from exile and the restoration of Torah-centered worship.
- **Chronicles:** Retells Israel's history, emphasizing faithfulness to YHWH and the importance of the Torah Law as the heart of covenant worship.

Example: Ezra Reads the Torah (Nehemiah 8:1–12)

- After returning from exile, Ezra reads the Torah aloud to the people.
- They weep, realizing how far they've drifted from God's commands.
- The people collectively recommit themselves to Torah obedience.

Takeaway: These narratives show us that alignment with Torah isn't just individual—it's communal. Restoration comes when a people collectively turn their hearts back to God.

The Emotional and Spiritual Heartbeat

The Writings are the **spiritual diary of covenant life**—they express the *human side* of obedience to God:

- The *joy* of worship.
- The *grief* of sin.
- The *confusion* of suffering.
- The *hope* of restoration.

They don't **replace** the Torah—they **reflect** it in action.

Takeaway for 3.2

Key Takeaway: The Writings are not abstract musings—they are deeply connected to Torah principles. They teach us how to:

- Worship with sincerity.
- Live with wisdom.
- Trust in God through suffering.
- Build faithful communities rooted in covenant alignment.

Together with the **Torah** and the **Prophets**, the **Writings** complete the structure of the Tanakh—a unified testimony of YHWH's covenant with His people.

Transition to 3.3

But something happened to how these sacred texts were understood in later Pauline Christian traditions.

- The structural understanding Jesus taught under was lost.
- The emphasis shifted from theological hierarchy to linear chronology.
- Jesus's understanding of the Torah, Prophets, and Writings was obscured.

As a result Christianity lost its ability to look at the Law, Prophets, and Writings through Jesus's scriptural lens.

In the next section, we'll examine how the **Christian loss of Jesus's scriptural lens** altered theological prioritization, and why it matters for understanding scripture today.

3.3 The Old Testament: Lost Priorities

Key Insight: Jesus's understood structure of the **Hebrew Bible**—Torah (Law), Prophets (Nevi'im), and Writings (Ketuvim)—wasn't arbitrary; it was a divinely inspired framework.

Losing it subtly, but profoundly, altered its message, purpose, and how it is understood today.

Commandment → Correction → Reflection: The Original Flow

In the **Hebrew structure Jesus taught**, the hierarchy was clear:

1. **Torah (Law):** The foundation—YHWH's commandments and covenant instructions.
2. **Prophets (Nevi'im):** The correction—prophets calling Israel back to covenant faithfulness.
3. **Writings (Ketuvim):** The reflection—songs, wisdom, and narratives showing life under the covenant.

This structure is not just linguistic—it's theological. Each building upon the previous, forming a seamless narrative and instructional arc.

When Christian tradition lost the structural understanding of these books, they lost a major lens of living-out God's Law according to Jesus's teachings.

3.4 How Modern Pauline Christian Understanding Alters the Focus

In modern Pauline Christianity, Jesus's understood hierarchy of the Hebrew Scriptures is largely extinct in practical teaching or application. Today, the fact Jesus most likely read a Septuagint Hebrew Bible is used to validate a sequence-based understanding, despite the clear structure Jesus himself understood and taught scripture with. As such, modern Christian understanding shifted from Jesus's:

- **Law → Prophets → Writings**

to one based merely on sequence

- **Pentateuch → History → Poetry → Prophecy**

This wasn't a **minor aesthetic shift** in understanding—it was a **fundamental recontextualization** of scripture's purpose.

Key Shifts in Emphasis:

1. **The Torah (Law)**
    - In Jesus's eyes, the Torah serves as the foundation of faith and practice.
    - In the Pauline Christian view, it became a distant historical record—"laws of the past" rather than an eternal covenant.
    - Torah Law became interpreted as an impossibility, a curse to be freed from even though Jesus called it the lightest of burdens and an easy yoke to bear. The Law Jesus's closest disciple described as the Law that gives Liberty and Prosperity.
2. **The Prophets (Nevi'im)**
    - In the Hebrew structure, the Prophets were covenant enforcers, calling Israel back to obedience.
    - In the Christian understanding, they are primarily seen as predictors of Jesus's coming—a prophecy manual rather than a covenant correction tool.
3. **The Writings (Ketuvim)**
    - In the Hebraic structural understanding, the Writings reflect life lived in covenantal alignment.
    - In the Christian understanding, they became abstract reflections, removed from their covenantal grounding.

Theological Consequences:

- The **Prophets** became understood as future-focused fortune-tellers, obscuring their original role as covenant watchdogs.
- The **Writings** became understood as inspirational but detached, offering comfort but little direction.
- The **Torah** became understood as a prelude rather than a foundation.

Takeaway: Even though Hebrew Bibles of Jesus's day were sequenced the same way our modern Old Testament is, the sequence of individual books alone was not how he understood, taught, or lived it out in his ministry.

3.5 How This Shift in Understanding Decontextualized Scripture

In the **Hebrew Tanakh structure:**

- **The Torah** establishes the foundational covenantal relationship with YHWH.
- **The Prophets** enforce that foundation, calling Israel back to alignment when they stray.
- **The Writings** reflect worship, wisdom, and practical faithfulness under the covenant.

In the modern **Pauline Christian understanding:**

- **The Torah** became historical background—relevant primarily as a setup for Jesus.
- **The Prophets** became fortune-tellers predicting Jesus, with their corrective function diminished.
- **The Writings** became abstract and detached wisdom literature, disconnected from covenantal living.

Subtle Shifts in Reader Perception:

- **From Covenant Relationship to Future Prediction:** The focus shifted from *living faithfully now* to *awaiting future fulfillment.*
- **From Practical Obedience to Abstract Morality:** Specific covenantal commands gave way to generalized moral lessons.
- **From Collective Accountability to Individual Devotion:** The community call to covenant living diminished in favor of a personal, individualistic faith.

Example:

- When Isaiah calls Israel to *"Cease to do evil, learn to do good; seek justice, correct oppression"* (Isaiah 1:16–17), the primary focus is covenant faithfulness.

- In a rearranged context, Isaiah is often read as a future-focused predictor of Jesus, rather than a present-focused call to repentance and obedience.

Takeaway: The loss of Jesus's scriptural lens altered how generations of readers approached scripture. Instead of guiding people back to covenant faithfulness to God, it became a fragmented anthology with shifting priorities.

3.6 Why This Matters Today

The consequences of the loss of Jesus's scriptural lens are still shaping modern Christianity:

- **Torah Misunderstood:** Many Christians view the Torah as obsolete laws for ancient Israel, not as an eternal covenantal foundation.
- **Prophets Misused:** Prophetic books are cherry-picked for end-times predictions rather than seen as calls to community repentance.
- **Writings Undervalued:** Psalms, Proverbs, and other wisdom texts are reduced to inspirational quotes rather than reflections on covenant living.

This has practical consequences:

- **Selective Obedience:** Moral laws are embraced while ritual and societal laws are dismissed.
- **Shallow Prophetic Engagement:** Prophets are often reduced to puzzle pieces in eschatological timelines.
- **Detached Worship:** Worship songs and prayers are sometimes disconnected from obedience and covenant alignment.

Restoring Jesus's Understanding

Understanding the **structure of the Hebrew Bible as Jesus did** isn't an academic exercise—it's a spiritual realignment:

1. **Torah:** The foundation of faith and obedience.
2. **Prophets:** The call to repentance and alignment.
3. **Writings:** The reflection on covenant life and worship.

When we read scripture through Jesus's lens:

- The **Torah** regains its place as the cornerstone of faith.
- The **Prophets** become relevant calls to modern repentance.
- The **Writings** become deeply practical guides for worship, wisdom, and faithfulness.

Final Takeaway for Section 3:

The loss of Jesus's scriptural lens was not neutral—it reshaped theology, worship, and faithfulness. Understanding how Jesus structured scripture allows us to **see the Bible as Jesus saw it**: a unified, cohesive testimony pointing to YHWH's covenant, justice, and love.

Transition to Section 4

With the **structure of scripture clarified**, we are now prepared to examine **how Jesus Himself approached, interpreted, and taught the Tanakh.**

- Did He treat the Torah as obsolete or foundational?
- Did He reduce the Prophets to predictors of Himself?
- Did He use the Writings as inspirational quotes or covenantal reflections?

In the next section, we'll uncover **Jesus's Scriptural Lens**—the lens through which He revealed God's heart and intent for humanity.

---

4. Jesus's Scriptural Lens

As we have established, Jesus didn't approach scripture as a fragmented set of isolated verses or disconnected books. He viewed it as a **unified,** living testimony of God's covenant, with **Torah Law as its foundation,** and the **Prophets and Writings reinforcing and reflecting** that foundation.

Modern readers often approach scripture with inherited biases—whether philosophical, cultural, or theological. But Jesus's lens was clear, consistent, and covenantal.

4.1 Jesus understood and taught scripture from the standpoint of an obediently observant Jew.

Key Insight: Jesus viewed scripture through a **Hebraic worldview,** not through **Greek dualism** or **Roman legalism.** This difference is crucial for understanding His teachings and actions.

Hebraic Worldview vs. Greek Dualism:

- **Hebraic Thought:** Holistic, cyclical, and relational. Focused on *"walking in obedience"* with YHWH through **covenantal faithfulness.** Time was seen as cyclical—marked by festivals, Sabbaths, and recurring divine patterns.
- **Greek Dualism:** Abstract, linear, and compartmentalized. Divides the world into material and spiritual realms, often elevating the spiritual while dismissing the physical.

Example of Cyclical vs. Linear Thought:

- In Hebraic thought, the **Sabbath and festivals** are recurring cycles that reflect God's ongoing relationship with His people.
- In Greek thought, time is linear—moving from one event to another, with little emphasis on recurring divine cycles.

Roman Legalism:

- The Roman Empire emphasized **law as a tool for control,** with rigid, inflexible applications of justice.

- Jesus's approach, by contrast, emphasized **justice, mercy, and faithfulness** over rigid adherence to human traditions (Matthew 23:23).

Biases in Modern Scripture Reading:

- Many modern readers unknowingly impose **Greek linearism** or **Roman legalism** on their reading of scripture.
- This results in fragmented interpretations, where the **relational, covenantal essence** of scripture is obscured.

Jesus's Lens:

- Jesus saw scripture not as isolated doctrinal points but as a **woven tapestry** of covenantal truth.
- He read the Torah as a **living foundation**, the Prophets as **covenant enforcers**, and the Writings as **reflections on faithfulness**.

Takeaway: Jesus's scriptural lens wasn't Greek, abstract or philosophical—it was Hebrew, **relational and covenantal**. He viewed scripture as a **guide to loving God, loving others, and walking in faithfulness**.

4.2 Jesus Quoted the Torah Law as His Foundation

When Jesus faced temptation in the wilderness (Matthew 4:1–11), He didn't rely on clever arguments, emotional appeals, or philosophical reasoning. Instead, He turned directly to **the Torah Law**—the foundation of His faith and authority.

The Wilderness Temptations:

1. **"Man shall not live by bread alone, but by every word that comes from the mouth of God."** *(Deuteronomy 8:3)*
   - Temptation: Prioritize physical needs over spiritual alignment.
   - Response: True life is found in obedience to YHWH's word.

2. **"You shall not put the Lord your God to the test."** *(Deuteronomy 6:16)*
   - Temptation: Manipulate God's promises for personal gain.
   - Response: Faith is about trust, not demands.
3. **"You shall worship the Lord your God and Him only shall you serve."** *(Deuteronomy 6:13)*
   - Temptation: Compromise worship and allegiance for power and control.
   - Response: Worship belongs to YHWH alone.

Why the Torah?

- Jesus didn't need new doctrines or novel interpretations—**the Torah was sufficient**.
- Each response demonstrated **deep alignment** with YHWH's commands.
- The Torah provided **spiritual clarity, moral authority, and covenantal grounding** in moments of crisis.

Beyond the Wilderness:

- Jesus consistently referenced the Torah throughout His ministry.
- Whether addressing religious leaders, teaching the crowds, or guiding His disciples, His authority came from the **divine foundation of the Torah**.
- **Example:** When asked about the greatest commandment, Jesus quoted from **Deuteronomy 6:5** (*"Love the Lord your God with all your heart, soul, and strength"*) and **Leviticus 19:18** (*"Love your neighbor as yourself"*).

Contrast with Modern Misuse:

- Many modern interpretations treat the Torah as obsolete or burdensome.
- Jesus demonstrated that it's neither—it's **essential** and **alive**.

Takeaway: The Torah wasn't peripheral to Jesus's teachings—it was **central**. It wasn't an outdated rulebook; it was **God's living covenantal guide**, and Jesus relied on it fully.

Transition to 4.3

Jesus didn't just reference isolated scriptures—He showed how the **entire Tanakh was a cohesive, unified testimony** pointing to God's covenantal plan.

On the **Road to Emmaus**, He gave His disciples a **masterclass in scripture interpretation**, revealing how every word of the Torah, the Prophets, and the Writings pointed to His ministry and mission.

In the next section, we'll walk that road together and uncover how Jesus revealed the **unified story of scripture** to His followers.

4.3 On the Road to Emmaus: A Unified Scriptural Testimony

Key Insight: On the road to Emmaus, Jesus didn't deliver a new revelation—He revealed the **unified testimony of scripture** that had always been there, waiting to be seen.

The Encounter on the Road to Emmaus

After His resurrection, Jesus appeared to two disciples walking along the road to Emmaus. They were disheartened, confused, and unable to reconcile recent events with their understanding of the Messiah.

In **Luke 24:27**, it's written:
"And beginning with Moses and all the Prophets, He explained to them what was said in all the Scriptures concerning Himself."

Later, in **Luke 24:44–45**, Jesus clarified:
"Everything must be fulfilled that is written about me in the Law of Moses, the Prophets, and the Psalms."

Notice the structure Jesus used:

- **Law (Torah)** → The foundation.
- **Prophets (Nevi'im)** → The enforcers and amplifiers of the Torah.
- **Writings (Ketuvim)** → The reflections and worship grounded in the Torah.

Jesus didn't isolate prophetic proof-texts or use Psalms as abstract poetry. He connected **all three sections** into a single narrative thread.

The Significance of the Emmaus Road Revelation:

- **A Cohesive Story:** Jesus showed how the Tanakh wasn't fragmented but a continuous, unified testimony.
- **Fulfillment, Not Replacement:** Jesus's life and mission weren't a deviation from scripture but a **satisfaction** of scripture—a core component of the Torah's covenantal arc, playing out before them: God keeping his promises to his people.
- **A Hermeneutic Blueprint:** Jesus gave His disciples a **template for reading scripture**—not as isolated verses, but as a hierarchical structure to illuminate YHWH's covenantal plan.

Modern Parallel:
Today, many Christians and nonbelievers alike see scripture as **fragmented, confusing, and disconnected from the modern world.**

The Emmaus Road story teaches us that to see scripture clearly, we must do as Jesus did:

- Begin with the **Torah as the foundation.**
- Let the **Prophets amplify God's message.**
- Reflect with the **Writings as wisdom and worship.**

Takeaway: Jesus viewed scripture as a **unified testimony of YHWH's covenantal plan.** Fragmentation leads to misunderstanding. Unity reveals the truth.

4.4 Jesus's Teachings Were Grounded in the Torah

Key Insight: Jesus didn't diminish or override the Torah—He upheld, clarified, and elevated it.

The Sermon on the Mount: A Torah Manifesto
In **Matthew 5–7**, often referred to as the Sermon on the Mount, Jesus

laid out a profound teaching rooted deeply in the Torah. He began with a crystal-clear statement:

> *"Do not think that I have come to abolish the Law or the Prophets; I have not come to abolish them but to fulfill them."(Matthew 5:17)*

Key Observations:

Not Abolish, but Fulfill: Jesus didn't see the Torah as outdated or burdensome. Instead, He lived it out perfectly, showing its **intended spirit and purpose**.

Depth Over Surface: Jesus clarified commandments that had become clouded by rigid legalism and empty ritual. For example:

- *"You have heard it said, 'Do not murder,' but I say anyone who is angry with his brother is subject to judgment."* (Matthew 5:21–22)
- *"You have heard it said, 'Do not commit adultery,' but I say anyone who looks at a woman lustfully has already committed adultery in his heart."* (Matthew 5:27–28)

These teachings weren't replacements for the Torah—they were **expositions of its heart and purpose**.

The Greatest Commandments:
When asked about the **greatest commandment**, Jesus responded without hesitation:

- *"Love the Lord your God with all your heart, soul, and mind."* (Deuteronomy 6:5)
- *"Love your neighbor as yourself."* (Leviticus 19:18)

Jesus quoted directly from the Torah. He didn't innovate; He illuminated. These two commandments serve as **summaries of the entire Torah:**

1. **Vertical Relationship:** Love and obedience to God.
2. **Horizontal Relationship:** Love and justice toward others.

Misinterpretation of Fulfillment:
Many modern readers interpret *"fulfillment"* in Matthew 5:17 as *"abolishment."*

- This misunderstanding leads to dismissing the Torah as outdated or irrelevant.
- In reality, *"fulfillment"* means **completion, embodiment, and perfect adherence** to YHWH's commandments.

Why the Torah Still Matters:

- The Torah teaches **justice, mercy, humility, and reverence for God.**
- Without the Torah, Jesus's teachings lose their context and authority.
- Ignoring the Torah while claiming to follow Jesus is like building a house without a foundation.

Takeaway: Jesus didn't redefine the Torah—He clarified it. His life and teachings illuminate its eternal value and purpose.

4.5 Why This Matters Today

Key Insight: The way Jesus viewed scripture isn't a historical footnote—it's a guide for us today.

A Fragmented Bible Leads to a Fragmented Faith:

- Modern Christianity often treats the **Old Testament** as background noise and the **New Testament** as the main event.
- But scripture was never meant to be divided this way.

The Foundation Matters:

- Without the Torah as the foundation, the **Prophets lose their authority**, and the **Writings lose their purpose**.
- Misreading scripture leads to shallow theology, legalism, and misaligned priorities.

Restoring the Unified Testimony:

- Seeing scripture through Jesus's lens restores **clarity, purpose, and unity**.
- Every book of the Tanakh contributes to the grand narrative of YHWH's covenant.

A Call to Modern Believers:

- Stop cherry-picking verses for convenience.
- Stop seeing the Torah as outdated rules.
- Start seeing scripture as **Jesus saw it**—a cohesive, living testimony of God's love and covenant.

Takeaway: If we want to follow Jesus, we must view scripture as He did—as a unified whole, with the Torah as its foundation, the Prophets as its enforcers, and the Writings as its reflections.

Section Takeaway: A Unified Testimony

Jesus didn't fragment scripture—He **unified it**.

- **Torah:** The foundation of faith and covenant.
- **Prophets:** The voice calling people back to that foundation.
- **Writings:** The reflections and worship inspired by that foundation.

To truly follow Jesus, we must **restore His lens**—seeing scripture as a **living covenant**, not a disjointed anthology.

With this clarity, we now transition to **Section 5: Table Contrasting Tanakh vs. Old Testament Book Order and Structure**—a visual aid that underscores these critical differences.

5: Table and Section-by-Section Breakdown

5.1 Table Comparing Law, Prophets and Writings & Old Testament

Category	Law, Prophets and Writings (Hebrew Bible)	Christian Old Testament
Structure	3 Sections: Torah (Law), Nevi'im (Prophets), Ketuvim (Writings)	5 Sections: Pentateuch, Historical Books, Wisdom Literature, Major Prophets, Minor Prophets
Purpose	Thematic and Covenantal: Covenant (Law) → Enforcement (Prophets) → Reflection (Writings)	Chronological and Historical: Creation → Patriarchs → Kingdoms → Exile → Prophecy
Final Focus	Chronicles: Restoration & Return	Malachi: Messianic Expectation

5.2 Section-by-Section Breakdown

Hebrew Bible	Christian Old Testament

Hebrew Bible

1. Torah (Law)

- Genesis

- Exodus

- Leviticus

- Numbers

- Deuteronomy

2. Nevi'im (Prophets)

- Joshua

- Judges

- Samuel (1 & 2)

- Kings (1 & 2)

- Isaiah

- Jeremiah

- Ezekiel

- The Twelve (Minor Prophets)

Christian Old Testament

1. Pentateuch (5 Scrolls)

- Genesis

- Exodus

- Leviticus

- Numbers

- Deuteronomy

2. Historical Books

- Joshua

- Judges

- Ruth

- Samuel (1 & 2)

- Kings (1 & 2)

- Chronicles (1 & 2)

- Ezra

- Nehemiah

- Esther

3. Wisdom Literature

- Job

- Psalms

- Proverbs

- Ecclesiastes

- Song of Solomon

3. Ketuvim (Writings)

- Psalms

- Proverbs

- Job

- Song of Songs

- Ruth

- Lamentations

- Ecclesiastes

- Esther

- Daniel

- Ezra-Nehemiah

- Chronicles (1 & 2)

4. Major Prophets

- Isaiah

- Jeremiah

- Lamentations

- Ezekiel

- Daniel

5. Minor Prophets

- Hosea

- Joel

- Amos

- Obadiah

- Jonah

- Micah

- Nahum

- Habakkuk

- Zephaniah

- Haggai

- Zechariah

- Malachi

6. Key Differences Summarized

Key Insight: The arrangement of scripture isn't trivial—it shapes how we understand God's story, His covenant, and our role within it.

6.1 Grouping and Purpose

The **Law, Prophets and Writings** (Modern Hebrew Bible) and the modern **Christian Old Testament** share the same books but arrange them differently, and this difference carries profound theological consequences.

Law, Prophets and Writings Structure:
- **Torah (Law):** The foundation of God's covenant and commandments.
- **Prophets (Nevi'im):** The enforcers and amplifiers of the Torah's message, calling Israel back to obedience.
- **Writings (Ketuvim):** Reflections, worship, and wisdom built on the Torah's foundation.

Christian Old Testament Structure:
- **Pentateuch:** The same first five foundational books, but often interpreted as historical curiosity rather than an eternal covenant.
- **History:** Books like Joshua, Judges, Samuel, and Kings are grouped as historical narratives rather than prophetic warnings rooted in the Torah.
- **Poetry:** Psalms, Proverbs, Ecclesiastes, and Song of Solomon are removed from their covenantal context and treated as isolated poetic or philosophical works.
- **Prophecy:** Divided into **Major Prophets** and **Minor Prophets**, placed at the end of the Old Testament as a prelude to the New Testament.

Why It Matters:

- The **Law, Prophets and Writings** maintains a theological flow: Commandment → Correction → Reflection.
- The **Christian Old Testament** shifts to a narrative emphasis: Law → History → Philosophy → Prediction.

Takeaway: The Law, Prophets and Writings emphasizes obedience, covenant faithfulness, and reflection, while the Christian Old Testament reorients the narrative toward prophetic fulfillment and messianic anticipation.

6.2 The Prophets Are Fragmented in the Old Testament

In the **Law, Prophets and Writings**, the Prophets (Nevi'im) form a **single cohesive section** that amplifies the Torah and calls Israel back to obedience. They are not treated as predictors of distant future events but as covenant enforcers operating within their historical contexts.

Prophets in Tanakh:

- Early Prophets (e.g., Joshua, Judges, Samuel, Kings)
- Later Prophets (e.g., Isaiah, Jeremiah, Ezekiel, and the Twelve Minor Prophets)

In the **Christian Old Testament**, the Prophets are split into two categories:

1. **Major Prophets:** Isaiah, Jeremiah, Lamentations, Ezekiel, Daniel.
2. **Minor Prophets:** Hosea, Joel, Amos, Obadiah, etc.

Consequences of Fragmentation:

- The **historical context** of prophetic books is often obscured.
- Prophets are viewed primarily as **fortune-tellers** rather than covenant watchdogs.

- Their connection to the **Torah** is weakened, and their role in calling Israel back to obedience is downplayed.

Takeaway: In the Law, Prophets and Writings, the Prophets are covenant enforcers; in the Christian Old Testament, they are often reduced to messianic predictors.

6.3 Ending Focus

The **final book** of a sacred text carries significant weight—it sets the tone for how the text is understood as a whole.

In the Hebraic Understanding and modern Tanakh: The final book is **Chronicles**, which ends with a **call to restoration** and an invitation to return to Jerusalem and rebuild the Temple.

- The focus is on **covenantal renewal** and the continuation of God's plan with His people.
- It emphasizes **reflection, hope, and responsibility.**

In the Christian Old Testament: The final book is **Malachi**, which ends with a **messianic expectation** and a warning of coming judgment.

- The focus shifts to **anticipation of a Savior** and the need for repentance before a coming divine intervention.
- It sets the stage for the **New Testament narrative** rather than closing with a call to covenantal reflection.

Why This Matters:

- The **Law, Prophets and Writings** concludes with an **invitation to action**—a responsibility to rebuild and return.
- The **Christian Old Testament** concludes with a **sense of waiting**—a passive anticipation of a messianic figure.

Takeaway: The Law, Prophets and Writings ends with **restoration and responsibility**; the Christian Old Testament ends with **waiting and expectation**. This subtle difference shapes the reader's relationship with the text.

Why It Matters

The understood structure of scripture isn't arbitrary—it's **theological architecture** designed to guide the reader toward YHWH's covenantal purpose.

- **The Law, Prophets and Writings' Structure:** Preserves the covenantal focus of scripture, with the Torah as its immovable foundation.
- **The Christian Old Testament's Structure:** Shifts focus toward prophecy fulfillment and messianic anticipation, subtly altering the overarching message.

Why This Matters for Us Today:

- **Misreading the Prophets:** Prophets are reduced to predictors of future events rather than voices calling for obedience.
- **Neglecting the Torah:** The Torah becomes an "old, obsolete law" rather than an eternal covenant.
- **Losing the Writings' Purpose:** Psalms and Proverbs become self-help quotes rather than reflections grounded in covenant living.

Final Takeaway: Loss of Jesus's scriptural lens hampered the reader's relationship with God's Word. Understanding these structural differences is essential for approaching the Bible as Jesus and His earliest followers understood it.

6.4 The Shift from Covenant to Creed

Key Insight: Hebraic faith emphasizes *covenantal obedience*—a life lived in alignment with God's commands. Rearrangement gradually shifted the emphasis toward *intellectual assent* and creedal formulas.

Covenant in Hebraic Thought:
- Faith is demonstrated through active, obedient living.
- God's people are judged not merely by their beliefs but by their actions, their alignment with His commandments, and their commitment to community holiness.

Creed in Hellenistic Influence:
- As Greco-Roman influence grew, faith became increasingly intellectualized.
- Belief became measured by creedal statements—doctrines codified into intellectual checklists rather than embodied obedience.

The Core Shift:
- **Covenant Obedience:** Faith is expressed by living in alignment with God's commands.
- **Creedal Assent:** Faith is expressed by subscribing to specific doctrinal statements.

Takeaway: When covenant is replaced by creed, obedience becomes optional instead of essential. Faith becomes something to *agree with*, rather than something to *live out*.

6.5 Theological Fog: Doctrine Over Obedience

Key Insight: Theology was never meant to replace obedience—it was meant to *inform* it.

When theology becomes an end in itself, it creates a fog that obscures the path of faith.

The Role of Theology in Hebraic Thought:
- Theology serves as a tool for better obedience to God.
- Scripture is approached as a guide for righteous living, not as a set of abstract philosophical puzzles.

The Role of Theology in Post-Rearrangement Christianity:
- Theology became an academic exercise.
- Faith became about *believing the right things* rather than *doing the right things*.

A Clear Example:

- **Hebraic Focus:** "Do this, and you will live." (Deuteronomy 30:16)
- **Modern Focus:** "Believe this, and you will be saved."

One emphasizes *action*, the other emphasizes *intellectual acceptance*. While both have a place, the rearranged emphasis leans heavily toward intellectual assent, creating an imbalance.

Takeaway: Theology should *serve* obedience, not replace it. Scripture was given to guide life, not to provide endless fodder for abstract debates.

6.6 Why This Matters Going Forward

Key Insight: The theological drift caused by rearrangement and misinterpretation wasn't an overnight event. It was a gradual unraveling that occurred over centuries. But unraveling is reversible. These distortions had cascading effects:

- **The Role of the Torah:** Reduced from an eternal covenant to a historical footnote.
- **The Purpose of the Prophets:** Distorted into fortune-telling rather than covenant enforcement.
- **The Context of the Writings:** Disconnected from their foundation in Torah obedience.

This unraveling isn't merely a historical curiosity—it impacts how we approach scripture today:

- Churches teach "grace vs. law" as if they are opposing forces.
- Prophetic books are used for speculative eschatology rather than moral accountability.
- Psalms are treated as comforting poetry, ignoring their covenantal context.

But this isn't where the story ends. Understanding *where* and *why* these shifts occurred equips us to retrace our steps:

- **Back to the Torah:** Rediscovering it as the living foundation of faith.
- **Back to the Prophets:** Hearing their calls to covenant faithfulness.
- **Back to the Writings:** Reflecting on life in alignment with God's commandments.

A Glimpse Ahead:
The following Inquiries will begin unraveling these distortions:

- **Inquiry 2:** Who Was Jesus—and Who Wasn't He?
- **Inquiry 3:** How do we Best Interpret the Prophets?

Takeaway: The path back begins with understanding *where* things went wrong, *why* they went wrong, and having the courage to retrace our steps to God's foundation.

Section 6 Takeaway

The loss of Jesus's understanding of scriptural hierarchy was not a neutral occurrence — it had profound implications in Pauline theology.

- **From Torah as foundation to historical curiosity.**
- **From prophetic correction to distant predictions.**
- **From reflective wisdom to isolated philosophy.**

This isn't about nostalgia—it's about rediscovering the *spiritual architecture* God designed for His Word. By identifying the structure Jesus followed in his teachings, we can begin to rebuild our understanding and return to God's original intent.

---

7. Translation and Interpretation Issues

Key Insight: Every translation introduces subtle shifts in meaning that, over time, reshape how scripture is understood and applied. The earliest major translation—the *Septuagint*—brought both accessibility and unintended philosophical influence, creating interpretive layers foreign to Hebraic thought.

The act of translating scripture is not neutral. Words are not mathematical equations—they carry cultural, emotional, and philosophical weight. When scripture is moved from one language to another, it doesn't simply shift letters and syllables; it shifts context, tone, and, sometimes, even intent. Nowhere is this more evident than in the translation of the Hebrew Bible into Greek, known as the *Septuagint*.

7.1 The Septuagint: Greek Translation and Influence

Key Insight: The *Septuagint* (LXX) represents a pivotal moment in the history of scripture. As the earliest translation of the Hebrew scripture into Greek, it made God's Word accessible to Greek-speaking Jews of the diaspora but also unintentionally introduced foreign philosophical influences into Hebraic theology.

By the 3rd century BC, the Jewish world was changing rapidly. Alexander the Great's conquests had spread Hellenistic culture and language across the known world. In Alexandria, Egypt—a major intellectual and cultural hub—many Jews had become more fluent in Greek than in Hebrew.

For these diaspora communities, the Hebrew scriptures were becoming increasingly inaccessible.

The *Septuagint* emerged as a solution. Tradition tells us that around 70–72 Jewish scholars (hence the name *Septuagint*, Latin for *seventy*) were commissioned to translate the Torah into Greek under the patronage of King Ptolemy II Philadelphus.

This initial translation of the Torah was later followed by translations of the Prophets and Writings.

The Dual Impact of the Septuagint:

- **Accessibility:** The translation made scripture available to Greek-speaking Jews, preserving their connection to their faith amidst linguistic and cultural assimilation.
- **Philosophical Drift:** Greek, as a language, carried with it cultural assumptions and philosophical frameworks. When Hebrew concepts were translated into Greek, they were filtered through a worldview shaped by Plato, Aristotle, and Stoic philosophy.

Takeaway: The *Septuagint* was a monumental achievement, making scripture accessible to diaspora Jews. But it also marked the beginning of subtle philosophical shifts in how core Hebraic concepts were understood and interpreted.

7.2 Why the Septuagint Was Created

Key Insight: The *Septuagint* was born out of necessity. It was a practical solution to the linguistic and cultural challenges faced by Jewish diaspora communities.

The Historical Context:

- **Hellenization:** Alexander the Great's empire spread Greek language and culture across the ancient Near East. Greek became the *lingua franca*—the common language of trade, governance, and intellectual life.
- **Diaspora Realities:** Many Jewish communities, particularly in Alexandria, were no longer fluent in Hebrew. Without access to scripture in a language they understood, the risk of spiritual and cultural disconnection grew.
- **Alexandria as a Hub:** Alexandria was home to one of the largest Jewish communities outside of Israel and boasted a renowned library. It was a center of learning, and Greek was its academic language.

The Motivation for Translation:

- **Preservation of Faith:** Jewish leaders recognized that without scripture in a comprehensible language, their communities would drift into cultural and spiritual assimilation.
- **Educational Utility:** The *Septuagint* became not just a spiritual tool but also an educational one, helping younger generations remain connected to their faith heritage.
- **Outreach:** The translation also made Jewish beliefs more intelligible to non-Jews, indirectly laying groundwork for future dialogues between Judaism and emerging Christian theology.

A Monumental Achievement, Yet an Unintended Shift:
The translators of the *Septuagint* were well-meaning, faithful scholars. Their work preserved access to scripture for countless generations.

However, no translation is perfect. The shift from Hebrew to Greek was not just linguistic—it was *philosophical*.

Takeaway: The *Septuagint* was a necessary adaptation to preserve scripture's accessibility. But its reliance on Greek language and thought created unavoidable interpretive distortions.

7.3 How Greek Philosophical Thought Influenced Translation Choices

Key Insight: Language isn't just about words—it's about worldview.

The Greek language brought linguistic precision but also philosophical biases that subtly reshaped Hebraic concepts.

Key Differences Between Hebraic and Greek Worldviews:

- **Hebraic Thought:** Holistic, relational, concrete. Life, faith, and creation are viewed as interconnected realities bound by covenant.
- **Greek Thought:** Abstract, dualistic, categorical. Spirit and body are often seen as separate realms, with spirit elevated above matter.

Linguistic Case Study: Nephesh vs. Psyche

- In Hebrew, the word *nephesh* is often translated as "soul," but its meaning is far more holistic. It refers to the entirety of a person—their body, breath, life force, and being.
- In Greek, *psyche* carries a more disembodied meaning. It suggests a soul or mind distinct from the physical body.
- The subtle shift from *nephesh* to *psyche* changed how generations of readers viewed the relationship between spirit and body. The holistic Hebraic understanding gave way to Greek dualism, which would later influence doctrines about the afterlife, resurrection, and even salvation.

Greek Abstraction vs. Hebraic Relationality:

- In Hebrew, concepts like *righteousness*, *faithfulness*, and *love* are not abstract ideals—they are expressed through action and relationship.
- In Greek, these same concepts often became intellectualized, detached from their relational roots.

Theological Consequences:

- The Hebrew understanding of *shalom* (peace) is deeply relational, encompassing wholeness and harmony in all areas of life.
- The Greek *eirene* (peace) carries a more static connotation, often reduced to the absence of conflict rather than the presence of covenantal wholeness.

The Lens of Translation:

Each translation is like a pair of glasses—it sharpens some details and blurs others. The *Septuagint* made scripture more widely accessible, but it also introduced subtle distortions shaped by Greek philosophical assumptions.

Takeaway: The *Septuagint* wasn't just a change in language—it was a change in worldview. These philosophical shifts have rippled across centuries, influencing not only Jewish thought but also the emerging Christian theology.

Why It Matters

The *Septuagint* was a monumental achievement, but it came with unintended consequences.

- Hebrew's relational, covenantal worldview was subtly filtered through Greek abstraction and dualism.
- Concepts like *soul*, *peace*, and *righteousness* took on new shades of meaning, influencing theological development for generations.

Understanding the strengths and limitations of the *Septuagint* equips us to approach scripture with both gratitude and discernment. We can appreciate its historical importance while being vigilant about the subtle shifts it introduced.

7.4 Example: Isaiah 7:14 "Virgin" vs. "Young Woman"

Key Insight: Small translation choices can have outsized theological consequences, reshaping entire doctrines over time. Isaiah 7:14 is one of the most famous examples of how a single word can carry profound implications.

The Original Hebrew: Context and Nuance

The "Great Isaiah Scroll", an archeological find in the Qumran caves and part of the Dead Sea Scrolls, dated to between 200 BC and 1 AD In the original Hebrew, reveals a control-text of Isaiah 7:14, showing that the word originally used in this verse was *"almah"*, which primarily means *"young woman"* or *"maiden."*

While the word *implies* virginity due to cultural expectations of a young, unmarried woman, it does not explicitly mean *"virgin."*

The verse in Hebrew reads:
"Behold, the young woman ("almah") shall conceive and bear a son, and shall call his name Immanuel."

The immediate context of Isaiah 7:14 was a prophecy delivered to King Ahaz of Judah during a time of political crisis.

The prophecy was meant to serve as a *sign* of hope and divine intervention within Ahaz's lifetime—a child born as a symbol of God's presence (*Immanuel* meaning *"God with us"*).

The Greek Translation: A Shift in Emphasis

When the Hebrew Bible was translated into Greek in the *Septuagint*, the word *'almah'* was rendered as *'parthenos'*, which explicitly means *"virgin."* This word choice introduced a significant theological shift:

- **In Hebrew:** A young woman would conceive, implying an immediate, contextual fulfillment of the prophecy.
- **In Greek:** A virgin would conceive, introducing a miraculous and messianic expectation into the prophecy.

The Greek rendering of *parthenos* became foundational in later Christian understandings of Isaiah 7:14 as a prophecy specifically foretelling the virgin birth of Jesus (*Matthew 1:23*).

Theological Consequences

This small linguistic shift has had profound theological ripple effects:

- **Doctrinal Debates:** Isaiah 7:14 became a cornerstone for doctrines surrounding the virgin birth of Jesus, leading to debates over the accuracy of translations and the nature of biblical prophecy.
- **Contextual Disconnect:** Many readers focus exclusively on the messianic interpretation of Isaiah 7:14, missing its original historical purpose as a sign to Ahaz.
- **Proof-Texting Pitfall:** The verse has often been wielded in apologetics as a "proof text" for Jesus's divinity, sometimes at the expense of engaging with the passage's original meaning and context.

Takeaway: Isaiah 7:14 is a case study in how translation choices can create theological weight beyond the original text's intent.

Both interpretations (immediate historical sign and messianic fulfillment) are valid, but they must be held together without distorting either.

7.5 Why This Matters Today

Key Insight: The *Septuagint* became the primary Old Testament text for early Christianity, shaping theological development for centuries. Its strengths and shortcomings continue to echo into modern biblical interpretation.

The Septuagint as a Double-Edged Sword

- **Accessibility:** The *Septuagint* made scripture widely available to Greek-speaking Jewish communities and later to early Christians. This was a tremendous blessing, preserving access to God's word amidst cultural and linguistic shifts.
- **Philosophical Layers:** The Greek language, while precise, brought with it philosophical assumptions that subtly redefined key Hebraic concepts. Words like *nephesh* (soul) became *psyche*, introducing dualism into theological interpretation.
- **Doctrinal Frameworks:** The *Septuagint's* word choices and interpretive shifts laid the groundwork for later theological constructs that sometimes drifted from Hebraic relational covenant into abstract philosophical speculation.

Inherited Interpretive Layers

Modern readers often inherit these interpretive layers without even realizing it:

- Many approach scripture with a Greek dualistic mindset, separating body and spirit in ways foreign to Hebraic thought.
- Prophetic texts are often read through a lens of predictive fortune-telling rather than covenantal correction.

- Complex doctrines are sometimes built on single translated words (*parthenos* vs. *'almah*) without acknowledging the context of those choices.

The Responsibility of Modern Readers

- **Context Awareness:** Understand the historical, cultural, and linguistic layers behind our modern translations.
- **Hebraic Mindset:** Seek to recover the relational and covenantal essence of scripture.
- **Integration, Not Division:** Avoid creating false dichotomies between Old Testament and New Testament, law and grace, or body and spirit.

Takeaway: The *Septuagint* was both a blessing and a cautionary tale. It preserved scripture for a scattered people but also introduced philosophical layers that continue to shape—and sometimes distort—our understanding of God's word.

7.6 Section Takeaway:

Key Insight: The *Septuagint* played a critical role in preserving and sharing scripture with Greek-speaking Jewish communities, but it also became a doorway for Greek philosophical thought to influence the interpretation of God's word.

- The *Septuagint* was a practical response to linguistic challenges in a Hellenized world.
- It introduced Greek philosophical categories into Hebraic theology, subtly reshaping key ideas.
- Examples like Isaiah 7:14 highlight how single word choices can create doctrinal ripples felt across millennia.

Why This Still Matters:

- Modern readers often approach scripture through inherited interpretive layers from the *Septuagint* and later theological traditions.
- Recovering a Hebraic mindset helps restore the relational, covenantal essence of God's word.

Final Takeaway: Understanding the strengths and limitations of the *Septuagint* allows us to approach scripture with clarity and discernment.

It's not about rejecting translations but about recognizing their influence and returning to the original relational framework intended by YHWH.

This foundation prepares us to examine the *Vulgate*—Latin's influence on scripture, theology, and Christian tradition.

---

8 The Vulgate: Latin Standardization and Transformation

Key Insight: Jerome's Latin Vulgate became the official Old Testament in the Bible of the Roman Church, but its translation choices and framing reflected Roman priorities rather than Hebraic covenantal intimacy. This shift further distanced Christianity from its Hebraic roots, emphasizing imperial majesty over relational covenant.

8.1 How Jerome's Translation Became the Church's Official Scripture

Jerome's *Latin Vulgate* was not merely a translation—it was a transformative moment in the history of scripture.

It centralized authority, solidified a standardized text, and unintentionally reinforced the growing distance between Christianity and its Hebraic roots.

The Commissioning of Jerome

In AD 382: Pope Damasus I recognized the fragmentation of biblical texts and interpretations within the Latin-speaking Western Church. Different regions used various Latin translations (*Vetus Latina*), many of which were inconsistent and riddled with translational errors. To address this, Damasus commissioned Eusebius Sophronius Hieronymus—better known as Jerome—to produce a single, authoritative Latin version of the Bible.

- **Why Jerome?** Jerome was one of the most skilled linguists and scholars of his time. He was fluent in **Latin, Greek, and Hebrew**, an incredibly rare combination among Western scholars.
- **The Goal:** Create a standardized, universally accepted Latin Bible that could be used across the Roman Empire, promoting doctrinal unity and liturgical consistency.
- **The Challenge:** Jerome had to navigate differences between the **proto-Masoretic texts**, the **Greek Septuagint (LXX)**, and the pre-existing **Old Latin translations** (Vetus Latina).

The Process of Translation

Jerome's approach combined scholarship, theological conviction, and, to some degree, political pragmatism.

- He began by translating the **Gospels** from Greek into Latin.
- He then turned his focus to the **Old Testament**, consulting both the **Septuagint** and **Hebrew texts** available to him.
- Jerome spent considerable time in **Bethlehem**, working closely with **Jewish rabbis** to improve his understanding of the original Hebrew texts.

However:

- While Jerome valued the Hebrew texts, he still leaned heavily on the *Septuagint* for many sections, especially where Hebrew manuscripts were unclear or unavailable.
- His translation choices were shaped not only by linguistic fidelity but also by the **theological and cultural expectations of the Roman Church**.

The Vulgate as the Official Bible

By **AD 405**, Jerome completed his monumental task, and the *Latin Vulgate* was born.

- The term *"Vulgate"* comes from the Latin word *vulgata*, meaning *"common"* or *"for the people."*
- It became the **official Bible of the Roman Catholic Church** and remained so for over **1,000 years**.
- The *Vulgate* was declared the **standard text at the Council of Trent (1545–1563)** in response to the Protestant Reformation.

Why the Vulgate Became So Influential

- **Linguistic Accessibility:** Latin was the *lingua franca* of the Western Roman Empire, allowing the Bible to be read and understood by clergy and educated elites across vast territories.
- **Institutional Authority:** By centralizing scriptural interpretation under an officially sanctioned text, the Church solidified its role as the *exclusive custodian of biblical truth.*
- **Liturgical Use:** The *Vulgate* became the foundation for Catholic liturgy, prayers, and theology.

Strengths of the Vulgate:

- It brought *consistency* and *unity* to scripture in the Western Church.
- Jerome's scholarship was rigorous, and his attempt to consult Hebrew sources was admirable.

Weaknesses of the Vulgate:

- Translation choices sometimes prioritized **Roman theological priorities** over Hebraic relational intent.
- Latin, while precise, couldn't always capture the relational nuances of Hebrew terms (e.g., *nephesh* vs. *anima*).
- The Vulgate reinforced the **centralization of authority**, limiting independent study and interpretation.

Jerome's Dilemma

Jerome was a complex figure—a bridge between two worlds:

- On one hand, he deeply respected the **Hebrew scriptures** and sought fidelity to their meaning.
- On the other hand, he operated within the framework of an **imperial church** that valued doctrinal uniformity and centralized control.

This tension is evident throughout the Vulgate. Some sections preserve Hebraic nuance, while others bear the mark of Roman institutional priorities.

Takeaway: Jerome's *Latin Vulgate* was a milestone in biblical history, making scripture accessible to the Western world while simultaneously embedding Roman theological and cultural priorities into its translation. It became both a triumph of scholarship and a tool of institutional control.

Transition to 8.2:

The *Vulgate* didn't just translate words—it reframed theological priorities. It carried the weight of Roman authority and became a pillar of the Western Church. But every translation carries its biases, and the Vulgate was no exception. In the next section, we'll explore how **Roman priorities shaped the theological framing of scripture**, subtly but powerfully reshaping Christianity's understanding of God's covenant.

8.2 How Roman Priorities Shaped Theological Framing

Key Insight: Language is not just a tool for communication—it's a carrier of culture, philosophy, and worldview. When the Bible transitioned from Hebrew (and Greek) to Latin, the words retained their shape, but their *tone* subtly shifted, reshaping how key theological principles were understood.

Latin vs. Hebrew: A Clash of Worldviews

The Hebrew language is deeply **relational** and **covenantal**.

- Words are action-oriented, emphasizing lived experience and ongoing relationship.
- The covenant between YHWH and His people is portrayed as a marriage, a familial bond, or a shepherd caring for sheep.
- The focus is on *"knowing God"* (a deeply intimate term in Hebrew) rather than *"understanding doctrine."*

Latin, by contrast, emerged from the legal and administrative backbone of the Roman Empire.

- Words carry connotations of **imperial authority**, **legal precision**, and **institutional hierarchy**.
- Latin prioritizes *command* and *compliance* over *intimacy* and *reciprocity*.
- The Roman worldview was one of **top-down governance**—order imposed from above rather than nurtured through relationship.

Theological Concepts Reframed

When scripture transitioned into Latin via the Vulgate, these cultural lenses subtly reframed key theological principles:

1. **Covenant → Contract**
    - **In Hebrew,** *berit* (covenant) is a sacred, relational agreement bound by love, loyalty, and mutual responsibility.
    - **In Latin,** *foedus* (contract) emphasizes legal terms, obligations, and consequences for breaches.
    - This shift made God's covenant with humanity feel less like a marriage and more like a legal contract—conditional, transactional, and enforceable by penalty.
2. **Faith → Intellectual Assent**
    - **In Hebrew,** *emunah* (faith) implies steadfast loyalty, trust, and active faithfulness.

- **In Latin,** *fides* often leans towards belief in doctrine—an intellectual acknowledgment of theological truths.
- Faith transitioned from *"living in trust with God"* to *"believing the right creeds."*

3. **Obedience → Institutional Compliance**
   - **In Hebrew,** *shema* (hear and obey) is a heart-oriented call to listen, internalize, and act out of love and devotion.
   - **In Latin,** *obedire* (to obey) implies following orders, adhering to regulations, and submitting to hierarchical authority.
   - Obedience became less about aligning one's heart with God's will and more about following church mandates and rules.

The Church's Growing Institutional Control

The shift from relational covenant to institutional contract didn't happen overnight, but the Vulgate played a key role in accelerating this transformation.

- The *Vulgate* became the **exclusive scriptural authority** within the Western Church.
- Access to scripture was centralized under **clergy and ecclesiastical courts**.
- Interpretation became **monopolized by scholars and priests**, removing scripture from the hands of the common people.

What was once a communal, participatory relationship with God's word became a **top-down transmission of doctrinal truth.**

- The average believer became a **passive receiver** rather than an **active participant** in covenantal living.
- Church leaders became the **gatekeepers** of scripture, determining what could or couldn't be questioned or interpreted independently.

The Consequences of Theological Framing

- **Sacraments replaced relational intimacy:** Ritual observance became a means of compliance rather than an expression of love.
- **Legalism overpowered spiritual renewal:** Rules, punishments, and institutional structures became more central than inward transformation.
- **Hierarchy overshadowed humility:** The majesty of Rome subtly replaced the humility of a shepherd-king God.

Not All Bad, But Not All Good

It's important to recognize that Jerome himself was not malicious in his intentions.

- He was a scholar doing his best under the constraints of his time and culture.
- The *Vulgate* preserved scripture for a vast population and prevented even greater fragmentation in the Western Church.

However, the unintended consequences of this linguistic and cultural shift are undeniable. The relational intimacy of scripture—its call to walk humbly with God—was buried under layers of imperial grandeur and institutional rigidity.

Takeaway: The *Vulgate* transformed scripture from a **living relational guide** into a **legalistic framework for institutional control**. Words that once called people into intimate covenant with YHWH became tools for maintaining ecclesiastical order. Understanding this shift helps us see how layers of institutional tradition have sometimes obscured the living heartbeat of scripture.

Transition to 8.3:

The transition from Hebraic intimacy to Latin majesty wasn't just about language—it was about *worldview*. The next section will explore how the relational warmth of Hebrew scripture was gradually replaced by the imperial grandeur of Latin framing. This shift had profound consequences for how God was portrayed, worshipped, and understood.

8.3 Hebraic Intimacy Became Latin Majesty

Key Insight: The transition from Hebrew to Latin didn't just change the words of scripture—it reshaped how people perceived their relationship with God. A relational, covenantal Father became a distant, imperial Sovereign.

Hebraic Intimacy: A Covenant of Relationship

In the Hebrew scriptures, the relationship between God (YHWH) and His people is portrayed through **deeply intimate metaphors** drawn from human experience:

- **A Father caring for His children:** *"As a father has compassion on his children, so the Lord has compassion on those who fear Him."* (Psalm 103:13)
- **A Husband devoted to His bride:** *"I will betroth you to Me forever; I will betroth you in righteousness and justice, in love and compassion."* (Hosea 2:19)
- **A Shepherd guiding His flock:** *"The Lord is my shepherd; I shall not want."* (Psalm 23:1)
- **A Redeemer rescuing the captive:** *"I am the Lord, your Holy One, Israel's Creator, your King."* (Isaiah 43:15)

These metaphors emphasize **tenderness, care, and personal devotion.** They invite believers to experience God not as a distant authority figure but as someone deeply invested in their lives.

The Hebrew word *chesed* beautifully encapsulates this relational warmth. It describes:

- **Loving-kindness:** God's active and faithful love for His people.
- **Steadfast loyalty:** An unbreakable covenant commitment.
- **Compassionate mercy:** God's willingness to forgive and restore.

In Hebrew thought, God's love isn't abstract—it's deeply **experiential, immersive, and relational.** It's a love expressed not just in lofty ideals but in tangible acts of faithfulness.

Latin Majesty: The Distant Sovereign

As scripture transitioned into Latin through Jerome's *Vulgate*, the relational intimacy of these Hebraic metaphors was subtly reshaped by the linguistic and cultural lenses of the Roman Empire.

- Latin was the **language of law, governance, and empire.**
- It carried a natural gravitation towards terms emphasizing **hierarchy, authority, and subjugation.**

Where Hebrew portrays YHWH as a Father or Shepherd, Latin often framed Him as:

- **A King ruling from an unreachable throne:** Majestic, sovereign, and distant.
- **A Magistrate enforcing divine law:** The final arbiter of guilt and innocence.
- **A Judge pronouncing unchallengeable decrees:** Authority was central, and relational intimacy became secondary.

The word *chesed*—so rich with relational warmth—lost some of its tenderness in translation. In Latin, it was often rendered as:

- *Misericordia* (mercy): Emphasizing pity and condescension from a position of authority.
- *Fidelitas* (faithfulness): Highlighting loyalty as an obligation rather than an act of love.
- *Justitia* (justice): Framing love within a legal and transactional paradigm.

These shifts weren't malicious, nor were they entirely avoidable—they were products of linguistic and cultural differences. However, their **cumulative effect** was profound:

- God felt **more distant** to the average believer.
- Worship became **more hierarchical and ritualistic.**
- Faith shifted from an **intimate covenant bond** to an **obedient legal contract.**

The Temple to the Throne: A Subtle Shift in Worship

Hebraic worship was grounded in the **Temple model**:

- A shared space where God's presence dwelled among His people.
- Priests acted as mediators, but they didn't monopolize access to God.
- The faithful approached God through sacrifice, prayer, and communal worship.

In the Latinized framework, worship began to reflect the **Imperial Throne Room model**:

- God became a **distant Emperor**, accessed through layers of intermediaries.
- The clergy became **gatekeepers of divine favor**.
- Rituals and sacraments became **legal obligations** rather than relational acts of love.

The *relational heart of faith*—trust, intimacy, and mutual devotion—was gradually replaced by an *imperial model of faith*—authority, compliance, and duty.

The Human Experience of Faith Was Transformed

Imagine two different relationships with a father:

1. **The Hebraic Father:** A dad kneeling down, arms open, welcoming his child to climb into his lap.
2. **The Latin Magistrate:** A judge seated on a high bench, sternly handing down decrees while the child trembles below.

The relationship is fundamentally different. One is built on **trust and vulnerability**, the other on **authority and fear**.

- **Hebraic Faith:** A dance of love, trust, and loyalty.
- **Latinized Faith:** A rigid march of compliance and obligation.

This transformation had ripple effects:

- **Theological Coldness:** God felt less like *Abba, Father* and more like *Deus, Dominus.*
- **Spiritual Distance:** Believers felt separated from God by layers of institutional authority.
- **Legalism Over Relationship:** Faith became more about rules than about love.

Restoring the Balance: Relational Majesty.
It's essential to clarify: God's majesty isn't the problem.

- **God *is* King.**
- **God *is* Sovereign.**
- **God *is* Ruler of all creation.**

But God is also:

- **Abba, Father.**
- **Shepherd of the sheep.**
- **The One who knows every hair on your head.**

Majesty and intimacy are not mutually exclusive. The problem arises when one **overshadows** the other. In the transition to Latin, majesty overwhelmed intimacy, and something vital was lost.

Takeaway: The transition from Hebraic intimacy to Latin majesty was not inherently evil, but it carried unintended consequences. It reframed God from being an intimate Father to a distant Emperor, from a relational Shepherd to an imposing Judge.

Faith became colder, more distant, and more legalistic. Today, rediscovering the **Hebraic intimacy of God's covenant** is not about rejecting His majesty—it's about balancing it.

God is both **King of Kings** and **Abba, Father.** To fully understand Him, we must hold both truths in harmony.

Transition to 8.4:

Translation is never neutral, and language carries worldview. As we move forward, we'll explore **further translation and interpretation issues**—subtle shifts and choices that have shaped how we understand scripture today. These aren't just academic points—they have profound spiritual consequences. Let's turn to **8.5 Further Translation and Interpretation Issues** and unpack these threads.

The long-term consequences of these shifts on key doctrines.

Key Takeaway: Language is not a neutral tool—it carries cultural and philosophical baggage.

8.4 Why This Matters Today

Key Insight: The Vulgate wasn't just a translation—it became the dominant *lens* through which scripture was understood for over a millennium. Its influence reshaped not only theology but also the average believer's relationship with God.

A Locked Book: Gatekeeping Scripture

When Jerome completed the Vulgate, it became the official Bible of the Roman Catholic Church. Over time, this translation wasn't merely *a version* of scripture—it became *the version.*

- **Language Barrier:** As Latin gradually ceased to be a common spoken language among the laity, scripture became increasingly inaccessible.
- **Centralized Control:** Only the clergy, trained in Latin, could read and interpret scripture.
- **Dependence on Authority:** Believers became dependent on institutional gatekeepers for their understanding of God's word.

Scripture was no longer something an individual or family could study and discuss—it was something delivered from the pulpit, mediated by institutional authority.

Key Shift: Faith transitioned from an *intimate covenant with YHWH* to *obedience to the institution that represented Him.*

The Shift from Participation to Passivity

In Hebraic tradition:

- Scripture was *recited, sung, discussed,* and *lived out* within communal settings.
- Every person—man, woman, child—was invited into the conversation of faith.

Under the Vulgate's reign:

- Scripture was *read aloud* by the clergy.
- The congregation became *passive listeners* rather than active participants.
- Discussion and dialogue gave way to ritual repetition and institutional enforcement.

Over time, the *dynamic relationship with God's word* was replaced with *static compliance to church teaching.*

The Loss of Relational Intimacy

The relational warmth of Hebraic scripture—the Fatherly love of YHWH, the Shepherd's care, the tender covenant bond—was gradually overshadowed by a colder, hierarchical dynamic:

- **YHWH became "Deus Rex" (God the King).**
- **Intimacy became formality.**
- **Love became obligation.**

The theological shift was subtle but profound:

- The focus moved from *knowing God* to *obeying the church.*

- Personal relationship gave way to corporate compliance.

While obedience to God and communal worship are essential, the relational **"why"** behind obedience was often lost.

Legalism Over Covenant

The legalistic overtones of Latin translated words reframed faith:

- **Sin** became less about *breaking a covenant* and more about *violating a law.*
- **Repentance** became less about *returning to relationship* and more about *performing penance.*
- **Worship** became less about *connection with YHWH* and more about *ritualized duty.*

This wasn't merely a theological abstraction—it was felt in the daily lives of believers.

- Worship felt distant.
- God felt unreachable.
- Faith felt transactional.

The result? Generations of believers experienced faith as a **cold institution** rather than a **living relationship.**

A Controlled Narrative

The institutional dominance of the Vulgate allowed for the creation of *a controlled narrative.*

- Select passages could be emphasized, while others were neglected.
- Interpretations were standardized, leaving little room for individual or community exploration.
- The Bible became an *authority to be enforced* rather than a *conversation to be shared.*

When scripture becomes a tool of institutional control, its *living, breathing power* is stifled.

The Reformation as a Reaction to the Vulgate

The Protestant Reformation wasn't merely about theological disagreements—it was a **response to centuries of institutional control over scripture.**

- Reformers like Martin Luther translated the Bible into vernacular languages, breaking the monopoly of the Latin Vulgate.
- The goal was to *return scripture to the people.*
- The battle cry was *"Sola Scriptura"*—Scripture alone as the highest authority.

However, while the Reformation restored access to scripture, it didn't fully restore *Hebraic relational intimacy.*

Much of Western Christianity remained shaped by:

- Theological abstraction.
- Doctrinal infighting.
- Legalistic interpretations.

The damage caused by centuries of institutional gatekeeping wasn't undone overnight.

Takeaway: The Vulgate's influence stretches far beyond historical curiosities—it shaped how scripture is read, understood, and experienced:

- **Scripture as Lawbook:** The relational intimacy of YHWH's covenant was overshadowed by legalism.
- **Clergy as Gatekeepers:** Institutional control replaced personal engagement with scripture.
- **God as Distant King:** The warmth of Abba, Father became obscured by the grandeur of Deus Rex.

But this isn't where the story ends.

- Today, we have access to tools, resources, and historical insights that allow us to *return to the roots.*

- We can rediscover scripture not as a cold legal document but as a *living covenant.*

The Vulgate's legacy offers us a valuable lesson: **When translation becomes gatekeeping, intimacy with God suffers.**

Section 8 Takeaway:
The Vulgate was a turning point in scriptural history—it brought consistency, but at the cost of relational intimacy. It centralized authority and replaced covenant relationship with institutional legalism.

Today, understanding this shift allows us to approach scripture differently—to peel back the layers of tradition, language, and cultural influence and rediscover the **intimate heart of YHWH's covenant.**

Transition to Section 9:

The Vulgate may have centralized scripture under institutional authority, but it was not the final word in translation history. Centuries later, the Protestant Reformation sought to undo that monopoly by returning to the original Hebrew texts. In their pursuit of authenticity, however, reformers overlooked an essential truth: not all Hebrew texts were created equal. By embracing the Masoretic Text, they unintentionally traded one layer of historical distortion for another. What they thought was a return to foundations was, in fact, an adoption of post-Temple Rabbinic innovations—a far cry from the Hebraic worldview of Jesus and His disciples.

---

9. The Masoretic Text: The Newest Translation.

The Protestant Reformation sought to restore scripture to its Hebraic roots, yet in doing so, it embraced the Masoretic Text—a product of Rabbinic Judaism developed centuries after the fall of the "Second Temple".

While the Masoretic Text offered precision and consistency, it reflected a later theological framework that often diverged from the scriptural traditions of Jesus's time. What the Reformers believed to be a return to the original foundation was, in reality, a step further from the covenantal richness preserved in earlier texts like the Septuagint.

9.1 Historical Development of the Masoretic Text

The Masoretic Text (MT) represents one of the most significant efforts in the history of biblical preservation, yet its origins tell a story deeply rooted in the upheaval and transformation of post-Temple Judaism.

The work of the Masoretes, spanning from the 6th to 10th centuries AD, was an ambitious endeavor to standardize the Hebrew scriptures in response to the challenges of a dispersed and fractured Jewish community.

However, this meticulous effort was not merely an exercise in preservation—it reflected the theological shifts of a post-Temple era, shaped by the necessity of redefining Jewish identity without a central sanctuary or sacrificial system.

Origins of the Masoretic Text

The Masoretes were Jewish scribes and scholars dedicated to ensuring the precision and uniformity of the Hebrew scriptures. Their work began in earnest following centuries of instability, as the destruction of the "Second Temple" in AD 70 by the Romans left the Jewish people without the physical and spiritual center that had defined their covenantal identity.

In this vacuum, Rabbinic Judaism rose to prominence, emphasizing the study and interpretation of scripture as the means of maintaining community cohesion and faithfulness to YHWH's covenant.

The Masoretes operated within this context, seeking to establish an authoritative Hebrew text that could unify Jewish practice across the diaspora. Their primary innovations included the development of a vocalization system—marking vowels and accents to guide pronunciation—and cantillation marks to preserve the oral tradition of scripture reading.

This effort culminated in the Leningrad Codex (c. AD 1008), the oldest complete manuscript of the MT, and the Aleppo Codex, an earlier but partially lost text. These codices became the foundation for the MT's later adoption as the authoritative Hebrew Bible.

The Masoretes' work was meticulous, driven by a near-sacred reverence for the text. They introduced rigorous scribal practices, counting every letter and word to ensure accuracy, yet their efforts did not exist in a theological vacuum.

The MT was shaped by the Rabbinic Judaism of its time, which had already begun narrowing interpretive frameworks to fit a post-Temple reality.

This narrowing is evident in the MT's deviations from older textual traditions, reflecting a move away from the broader and more diverse scriptural interpretations of the "Second Temple" period.

The Babylonian Talmud and Rabbinic Influence

The development of the MT cannot be separated from the influence of the Babylonian Talmud, completed between AD 200–500 in Persia (modern-day Iran). The Talmud served as the central authority of Rabbinic Judaism, providing extensive commentary on the Torah and codifying oral traditions into a coherent legal and theological system.

The Talmud's theological priorities significantly influenced the scribal choices reflected in the MT. Where earlier Second Temple traditions, such as those preserved in the Septuagint, emphasized messianic prophecies and covenantal themes, the Rabbinic framework often redirected focus toward halakhic (legal) interpretations and communal identity.

For example:

- Textual variants that supported messianic expectations, prominent in the Septuagint and Dead Sea Scrolls, were softened or omitted in the MT.
- The divine council imagery of Deuteronomy 32:8—rendered in the Septuagint as "sons of God"—was replaced with "sons of Israel" in the MT, aligning with Rabbinic efforts to center national identity.

This shift represents a departure from the textual diversity of the "Second Temple" period, where multiple traditions coexisted, including those reflected in the Dead Sea Scrolls and the Septuagint. By contrast, the MT solidified a single, post-Temple interpretation of scripture, shaped by the theological and cultural priorities of Rabbinic Judaism.

The Historical Context of the Masoretic Text

The centuries following the Temple's destruction were marked by profound upheaval for the Jewish people. As communities scattered across the Roman and Persian empires, the question of how to maintain covenantal faithfulness without a central altar or sacrificial system became paramount. Rabbinic leaders, through the Talmud and the MT, sought to answer this question by reimagining the covenant as one centered on study, prayer, and the observance of Torah laws.

The Masoretic Text emerged from this environment as a text both preserved and shaped by its time. Its precision and uniformity made it a valuable tool for maintaining Jewish identity in the diaspora, yet its theological framework bore the imprint of Rabbinic priorities that diverged from earlier Hebraic traditions.

9.2 The Dead Sea Scrolls as a "Control Text"

Discovered in the mid-20th century, the Dead Sea Scrolls (DSS) have revolutionized our understanding of biblical textual traditions. Dating from approximately 200 BC to AD 70, these ancient manuscripts provide a snapshot of "Second Temple" scriptural diversity, offering an invaluable comparison point for later texts such as the Masoretic

Text (MT). The DSS not only predate the MT by over a millennium but also often align more closely with the Septuagint (LXX), revealing how textual traditions evolved over time.

A Window into "Second Temple" Textual Diversity

The Dead Sea Scrolls include a wide array of biblical and extrabiblical texts, representing multiple textual traditions that coexisted during the "Second Temple" period. This diversity challenges the perception of a singular, unified scripture during Jesus's time. Instead, it confirms that early Jewish communities engaged with multiple versions of key texts, reflecting a broader, more dynamic understanding of God's covenant and prophetic revelation.

Key examples from the DSS demonstrate their alignment with the Septuagint and their divergence from the MT, underscoring the MT's later narrowing of theological themes:

1. Deuteronomy 32:8 – "Sons of God" vs. "Sons of Israel":
- **The DSS and Septuagint** read, *"according to the number of the sons of God,"* preserving a vision of divine council imagery and highlighting the cosmic scope of God's covenantal order.
- **The MT,** however, replaces this phrase with *"sons of Israel,"* shifting the focus inward to the nation of Israel and reflecting the Rabbinic emphasis on national identity post–Temple.
2. Isaiah 53 – The Suffering Servant:
- **The DSS** version of Isaiah 53 aligns closely with the Septuagint in emphasizing the suffering servant's sacrificial role, reinforcing messianic typology that Christians would later associate with Jesus.
- **The MT,** while retaining the passage, reflects subtler phrasing that diminishes its explicit messianic interpretation, consistent with Rabbinic Judaism's post–Jesus theological priorities.

These examples illustrate how the DSS provide a vital benchmark for understanding how scripture was interpreted and transmitted before the theological shifts of Rabbinic Judaism shaped the MT.

Confirming the MT as a Later Tradition

The DSS reveal that the MT represents a narrower textual tradition, reflecting the theological and cultural realities of post-Temple Judaism. By comparing the DSS to the MT, several key patterns emerge:

- **Messianic De-Emphasis:** Texts like Isaiah 53 and Deuteronomy 32:8 in the MT often obscure themes of cosmic significance or messianic anticipation present in the DSS and Septuagint.
- **Standardization vs. Diversity:** While the MT sought uniformity, the DSS reflect a living, breathing tradition with multiple textual strands coexisting. This diversity aligns more closely with the scriptural landscape Jesus and His disciples would have known.

The DSS act as a "control text," allowing scholars and believers alike to assess the fidelity of later translations like the MT.

They confirm that the MT is not the original foundation it is often assumed to be, but rather a later, narrower version shaped by the Rabbinic priorities of its time.

Implications for Understanding Scripture

For modern readers seeking to approach scripture as Jesus and His disciples understood it, the DSS offer a powerful corrective. They remind us that the Bible is not a static document but the product of centuries of faithful transmission and interpretation.

By examining the DSS alongside the Septuagint and the MT, we gain a fuller picture of God's covenantal narrative—a narrative that transcends the confines of any single textual tradition.

9.3 Protestant Adoption of the Masoretic Text for Old Testament

The Protestant Reformation and the KJV

The Protestant Reformation sought to free scripture from institutional control and return it to the people. Reformers like Martin Luther believed that reconnecting with the Hebrew texts would restore the authenticity of the Old Testament as understood in its original context. However, the Hebrew scriptures they embraced were not the same ones Jesus and His disciples relied upon during the "Second Temple" period. Instead, they adopted the Masoretic Text (MT), a Rabbinic compilation developed centuries after the destruction of the Temple.

The MT, while preserving meticulous textual consistency, reflects the theological priorities of post-Temple Rabbinic Judaism. It replaced earlier textual traditions, such as those found in the Septuagint and Dead Sea Scrolls, which were far closer to the scriptures of Jesus's time.

The Reformers, in their desire for a "return to the roots," inadvertently turned to a text that reflected a later and narrower framework—one shaped by the realities of Jewish life in exile.

This adoption of the MT was institutionalized in Protestant translations such as the King James Version (KJV), which relied heavily on the Textus Receptus, a compilation derived from the MT.

While this choice was seen as a move toward "Hebrew authenticity," it created a theological disconnect from the diverse and dynamic scriptural traditions Jesus would have engaged with in His teachings.

Impact on Theology and Interpretation

The reliance on the MT led to significant shifts in how key passages were understood, particularly those relating to prophecy and covenantal themes. While the MT preserves certain Hebraic elements, its post-Temple origins introduced a narrower interpretive lens that often obscured earlier "Second Temple" insights.

Examples of Increased Theological Accuracy:

Isaiah 7:14 – "Young Woman" vs. "Virgin":
- The MT organizes the respective books of the Hebrew Bible in the structure by which "Second Temple" Jews understood the narrative arc of scripture: Law, Prophets, Writings – exactly how Jesus and his direct disciples taught them, lived them, and instructed us to see them..
- The MT renders *almah* as "young woman," which is more faithful to the Hebraic understanding of the text in its original context as opposed to the Septuagint's Hellenized influence.
- This distinction highlights the MT's attempt to preserve a more grounded, Hebraic understanding of prophecy.

Messianic Psalms – Subtle Shifts in Imagery:

- The MT reflects Rabbinic priorities in downplaying certain messianic associations, though it retains clear typologies in many passages. For example:
- Psalm 22:16: The MT renders this as *"Like a lion, they are at my hands and feet,"* compared to the Dead Sea Scrolls and Septuagint, which read *"They pierced my hands and my feet."*
- While the MT preserves the poetic and Hebraic essence of the text, it reflects a reluctance to emphasize messianic suffering.

These examples underscore how the MT diverged from the textual traditions Jesus's disciples would have recognized, such as the Septuagint and Dead Sea Scrolls, which preserved broader covenantal themes and messianic anticipation.

A Narrower Hebraic Tradition

While the MT represents a carefully preserved text, its theological framework reflects the challenges of Rabbinic Judaism's post-Temple evolution.

- The destruction of the Temple and subsequent exile prompted a reevaluation of scripture's role in maintaining Jewish identity.
- The MT's development during this period prioritized legal and communal cohesion, often at the expense of the broader textual diversity that characterized the "Second Temple" period.

This narrower framework shaped how scripture was understood in Protestant traditions. By adopting the MT, the Reformers unintentionally aligned themselves with a Rabbinic interpretation of the Old Testament that had already diverged from the broader Hebraic worldview of Jesus's time.

9.4 The Logical Error in Christian Adoption of the MT

Not a Return, but a Farther Departure

When the Protestant Reformers adopted the Masoretic Text (MT) as the foundation for their Old Testament translations, they believed they were returning to the authentic Hebraic scriptures of Jesus's time. This decision was driven by a sincere desire to strip away centuries of institutional distortion and recover the purity of scripture. However, this well-intentioned choice resulted in a profound theological misstep: rather than returning to the textual traditions Jesus and His disciples would have known, the Reformers embraced a later, narrower tradition shaped by post-Temple Rabbinic Judaism.

The MT emerged centuries after the destruction of the "Second Temple", during a period when Jewish leaders were redefining their faith in response to the loss of their principal place of worship. This redefinition prioritized legalism, halakhic interpretations, and the preservation of national identity over the covenantal breadth and diversity of earlier traditions.

By contrast, the Septuagint (LXX) and the Dead Sea Scrolls (DSS) offer a closer window into the textual diversity of the late "Second Temple" period—a diversity that Jesus Himself would have engaged with in His teachings.

The adoption of the MT represents not a recovery of Hebraic foundations but a departure from them. It reflects a failure to recognize the richness of "Second Temple" textual traditions, where multiple strands of scripture coexisted and messianic prophecies were given prominence. The Reformers, in their zeal to "return" to Hebrew authenticity, unwittingly aligned themselves with a text that had been shaped to distance Judaism from the emerging Christian movement.

A Theological Misstep with Lasting Consequences

By favoring the MT over the Septuagint or the textual evidence of the DSS, Protestant traditions embedded into their theology a framework that was already far removed from the covenantal worldview of Jesus's era.

Key aspects of this divergence include:

- **Messianic Interpretation:** The MT's revisions often downplayed or obscured messianic themes, particularly in passages like Isaiah 7:14 and Psalm 22:16, which the Septuagint and DSS preserved with greater clarity.
- **Loss of Diversity:** The MT's standardization narrowed the scriptural witness, excluding textual variants that illuminated the broader theological and prophetic landscape of the "Second Temple" period.

This misstep highlights the importance of understanding the historical and theological contexts in which scripture was transmitted.

Without this awareness, well-meaning efforts to restore scripture can inadvertently lead to greater distortion.

9.5 Implications for Modern Scripture and Faith

Why It Matters

The adoption of the MT as the foundation for modern English Bibles has far-reaching implications for how scripture is read, understood, and experienced today. While the MT represents a remarkable achievement in textual preservation, its theological framework reflects the priorities of Rabbinic Judaism in the centuries after Jesus's ministry. As a result, modern translations often reflect a Rabbinic lens rather than the broader Hebraic worldview of the "Second Temple".

This shift has profound consequences for how key themes in scripture are interpreted:

- **Messianic Prophecies:** Texts that Jesus's disciples saw as clear messianic signposts—such as Isaiah 53 or Deuteronomy 32:8—are often rendered more ambiguously in the MT, obscuring their covenantal significance.
- **Covenantal Breadth:** The MT's emphasis on legalism and national identity can overshadow the relational intimacy and universal scope of God's covenant, themes that are preserved more clearly in the Septuagint and DSS.

By relying on the MT, modern believers may unintentionally adopt a theological framework that limits their understanding of God's covenant and the messianic mission. To fully grasp scripture as Jesus and His disciples did, it is essential to also engage with earlier textual traditions that preserve the diversity and depth of "Second Temple" Judaism.

Recovering Earlier Traditions

The discovery of the Dead Sea Scrolls has provided modern scholars and believers with an unprecedented opportunity to bridge the gap between the textual traditions of Jesus's time and those of today.

These ancient manuscripts confirm the richness and diversity of "Second Temple" scripture, offering a corrective to the narrowing tendencies of the MT.

Similarly, the Septuagint, as the Greek translation of the Hebrew Bible used by early Christians, provides a valuable window into how Jesus and His disciples understood and interpreted scripture.

By recovering these earlier traditions, modern believers can:

- **Rediscover Messianic Depth:** Engage with the prophetic and covenantal themes that the MT often obscures.
- **Restore Relational Intimacy:** Reconnect with the relational essence of God's covenant, moving beyond the legalistic framework of post-Temple Rabbinic Judaism.
- **Enrich Biblical Understanding:** Appreciate the diversity of textual traditions that shaped the faith of Jesus and His disciples.

A Call to Reflection

The implications of the MT's adoption extend beyond scholarly debate—they shape how millions of believers encounter God's Word. To approach scripture as Jesus did, we must be willing to peel back the layers of tradition and translation that have accumulated over centuries. By engaging with earlier textual traditions like the Septuagint and Dead Sea Scrolls, we can rediscover the covenantal richness that lies at the heart of God's Word.

This section's exploration of the Masoretic Text serves as a reminder that scripture is not static—it is a living conversation shaped by the hands that transmit it. Jesus and His disciples understood scripture within the context of "Second Temple" textual diversity, engaging with traditions that reflected the fullness of God's covenant. Modern believers have the tools to do the same, returning to the richness of earlier traditions to uncover the true essence of God's Word.

9.6 Transition to Section 10: The Long-Term Consequences of Translation Divergences

The journey of scripture.

Transitioning from Ancient Hebrew to Greek to Latin, and finally to the English translations familiar to most Christians today—was far more than a linguistic exercise. It was a journey of worldview, theology, and, ultimately, power.

Each translation brought with it cultural assumptions, theological priorities, and, in some cases, significant shifts in the way God's covenant was understood and practiced.

The adoption of the Masoretic Text in Protestant traditions added another layer to this complex story. By embracing a post-Temple Rabbinic text as their foundation, Reformers believed they were reclaiming the authenticity of Jesus's time.

Instead, they unknowingly incorporated theological adjustments that reflected a later worldview—one focused on preserving Jewish identity after the Temple's destruction rather than the broader covenantal truths of the "Second Temple" period.

As we look at the long-term consequences of these translation divergences, we see how they shaped doctrine, worship, and daily faith practice. The loss of messianic emphasis, the narrowing of God's covenantal vision, and the drift toward theological abstraction are not simply historical curiosities—they are obstacles to reclaiming the relational intimacy YHWH always intended.

Understanding these consequences is not about assigning blame, but about gaining clarity. Only with clarity can we begin to reverse the drift and return to the covenantal relationship that lies at the heart of scripture.

10. The Long-Term Consequences of Translation Divergences

Key Insight:
Every translation carries cultural and theological assumptions that shape how scripture is understood and lived out.

Over time, these assumptions have had cumulative effects, leading to theological misunderstandings, a loss of covenantal focus, and a shift away from obedience toward abstract notions of grace.

The Role of Translation in Shaping Theology
The act of translation is never neutral. From the Septuagint to the Vulgate, and later the Masoretic Text, each version of scripture was influenced by the worldview of its translators and the priorities of its era.

For example:
- **The Septuagint**, created for a Greek-speaking Jewish diaspora, expanded messianic themes and universalized the covenant's scope, aligning closely with the theological framework of Jesus and His disciples.
- **The Vulgate**, reflecting the priorities of the early Church, emphasized institutional authority and doctrinal consistency, shifting the focus toward the centralization of power.
- **The Masoretic Text**, shaped by post-Temple Rabbinic Judaism, narrowed the scriptural witness to focus on halakhic interpretations and national identity, often at the expense of messianic anticipation and universal covenantal themes.

These shifts were not inherently malicious but reflected the evolving priorities of their respective communities. Yet, their cumulative impact has profoundly influenced how scripture is read, taught, and experienced today.

10.1 Theological Misunderstandings Born from Translation Choices

One of the most significant consequences of translation divergences has been the emergence of theological misunderstandings that distort the original intent of scripture. These misunderstandings have altered key doctrines, reshaped worship practices, and created gaps in covenantal obedience.

Recovering the Original Vision

Theological misunderstandings born from translation choices are not insurmountable obstacles. By studying earlier textual traditions, such as the Septuagint and the Dead Sea Scrolls, believers can recover a richer, more authentic understanding of scripture. This recovery involves:

- **Rediscovering the Messianic Narrative – In Context:** Engaging with texts that preserve the fullness of messianic anticipation, but do so without attributing prophecies to Jesus that were explicitly written about other biblical figures. False attributions borne of proof-texting do nothing to honor Jesus, they only confuse readers on his pivotal role in upholding God's Law and Prophets.
- **Restoring Relational Intimacy:** Recognizing God's covenant as a living relationship, not a static legal framework.
- **Reclaiming the Universal Covenant:** Understanding God's plan for humanity as one that encompasses all his children, not just a single nation or sect.

10.2 Theological Misunderstandings Born from Translation Choices

Key Insight: Every translation carries the fingerprints of its translators—their cultural biases, theological priorities, and linguistic limitations. These fingerprints have left indelible marks on how scripture is understood and practiced.

The Power of a Word: Language isn't a neutral tool—it shapes how we think, feel, and understand reality. Each word carries cultural weight, subtle connotations, and unspoken implications.

- In **Hebrew**, words are deeply relational and covenantal. They are tied to action, embodiment, and lived experience.
- In **Greek**, words often lean toward abstraction, intellectual categories, and philosophical ideals.
- In **Latin**, words are shaped by legal, hierarchical, and imperial overtones.

These linguistic lenses didn't just translate scripture—they reinterpreted it.

Examples of Doctrinal Shifts Through Translation

Nephesh → Psyche → Anima (Soul)
- In **Hebrew (Nephesh)**: The soul is not a disembodied spirit—it's the whole person. It encompasses physical, emotional, and spiritual life.
- In **Greek (Psyche)**: The soul became something separate from the body, introducing a dualistic view of humanity.
- In **Latin (Anima)**: The soul became even more abstract, associated with eternal reward or punishment after death.

Impact: This shift created theological frameworks where the physical world was seen as lesser, temporary, or even corrupt, while the spiritual world was elevated as pure and eternal.

Chesed → Pietas (Loving-Kindness → Duty/Obligation)
- In **Hebrew (Chesed)**: Chesed embodies steadfast love, relational loyalty, and covenant faithfulness—it's deeply emotional and deeply active.
- In **Latin (Pietas)**: Chesed was translated into terms of duty, obligation, and loyalty to authority.

Impact: The relational warmth of chesed was diminished. Obedience became less about love and more about fulfilling legal or institutional obligations.

Theological Fault Lines

Each translational shift created **doctrinal fault lines**—subtle fractures in understanding that widened over time:

- **Faith became belief.** Instead of trust and obedience, faith was reduced to intellectual agreement.
- **Grace became abstraction.** It shifted from God's covenantal loyalty to an unconditional legal pardon.
- **Sin became crime.** Rather than a relational breach, sin became a violation of a cosmic legal code.

These fault lines didn't appear overnight—they were compounded with each generation, each doctrinal debate, and each theological council.

Key Takeaway: Translation isn't a mirror—it's a lens. And every lens has distortions. Understanding these distortions isn't about dismissing translations but about being mindful of their influence.

10.3 Loss of Covenantal Focus in Favor of Abstract Grace

Key Insight:

Hebraic faith was a covenant—an active, relational partnership with YHWH. Greek and Latin thought shifted this into an abstract framework of belief and grace, a transition exacerbated by the narrowing influence of the Masoretic Text.

Faith: An Active Partnership vs. Intellectual Assent

In Hebraic thought, **faith (emunah)** is inseparable from action. To believe in YHWH is to do what He commands. It's not simply a mental acknowledgment but a lived expression of loyalty, trust, and steadfastness. This relational partnership is woven through the Torah and emphasized by the prophets, whose messages the MT preserves but often narrows by focusing on national identity and legal minutiae over broader covenantal themes.

In contrast, the transition to Greek **faith (pistis)** introduced a more abstract understanding. While pistis retained elements of trust, it began to lean toward intellectual belief—faith in propositions or doctrines rather than in a living, relational partnership with God. This framework, adopted by the Septuagint translators for Hellenistic audiences, reflected a shift in worldview but still preserved the covenantal themes more robustly than the MT.

By the time scripture was filtered through Latin **faith (fides)** during the Vulgate era, faith had become heavily institutionalized. Fides implied allegiance to the institution that represented God rather than direct loyalty to YHWH Himself. This shift further distanced faith from its Hebraic roots, where obedience and active participation in the covenant were central.

Impact:
Faith transitioned from "a way of living" to "a way of thinking." In the process:

- **Emunah** (active loyalty) was replaced by intellectual assent.
- Obedience became optional, often seen as secondary to belief.

This redefinition of faith, shaped by translation and cultural divergence, weakened the relational intimacy that YHWH intended to have with His people.

Grace: Relational Loyalty vs. Abstract Pardon

In Hebrew, **grace (chesed)** is deeply relational. It represents God's steadfast loyalty to His covenant—His unfailing love, patience, and forgiveness toward those who uphold their end of the covenant. Chesed is not a one-sided gift but a mutual partnership, where YHWH's faithfulness inspires reciprocal faithfulness from His people.

However, in Greek thought, **grace (charis)** shifted toward a broader cultural understanding of favor and kindness. While still reflecting divine generosity, charis became less tied to covenant loyalty and more abstract—a one-sided gift disconnected from relational reciprocity. This Greek influence, while present in the Septuagint, became dominant in Christian theology, emphasizing grace as unearned favor rather than steadfast relational commitment.

Latin thought further institutionalized this concept with **grace (gratia)** as a theological currency. Gratia emphasized God's legal pardon over His covenantal faithfulness, reducing grace to a transactional guarantee of salvation rather than an active, living relationship.

Impact:

- Grace transitioned from a relational promise to a doctrinal guarantee.
- Chesed's covenantal faithfulness was sidelined, replaced by a focus on receiving pardon without responsibility.

Faith Without Works? Grace Without Covenant?

When faith becomes belief and grace becomes pardon, the covenantal relationship at the heart of scripture begins to fade. The Masoretic Text, by emphasizing halakhic interpretations and national identity, further contributed to this narrowing by prioritizing legal frameworks over relational intimacy. Combined with the theological shifts of Greek and Latin thought, this transition created a theological landscape where:

- Faith became passive, defined by mental assent rather than active obedience.
- Grace became entitlement, a promise of pardon disconnected from covenantal faithfulness.
- Obedience became secondary, even optional, as theological abstraction replaced the relational demands of the covenant.

This misunderstanding fueled centuries of theological debates, schisms, and distortions, as faith communities struggled to reconcile the relational covenant of scripture with a framework increasingly dominated by abstract grace and intellectual belief.

Key Takeaway:

A focus on abstract grace without covenantal obedience distorts the relationship YHWH intended to have with His people. To recover the fullness of scripture, modern believers must return to the Hebraic foundation of faith as an active partnership and grace as relational loyalty. Only by embracing the covenantal intimacy of **emunah** and **chesed** can we begin to repair the drift caused by centuries of theological abstraction.

10.4 The Cumulative Effect Across Centuries

Key Insight:

Theological shifts from translation choices didn't occur in isolation— they accumulated across centuries, creating cascading effects on doctrine, worship, and daily faith.

The Butterfly Effect of Translation

A single word or choice in translation can ripple across history. Words are not static; they carry cultural weight, theological intent, and linguistic nuance. A seemingly minor shift can lead to profound consequences over time.

Examples of Linguistic Shifts and Their Impact

1.   **Nephesh → Psyche → Anima (Soul):**
     - **In Hebrew (Nephesh):** The soul is holistic, encompassing the entire being—physical, emotional, and spiritual.
     - **In Greek (Psyche):** The soul became separate from the body, introducing dualism into theological thought.

- **In Latin (Anima):** The soul became an abstract entity, reduced to an eternal, disembodied essence.
- **Impact:** This redefinition shaped doctrines on life, death, resurrection, and the afterlife, shifting from a Hebraic focus on resurrection and embodied life to abstract notions of an immortal, disembodied soul.

2. **Chesed → Pietas (Loving-Kindness → Duty/Obligation):**
   - **In Hebrew (Chesed):** Chesed conveys steadfast love, relational loyalty, and covenant faithfulness.
   - **In Latin (Pietas):** Chesed was translated in terms of loyalty to authority and dutiful obligation.
   - **Impact:** The relational warmth of chesed was diminished, replaced by cold, legal duty. This shift mirrors the MT's post-Temple legal emphasis, which framed covenantal faithfulness in terms of national identity and legal precision rather than relational intimacy.
3. **Emunah → Pistis → Fides (Faith):**
   - **In Hebrew (Emunah):** Faith implies loyalty, trust, and action. It is deeply relational and active.
   - **In Greek (Pistis):** Faith leaned toward intellectual belief and mental assent.
   - **In Latin (Fides):** Faith became institutional allegiance rather than relational trust.
   - **Impact:** Faith transitioned from active obedience to passive belief. The MT's narrower framework, focused on halakhic observance, further distanced faith from its relational foundation by prioritizing legalistic interpretations.

Each linguistic shift, small on its own, built a theological framework increasingly disconnected from the relational, covenantal foundation YHWH established.

Generational Drift

Each generation inherited these frameworks without realizing they were built on subtle linguistic and cultural shifts. Over centuries, the cumulative effect was profound:

- **Worship:** Shifted from relational intimacy to ritual duty.
- **Theology:** Focused more on abstract debates than covenant obedience.
- **Faith Communities:** Became defined by doctrinal alignment rather than lived covenant loyalty.
- **The Prophets:** Once covenantal watchdogs, were reduced to fortune-tellers.
- **The Writings:** Once worshipful reflections on the Torah, became isolated poetic musings.
- **The Torah:** Once the bedrock of covenantal faith, became an archaic historical document.

Even the Masoretic Text, while preserving critical aspects of scripture, contributed to this drift by emphasizing national and legalistic frameworks over the broader covenantal themes evident in the Septuagint and Dead Sea Scrolls.

What began as small stones thrown into the river of theological understanding eventually carved entirely new channels, leading to the fragmented theological landscape of modern Christianity.

Reclaiming the Foundation

Understanding these shifts isn't about vilifying translators or dismissing past generations—it's about discernment, humility, and clarity.

- **Recognize where shifts occurred:** Identify key areas where translations diverged from the Hebraic worldview of Jesus's time.
- **Understand how they shaped theology and worship:** Examine the cumulative impact of these shifts on doctrine and daily faith.
- **Return to YHWH's covenantal intimacy:** Recover the relational focus of scripture, where faith is active, grace is relational, and covenant obedience is central.

The goal isn't simply academic—it's deeply spiritual. Recognizing these shifts allows us to approach scripture not as a fragmented text but as a unified testimony to YHWH's covenant, love, and purpose.

Takeaway:

Translation is never neutral—it reflects the cultural, theological, and political context of its translators. By understanding these influences, we can discern the difference between interpretive bias and divine intent. Reclaiming the relational covenant YHWH intended requires peeling back layers of linguistic and cultural distortion to rediscover the unity and intimacy of His Word.

10.5 Why This Matters Today

Key Insight:

Modern Christianity still carries the weight of these cumulative shifts. Many believers are unaware of how deeply translation choices—shaped by cultural, theological, and political biases—have influenced their faith, often steering it away from the relational covenant YHWH intended.

Inherited Assumptions

Over centuries, the theological shifts introduced by translation choices have become deeply ingrained in Christian thought.

Many believers inherit these assumptions without questioning their origins or recognizing their impact:

Grace:
- Often understood as a one-sided pardon rather than covenantal loyalty, a shift shaped by Greek and Latin interpretations of **chesed**.
- The MT, with its narrower legal focus, reinforced this abstraction by emphasizing halakhic obligations over relational intimacy.

Faith:
- Frequently reduced to intellectual agreement rather than lived trust.

- The MT's prioritization of precise legal observance over broader covenantal themes contributed to this misunderstanding.

Obedience:
- Viewed by many as legalism rather than relational fidelity.
- By sidelining messianic anticipation and universal covenantal promises, the MT narrowed the scope of obedience to national and legal frameworks, which later translations often misunderstood or overly institutionalized.

These inherited assumptions do more than shape individual belief— they influence communal worship, institutional priorities, and societal norms, creating a theological framework that can obscure the covenantal relationship YHWH intended to have with His people.

Scripture Deserves Thoughtful Engagement

Translation is not a neutral act—it's an interpretive process influenced by the context and priorities of its translators.

The Masoretic Text, like the Septuagint and Vulgate, reflects the theological and cultural environment in which it was produced. Recognizing this allows modern readers to engage scripture more thoughtfully and with greater clarity.

Approach Scripture with Humility:
- Acknowledge that translation choices can shape theological assumptions.
- Recognize that scripture is more than a collection of texts—it's a living testimony to YHWH's covenantal love and purpose.

Discern Theological Biases:
- Study where translation decisions—whether in the MT, Septuagint, or Vulgate—may have shifted the relational intent of the text.
- Question inherited frameworks that reduce faith to belief, grace to pardon, and obedience to legalism.

Engage with Covenantal Intent:
- Return to the relational foundation of scripture, where faith is active, grace is loyal, and obedience is an act of love.

- Seek out the broader textual traditions preserved in the Septuagint and Dead Sea Scrolls to recover the richness of YHWH's covenant.

The Bible isn't a stagnant artifact—it's a living, breathing testimony. To honor it, we must approach it with clarity, humility, and a commitment to understanding its original relational intent.

Section 10 Takeaway

Translation isn't a neutral act—it's a process shaped by language, culture, and theology. Over centuries, these shifts compounded, creating profound changes in how scripture is understood and lived out:

- Faith became belief.
- Grace became pardon.
- Obedience became optional.

These shifts are not just historical curiosities—they are living assumptions that continue to shape modern theology, worship, and faith communities.

To reclaim the heart of scripture, we must not only return to the text itself but also peel back the layers of linguistic, cultural, and theological distortions that have built up over time. This process isn't about blame—it's about recovering the covenantal relationship YHWH intended for His people.

Transition to Section 11:

The Diaspora wasn't just a physical scattering of people—it was a scattering of thought, practice, and interpretation. As Jewish communities spread across the ancient world, they carried scripture with them, adapting it to new cultural and linguistic contexts. These adaptations further shaped how scripture was understood, influencing not only Jewish theology but also the development of Christian thought.

In the next section, we'll explore how the Diaspora's theological impact reverberated across centuries, reshaping the way scripture was interpreted and lived out in diverse communities.

---

11. The Diaspora and Its Theological Impact

Key Insight: The scattering of God's people across the ancient world didn't just change their geography—it changed their relationship with scripture. Each wave of diaspora (dispersion) introduced new cultural, linguistic, and theological influences, shaping how God's word was preserved, interpreted, and applied.

Waves of the Diaspora

The history of Israel is marked by waves of diaspora, each with its own consequences for the preservation and interpretation of scripture. While these events were often seen as punishment for disobedience, they also became opportunities for reflection, preservation, and adaptation.

11.1 Assyrian Exile: The Loss of the Ten Tribes

Key Insight: The Assyrian conquest of the northern Kingdom of Israel didn't just scatter a people—it fractured their cultural, spiritual, and covenantal identity.

The Historical Event

In 722 BC: the northern Kingdom of Israel fell to the Assyrian Empire under King Shalmaneser V and later Sargon II. The Assyrians implemented their policy of mass deportation, forcibly relocating substantial portions of the Israelite population to distant regions of the empire.

- **Assimilation and Cultural Dilution:** The Ten Tribes were scattered across Assyrian territories, where they gradually assimilated into foreign cultures. Their language, traditions, and covenantal practices were diluted over generations.

- **Oral Tradition Undermined:** The northern tribes relied heavily on oral tradition for preserving their identity and faith. Without cohesive communities or central places of worship, these traditions began to fade.
- **Remnants of Faith:** While most northern Israelites lost their distinct identity, some fragments of their faith and practices survived. Small communities clung to their worship of YHWH in obscurity.

The Spiritual Impact

The Assyrian exile represented more than just a geopolitical defeat—it was a **spiritual rupture**:

- **Loss of Unity:** The northern tribes were no longer a cohesive people with a shared sense of covenant purpose.

- **Breakdown of Worship Practices:** Without the centralization of worship in Jerusalem or Samaria, ritual observance became fragmented or abandoned.

- **A Lost Heritage:** Many covenantal laws, traditions, and historical narratives were forgotten by the scattered northern tribes.

However, amidst the devastation, a critical shift began:

- **Written Scripture as a Lifeline:** With oral tradition destabilized, the preservation of **written texts** became even more critical.

- **Survival Through Writing:** Prophetic warnings, covenantal laws, and historical accounts gained renewed importance as tools for remembrance and survival.

Theological Reflection

Prophets like **Hosea** and **Amos** had warned the northern kingdom repeatedly about their idolatry, injustice, and disobedience. Their voices echoed in the aftermath of exile:

- **God's Faithfulness Endures:** Despite Israel's unfaithfulness, YHWH's covenant promises remained.
- **Repentance and Return:** The exile underscored the need for repentance and covenant renewal.

Takeaway: The Assyrian exile marked a devastating loss of cultural and spiritual continuity, but it also forced a critical reliance on **written scripture** as the primary means of preserving identity. The surviving voices of the Prophets became beacons of hope and reminders of YHWH's enduring faithfulness.

11.2 Babylonian Exile: Codification and Reflection

Key Insight: The Babylonian exile was not just a period of loss—it was a crucible where scripture, identity, and worship were refined and preserved under immense pressure.

In **586 BC**, the southern Kingdom of Judah fell to King Nebuchadnezzar II of Babylon. Jerusalem was sacked, the Temple was destroyed, and the Jewish people were carried off into exile.

The Loss of the Temple: For Judah, the Temple wasn't just a building—it was the heart of their worship and the dwelling place of YHWH's presence.

Spiritual Crisis: Without the Temple, the sacrificial system, and a centralized priesthood, the people faced profound theological and spiritual questions:
- *How can we worship without a Temple?*
- *Are we still God's people in a foreign land?*
- *Has YHWH abandoned us?*

The Rise of Written Scripture

In the absence of the Temple and land, **scripture became the sanctuary**:

- **Codification of the Torah:** During the Babylonian exile, the Torah became central to Jewish life. The teachings of **Moses** were meticulously preserved, written down, and studied with renewed focus.
- **The Role of the Synagogue:** With no Temple, synagogues emerged as centers for worship, teaching, and community gatherings.
- **Prophetic Reflection:** Prophets like **Jeremiah, Ezekiel, and Daniel** provided theological clarity, reminding the people of YHWH's promises and calling them to faithfulness even in captivity.

Spiritual and Theological Growth

The exile wasn't just a period of survival—it was a time of profound reflection:

- **Obedience Beyond Geography:** The Jewish people learned that faithfulness to YHWH wasn't confined to the land of Israel. Obedience could—and must—be practiced in exile.
- **Covenant Renewal:** Prophetic messages emphasized repentance, hope, and the promise of restoration.
- **A Portable Faith:** The Torah and the teachings of the Prophets became portable sanctuaries, allowing the Jewish people to carry their faith wherever they went.

Key Example:

- **Ezekiel's Vision of the Valley of Dry Bones (Ezekiel 37):** A vivid picture of hope and restoration, symbolizing the renewal of a spiritually dead nation.

Theological Legacy

The Babylonian exile planted seeds of resilience:

- **Scripture as a Lifeline:** The written Torah became a non-negotiable cornerstone of faith.
- **Synagogue Worship:** The roots of synagogue worship as a community-focused expression of faith trace back to this period.
- **Prophetic Tradition Endured:** The words of the prophets transcended geography, resonating across time and place.

Takeaway: The Babylonian exile was both a **spiritual crisis** and a **spiritual rebirth**.

Through loss and lamentation, the Jewish people rediscovered the centrality of **scripture**, the resilience of covenantal faith, and the enduring hope of restoration.

Transition to 11.3 & 11.4

The Assyrian and Babylonian exiles reshaped Jewish identity, worship, and the role of scripture. However, these exiles were only the beginning.

In the following sections, we'll explore how the **Hellenistic Diaspora** brought Greek cultural influences into Jewish theology and how the **Roman Diaspora(s)** scattered the Jewish people even further, setting the stage for theological divergence that would echo into Christianity and beyond.

11.3 Hellenistic Diaspora: Greek Influence and Cultural Blending

Key Insight: The Hellenistic diaspora didn't just scatter the Jewish people geographically—it introduced a fusion of Hebraic covenantal faith and Greek philosophical reasoning that would echo into both Judaism and early Christianity.

Historical Context: The Age of Alexander the Great

In the **4th century BC**, **Alexander the Great** conquered much of the known world, creating the vast **Hellenistic Empire**. Greek culture—language, philosophy, art, and education—spread across the ancient Near East, including Judea and major diaspora centers like **Alexandria**.

- **Greek as the Lingua Franca:** Greek became the universal language of commerce, scholarship, and diplomacy. Even many Jews began to speak Greek more fluently than Hebrew or Aramaic.

- **Alexandria as a Cultural Epicenter:** The city became home to one of the largest and most influential Jewish diaspora communities, blending Greek intellectualism with Jewish religious traditions.

- **The Birth of the Septuagint:** In **the 3rd century BC**, Jewish scholars in Alexandria translated the Hebrew scriptures into Greek, creating the **Septuagint (LXX)**.

Theological and Philosophical Influence

Greek philosophical ideals began to seep into Jewish theological thinking:

- **Abstract vs. Relational Thought:** Hebrew thought was deeply covenantal and relational, centered on obedience, family, and community. Greek philosophy leaned toward abstraction, universal ideals, and intellectual reasoning.

- **Body-Soul Dualism:** Greek dualism (e.g., Plato's philosophy) introduced a division between the material and spiritual worlds. This was foreign to Hebraic holistic thinking, where the body and soul are seen as integrated.

- **Moral Philosophy vs. Covenantal Obedience:** Greek ethics emphasized moral ideals abstracted from divine covenant, while Jewish ethics remained rooted in obedience to YHWH's commandments.

Jewish Faith in a Hellenistic World

For many diaspora Jews, faith became a balancing act between preserving their Hebraic covenantal identity and adapting to Greek cultural norms:

- **Synagogues as Community Anchors:** Synagogues emerged as crucial centers for maintaining Hebraic identity in foreign cities.
- **Cultural Blending:** While some Jews resisted Hellenization (e.g., the Maccabean Revolt), others embraced elements of Greek culture, leading to varying degrees of assimilation.
- **Philo of Alexandria:** A key Jewish philosopher in Alexandria, Philo attempted to harmonize Jewish scripture with Greek philosophy, blending Platonic ideals with Hebraic theology.

The Impact on Early Christianity

The Hellenistic diaspora created fertile ground for the early spread of Christianity:

- **Greek as a Common Language:** The New Testament was written in Greek, ensuring accessibility across the Hellenistic world.
- **Greek Thought in Christian Theology:** Early Christian theologians, including Paul (Saul of Tarsus), often framed their arguments using Greek philosophical categories.
- **A Hybrid Faith Emerged:** Christianity inherited both Hebraic covenantal roots and Hellenistic philosophical frameworks, creating a unique theological synthesis.

Takeaway: The Hellenistic diaspora introduced a **Greek lens** into the interpretation of scripture and faith. While it made scripture more accessible to a broader audience, it also subtly reshaped Hebraic covenantal concepts into more abstract philosophical ideas—a shift that would reverberate through Jewish and Christian thought for centuries.

11.4 Roman Destruction of the Temple: Final Scattering

Key Insight: The destruction of the "Second Temple" in **AD 70** and the subsequent Jewish revolts scattered the Jewish people even farther, turning synagogue worship and scripture study into the permanent pillars of Jewish identity.

The First Roman-Jewish War (AD 66–73)

In **AD 70**, after a prolonged rebellion, the Roman general **Titus** besieged **Jerusalem** and destroyed the **"Second Temple"**.

- **The Loss of the Temple:** With the Temple gone, the sacrificial system, centralized worship, and priestly authority ended.

- **Diaspora Accelerated:** Thousands of Jews were killed, enslaved, or forcibly relocated across the Roman Empire.

- **Religious Crisis:** Judaism had to redefine itself without a physical center of worship.

The Bar Kokhba Revolt (AD 132–136)

A second major revolt erupted under **Simon bar Kokhba** in **AD 132**.

- **Further Scattering:** After crushing the revolt in **AD 136**, Emperor **Hadrian** expelled most remaining Jews from **Jerusalem**, renaming the city **Aelia Capitolina** and Judea as **Syria Palaestina**.

- **Cultural Suppression:** Jewish practices, including circumcision and Torah study, were outlawed in many regions.

- **Diaspora Deepened:** The Jewish people were now scattered across **Europe, North Africa, and the Middle East.**

The Shift to Synagogue and Scripture

With the Temple permanently gone and Jerusalem largely inaccessible, Judaism adapted:

- **Synagogue as the New Center:** Synagogues became the primary places of worship, community, and Torah study.
- **Torah as the Anchor:** The written Torah took on even greater significance as the unifying force of Jewish identity.
- **Regional Interpretations:** Without a central Temple authority, Jewish communities developed regional variations in traditions, customs, and theological emphasis.

Impact on Early Christianity

The Roman diaspora also had significant implications for the emerging Christian movement:

- **Decentralized Worship:** Early Christian gatherings mirrored synagogue worship, centered around scripture reading, prayer, and communal meals.

- **Theological Diversity:** Just as regional Jewish interpretations developed, early Christian communities also developed distinct theological emphases based on local contexts.

- **The Separation Begins:** As Christianity spread among Gentile communities, the roots shared with Judaism began to fade in favor of new theological frameworks.

Takeaway: The destruction of the "Second Temple" and the Roman diasporas didn't just scatter the Jewish people—they transformed worship, identity, and scriptural engagement forever.

Synagogue worship, Torah study, and decentralized community structures became the enduring legacy of this era.

The Assyrian, Babylonian, Hellenistic, and Roman diasporas weren't just historical events—they were **pivotal turning points** that reshaped Jewish and Christian identities, worship practices, and scriptural interpretations.

- **From Centralized to Decentralized Faith:** Worship transitioned from Temple rituals to synagogue and scripture study.
- **From Unified to Regional Practices:** Faith traditions became regionally diverse.
- **From Relational to Philosophical Lenses:** Greek and Roman influences reframed Hebraic covenantal thought into abstract theological categories.

In the next section, we'll explore why these historical diasporas still matter today and how their consequences continue to shape the spiritual landscape of Judaism and Christianity.

11.5 Why This Matters Today

Each wave of diaspora left an **indelible mark on how scripture is read, understood, and applied.**

- The **loss of the Ten Tribes** highlighted the fragility of oral tradition.
- The **Babylonian exile** cemented scripture as the **center of worship and identity.**
- The **Hellenistic diaspora** introduced philosophical layers that persist in Christian theology today.
- The **Roman destruction of the Temple** decentralized worship and set the stage for **modern Jewish and Christian traditions.**

These events didn't just affect history—they shaped the **spiritual DNA of both Judaism and Christianity.**

Every diaspora added cultural, linguistic, and theological layers to scripture interpretation. Recognizing these influences helps us untangle cultural assumptions from divine revelation and return to the covenantal focus at the heart of God's word.

Section 11 Takeaway:
The diaspora wasn't just a historical tragedy—it was a transformative force that shaped how scripture was preserved, interpreted, and applied. Each wave added layers of influence, and those layers still impact how we understand God's word today.

To reclaim clarity, we must acknowledge these influences and return to the foundation YHWH established.

---

12 Desanctification and Diaspora

Key Insight: Diaspora wasn't just a historical event—it was a **spiritual consequence** of rebellion and disobedience. Time and again, when God's people turned away from His commandments, they found themselves scattered among the nations. Yet, diaspora wasn't merely a punishment—it was also a **call to repentance and resanctification in God's grace**, a chance to return to YHWH with humble obedience.

12.1 How Exile Followed Spiritual Disobedience

Key Insight: Exile was never arbitrary—it followed clear patterns of rebellion, idolatry, and disregard for YHWH's commandments.

Patterns of Spiritual Rebellion Leading to Exile

Throughout scripture, a consistent pattern emerges: **Spiritual rebellion → Prophetic warning → Continued disobedience → Diaspora.**

The Northern Kingdom (Assyrian Exile, 722 BC)
- The Ten Tribes of Israel engaged in **idolatry, social injustice, and covenantal unfaithfulness** (2 Kings 17:7–23).
- Despite repeated prophetic warnings from figures like **Elijah, Elisha, and Amos**, the people refused to turn back to YHWH.
- The Assyrians conquered the Northern Kingdom, scattering the ten tribes across the empire.

The Southern Kingdom (Babylonian Exile, 586 BC)

- Judah followed a similar path: **idol worship, social corruption, and ignoring prophetic warnings** (2 Chronicles 36:15-19).
- Prophets like **Jeremiah and Ezekiel** warned of impending exile, yet their messages were dismissed.
- Nebuchadnezzar's Babylonian army destroyed Jerusalem and the Temple, leading to mass deportation.

These exiles weren't just geopolitical events—they were **spiritual turning points**, moments where rebellion reached a breaking point, and YHWH allowed His people to experience the consequences of their actions.

The Spiritual Concept of Desanctification

- **Holiness Lost:** When God's people abandoned His commandments, the land, the Temple, and their worship lost their sanctity.
- **The Land Spewed Them Out:** In **Leviticus 18:28**, YHWH warns, *"If you defile the land, it will vomit you out as it vomited out the nations before you."*
- **Desanctification isn't just external—it's internal:** Hearts became hardened, worship became ritualistic, and obedience became selective.

Modern Reflection: Desanctification Today

This pattern isn't confined to ancient Israel.

- **Spiritual Apathy:** When individuals or communities abandon foundational principles, spiritual vitality erodes.
- **Cultural Exile:** In many ways, the modern world reflects a spiritual diaspora—a scattering away from moral and ethical anchors.

Takeaway: Diaspora isn't just political exile—it's spiritual desanctification. When God's people abandon His commandments, they lose the sanctity of their worship, community, and identity.

12.2 How Return Symbolized Repentance and Resanctification

Key Insight: Diaspora wasn't the end of the story. YHWH always left the door open for **repentance, return, and resanctification.**

Return as a Spiritual Homecoming

Return from exile was never just about geography—it was about the heart.

Spiritual Renewal: The true return began with repentance, humility, and a renewed commitment to God's commandments.

Nehemiah and Ezra:
- Nehemiah rebuilt Jerusalem's walls, but his focus wasn't just physical restoration—it was spiritual accountability.
- Ezra reintroduced Torah-centered worship and community living.

2 Chronicles 7:14 – God's Invitation to Return

"If my people, who are called by my name, will humble themselves and pray and seek my face and turn from their wicked ways, then I will hear from heaven, and I will forgive their sin and will heal their land."

- **Humility:** Recognizing spiritual rebellion.
- **Prayer:** Seeking God earnestly.
- **Repentance:** Turning away from disobedience and back to God's covenant.
- **Restoration:** God promises forgiveness and healing.

The Concept of Resanctification

- **Sanctity Restored:** Resanctification isn't just rebuilding physical spaces—it's about realigning hearts and communities with God's will.

- **Obedience as Worship:** Following God's commandments isn't about legalism—it's about love and loyalty.

- **Community Accountability:** Return and restoration weren't individual endeavors—they were communal acts of repentance and renewal.

Modern Reflection: What Does Return Look Like Today?

- **Personal Return:** Individually seeking alignment with God's commandments and principles.

- **Communal Return:** Faith communities prioritizing holiness, obedience, and love.

- **Global Reflection:** Humanity recognizing its moral drift and humbly turning back to foundational truths.

Takeaway: True restoration isn't merely about returning to a place—it's about returning to God's commandments with humility, obedience, and love. Diaspora wasn't solely a punishment—it was also an invitation.

- An invitation to **pause, reflect, and realign.**
- An invitation to **turn back to God with humility and sincerity.**
- An invitation to **see the exile not just as an end, but as a beginning.**

In the next section, we'll explore how diaspora functions **both as divine judgment and as a gracious invitation** to return to YHWH with renewed hearts.

12.3 Diaspora as Both Judgment and Invitation

Key Insight: While diaspora serves as a consequence of rebellion, it is also a divine invitation to return.

It is not merely punitive—it is restorative, offering a pathway back to covenantal faithfulness.

Diaspora as Judgment: Consequences of Rebellion

Diaspora serves as a **spiritual and physical consequence of repeated disobedience** to God's commandments.

- **Justice Demands Consequences:** YHWH's justice cannot ignore persistent rebellion and idolatry.
- **The Land Itself Reacts:** As seen in **Leviticus 18:28**, the land "vomits out" those who defile it, showing that rebellion has natural, built-in consequences.
- **Prophetic Warnings Fulfilled:** Time and again, prophets warned Israel and Judah about the consequences of turning away from God (e.g., Jeremiah, Isaiah, Ezekiel).

Yet, even within this judgment, there is **a spark of mercy, a doorway of hope**.

Diaspora as Invitation – A Call to Return: While exile is a consequence, it is never without hope:

- **Nehemiah 1:9** captures this paradox beautifully:
  "But if you return to me and obey my commands... then even if your exiled people are at the farthest horizon, I will gather them from there and bring them to the place I have chosen as a dwelling for my Name."
- **God's Invitation Remains Open:** The prophets consistently conveyed that God's desire is not punishment but repentance and restoration.
- **A Spiritual Homecoming:** Diaspora creates a longing—a homesickness—for God's presence, His commandments, and His sanctuary.

The 2 Choices Presented in Every Diaspora:

1. **Remain scattered and spiritually desanctified:** Stay distant, fragmented, and lost.

2. **Return, repent, and be resanctified in obedience to YHWH:** Step back into alignment, obedience, and intimate relationship with God.

The Paradox of Diaspora: Justice and Mercy Interwoven

Diaspora reveals the **paradoxical nature of God's justice and mercy**:

- **Justice:** God cannot overlook rebellion without undermining His holiness and covenant.
- **Mercy:** Even in judgment, God's hand is extended in invitation.

Prophets Highlighted Both Sides:

- **Jeremiah 29:11** (often taken out of context) is a message spoken in the middle of exile: *"For I know the plans I have for you... plans to prosper you and not to harm you, plans to give you hope and a future."*
- **Hosea 14:1-2:** *"Return, Israel, to the Lord your God. Your sins have been your downfall! Take words with you and return to the Lord."*

Takeaway: Diaspora is not an end—it's a crossroads. It is both a judgment for disobedience and a loving call to return to God.

12.4 Diaspora Demonstrates Both God's Justice and Mercy

Key Insight: Every diaspora carries a dual message—God's unwavering justice and His boundless mercy.

Justice: God Cannot Ignore Rebellion

- God's justice demands that covenant violations carry consequences.
- Sin, when left unaddressed, festers into systemic corruption.
- The exile was not arbitrary; it was the fulfillment of prophetic warnings and covenantal consequences outlined in **Leviticus 26** and **Deuteronomy 28**.

Mercy: The Door to Return is Always Open

- Despite rebellion, God always preserved a **remnant**—a group who would carry the covenant forward.

- The return from Babylon, led by leaders like **Ezra and Nehemiah**, showed God's willingness to forgive and restore.
- God's character, as described in **Exodus 34:6-7**, is *"compassionate and gracious, slow to anger, abounding in love and faithfulness."*

The Lesson of Diaspora:

Diaspora is not God abandoning His people—it is God refining them.

- **In the Furnace of Exile:** Spiritual impurities are burned away.
- **In the Silence of Scattering:** God's voice becomes clearer to those who listen.
- **In the Longing for Return:** The heart softens and remembers the covenant.

Takeaway: Diaspora stands as both a symbol of God's justice and a banner of His mercy. It declares: *"Return, and you will be welcomed."*

12.5 Why This Matters Today

Key Insight: The pattern of desanctification and diaspora isn't just historical—it's a recurring spiritual reality in every generation.

Spiritual Diaspora in Modern Life

- Many believers today live in **spiritual exile**, disconnected from God's commandments and His appointed ways of worship.
- Cultural pressures, theological distortions, and personal rebellion often lead to a scattering of spiritual focus and obedience.
- **Desanctification Today:** Worship becomes routine, prayer becomes hollow, and obedience becomes optional.

The Invitation Still Stands: The call to return to YHWH is universal and timeless:

- **Repentance isn't punishment—it's restoration.**
- **Obedience isn't a burden—it's alignment.**
- **Sanctity isn't about ritual—it's about relationship.**

Three Lessons from Diaspora for Modern Believers:

1. **Identify Rebellion in Our Lives:** Recognize where disobedience has caused spiritual drift.
2. **Accept the Consequences with Humility:** Understand that consequences are opportunities for refinement, not rejection.
3. **Respond to God's Invitation:** Return to God with sincerity, humility, and obedience.

Hope in the Pattern of Return

- Every moment of scattering can become a moment of gathering.
- Every act of repentance can become a doorway to restoration.
- Every spiritual exile can end with a spiritual homecoming.

Takeaway: Diaspora isn't the final word—it's an opportunity for renewal. The path back to God is always open, paved with humility, repentance, and obedience.

Section 12 Takeaway:

Diaspora isn't merely a historical event—it's a **spiritual reality** that carries profound lessons. It serves as both **judgment for rebellion** and **an invitation to return to God's covenantal embrace.** Understanding this pattern helps us see our own spiritual exiles, hear God's call to return, and respond with humility and obedience.

13. Hierarchy of the New Testament:

Key Insight: The New Testament is not a flat text—it follows an intentional structure that mirrors the hierarchy of the Old Testament.

At its peak stand the Gospels, containing the words, actions, and teachings of Jesus Himself.

These must be interpreted in submission to the Torah and Prophets, as Jesus explicitly affirmed in Matthew 5:17-19.

The structure of the New Testament reflects divine prioritization:

1. **The Gospels:** The foundation—Jesus's life, teachings, and fulfillment of the Torah.
2. **The Judaic Epistles:** The bridge—written by those who intimately walked with Jesus and carried forward His teachings.
3. **The Pauline Epistles:** Commentary—letters addressing specific **gentile** communities with context-dependent advice.

This hierarchy must be respected to preserve clarity and prevent distortion.

13.1 The Gospels: The Foundation of the New Testament

Key Insight: The Gospels (Matthew, Mark, Luke, and John) are not just biographical accounts of Jesus—they are the foundational cornerstone of the New Testament, recording His direct teachings, actions, and mission.

The Authority of the Gospels:

The Gospels are unique because:

- They contain **direct teachings** from Jesus Himself.
- They provide **firsthand accounts** of His actions and ministry.
- They establish the **standard of obedience** and **the heart of God's commandments** lived out in real time.

Why the Gospels Hold Primacy:

- **Direct Record of Jesus's Words:** These texts contain the teachings and parables spoken by Jesus Himself.
- **Jesus as the Fulfillment of the Torah and Prophets:** His life represents the perfect embodiment of Torah obedience.
- **Covenantal Restoration:** Jesus wasn't establishing a new religion— He was calling people back to YHWH's original covenant.

What Happens When the Gospels Are Diminished in New Testament understanding?

When the Gospels are treated as just one set of writings among many:

- The **core teachings of Jesus** are filtered or overridden by later commentary.
- The **Hebraic foundation** of Jesus's ministry is ignored or diminished.
- Christianity drifts from a **living covenantal relationship** with God into a doctrinal system focused on abstraction and intellectual assent.

Restoring the Gospels' Place:

The Gospels must remain the **highest authority** in the New Testament. Every doctrine, every epistle, every interpretation must align with and submit to them.

Takeaway: The Gospels are **not commentary—they are the foundation.** Everything else in the New Testament must align with and submit to their message.

13.2 The Words, Actions, and Teachings of Jesus Himself

Key Insight: The Gospels are not theological reflections or secondhand commentary—they are **firsthand accounts of Jesus's life, teachings, and actions to uphold Torah and Prophets.**

The Teachings of Jesus:

- Jesus didn't speak abstract theology—He taught **practical obedience** to YHWH's commandments in Torah Law.
- His words consistently pointed people back to **Torah faithfulness** and **heart-level obedience**.
- He opposed traditions and doctrines of men that contradicted God's commandments (**Mark 7:6-13**).

The Actions of Jesus:

- **Jesus Kept the Sabbath:** *"He went to Nazareth, where he had been brought up, and on the Sabbath day he went into the synagogue, as was his custom."* (**Luke 4:16**)
- **Jesus Honored the Torah:** *"Do not think that I have come to abolish the Law or the Prophets; I have not come to abolish them but to fulfill them."* (**Matthew 5:17**) : fulfill means "uphold", much more-so than it means "override", or "contradict", each of those being nothing more than abolishment under a different name.
- **Jesus Defended God's Commandments:** When traditions undermined the Torah, Jesus called them out directly (**Mark 7:8-9**).

Examples of Scriptural Alignment in Jesus's Teachings:

- In the wilderness, Jesus rebuked Satan using **Deuteronomy 8:3, 6:16, and 6:13**—demonstrating reliance on the Torah as the moral and spiritual standard.
- In the **Sermon on the Mount** (Matthew 5–7), Jesus elevated the Torah's commandments to their spiritual core, showing that obedience begins in the heart.
- In **Matthew 22:37-40**, Jesus summarized the Torah into two commandments:
  - *"Love the Lord your God with all your heart, soul, and mind."* (**Deuteronomy 6:5**)
  - *"Love your neighbor as yourself."* (**Leviticus 19:18**)

These were not new commandments—they were the distilled essence of the Torah.

The Consistency of Jesus's Message: Jesus's ministry was never about replacing the Torah—it was about fulfilling it.

- He clarified its deeper spiritual intent (**Matthew 5−7**).
- He demonstrated obedience in His own life.
- He called His followers not to vague spirituality but to **tangible obedience** to YHWH's commandments.

The Authority of Jesus's Words:

- Jesus taught his followers to uphold Law and Prophets and teach others to do the same so long as Heaven and earth exist − to the least stroke of the pen. This is because that is the source of any power and authority he ever exercised.

- Christians should view Jesus's teachings as **non-negotiable directives**, not optional musings. To paraphrase Ezekiel "If you think Jesus is messiah, follow Jesus. If you think Saul is messiah, follow Saul". One cannot serve two masters.

- Every word spoken by Jesus carries **the weight of divine authority** because He perfectly embodied the Torah.

Takeaway: Jesus wasn't creating a new system of belief—He was **restoring people to the covenant** they had drifted away from. His words and actions remain **the highest authority** in the New Testament while staying **submissive** to the **Law and Prophets** which Jesus upheld and expected us to as well.

- **Gospels are the foundation** because they contain Jesus's life, words, and mission.
- The **words and actions of Jesus** are not suggestions—they are **living instructions for covenantal faithfulness.**

Everything else in the New Testament—every epistle, every letter, every doctrine—must align with and submit to these foundational truths. At the same time, everything in the New Testament has to be read and understood in compliance with the covenantal framework of the Law, Prophets, and Writings.

13.3 The Cornerstone of the New Testament – Not the Foundation of Law.

Key Insight: The Gospels are not just one part of the New Testament—they are its **cornerstone**. While they carry authority over other books in New Testament because they contain the **direct words, actions, and teachings of Jesus Himself**, who spoke as a both a prophet, calling us back to relational covenant with YHWH under Torah Law, and as **a messianic embodiment of God's will and Torah faithfulness** lived out in example.

- *"My yoke is easy and my burden is light"* Jesus saw God's Law as wings, not shackles.
- *"Take up your cross and follow me"* Jesus expects us to follow his example, embodying God's Law, personally and in community, in both thought and action.

This contradicts the common Pauline doctrine of today that says "Jesus did the impossible so you don't have to".

Jesus showed upholding the Law and Prophets was not only possible, he said it was easy, barely a burden at all..

Why Torah Submissive Gospels Must Govern the New Testament

The preeminence of the Gospels in New Testament isn't a matter of preference—it's a matter avoiding theological inversion moving forward. This is the same understanding the same reason the Gospels must remain submissive to Law & Prophets they are predicated upon, also to avoid theological inversion looking back.

- **Direct Teachings of Jesus:** Every word spoken by Jesus carries divine weight (*"For I did not speak on my own, but the Father who sent me commanded me to say all that I have spoken."* – John 12:49).
- **The Foundation of Faith:** Jesus's words clarify, elevate, and fulfill the Torah and Prophets.
- **Divine Example:** Jesus not only spoke but lived out God's commandments perfectly, setting an eternal standard for covenant faithfulness.

The Problem of Reversed Priorities

Much of modern Christianity has reversed the intended hierarchy:

- The **epistles of Paul** are often treated as the lens through which the Gospels are understood.
- Doctrines derived from the Pauline epistles are used to reinterpret or even override Jesus's direct teachings.
- This creates theological systems where grace becomes abstract, obedience becomes optional, and the Torah is seen as irrelevant.

Example of Reversed Priorities:

When Jesus says:

> - *"Do not think that I have come to abolish the Law or the Prophets; I have not come to abolish them but to fulfill them."* (**Matthew 5:17**)

And Paul is interpreted to mean:

> - *"You are not under the Law but under grace."* (**Romans 6:14**)

Instead of harmonizing these teachings, many prioritize Paul's words over Jesus's, creating a theological imbalance.

The Proper Framework:

- The Gospels must serve as the **interpretive foundation** for every epistle and teaching in the New Testament.
- When there appears to be tension between Paul and Jesus, **Jesus's words must prevail**—not as a preference, but as a divine mandate.

The Risk of Misplaced Priorities

When the Gospels are de-emphasized:

- Jesus becomes a symbolic figure rather than the active teacher and example of faith.
- Theology becomes abstract and disconnected from covenantal obedience.

- The Torah is dismissed as a historical relic rather than an enduring guide.

A Practical Example:

When Jesus says:

- *"If you love me, keep my commandments."* (**John 14:15**)

This cannot be reinterpreted to mean:

- "If you believe in me, obedience is optional."

Restoring the Gospels as the Cornerstone

Three steps to reclaim the integrity of scripture:

1. **Prioritize the Gospels** as the highest authority in the New Testament.
2. **Interpret all epistles through the teachings of Jesus**, not the other way around.
3. **Reject contradictions:** If an interpretation of Paul conflicts with Jesus's words, the error lies in the interpretation—not in Jesus's authority.

Takeaway: The Gospels are **not commentary—they are the cornerstone**. Every epistle, doctrine, and teaching must submit to the direct words and actions of Jesus.

13.4 Submission to the Law and the Prophets

Key Insight: The Gospels don't exist in isolation—they are firmly rooted in the **Torah and the Prophets**. Jesus Himself made this abundantly clear in **Matthew 5:17-19**.

Jesus's Alignment with the Torah and Prophets:

> *"Do not think that I have come to abolish the Law or the Prophets; I have not come to abolish them but to fulfill them. For truly I tell you, until heaven and earth disappear, not the smallest letter, not the least stroke of a pen, will by any means disappear from the Law until everything is accomplished."* (**Matthew 5:17-18**)

Jesus's relationship with the Torah and Prophets can be summarized as:

1. **Teaching from the Torah:** Every one of Jesus's core teachings aligns with the Torah's foundational principles.
2. **Clarifying Misunderstandings:** Jesus frequently rebuked religious leaders for distorting God's commandments with man-made traditions (**Mark 7:6-13**).
3. **Living in Perfect Obedience:** Jesus was not just a teacher of the Torah—He was its **perfect embodiment**.

How Misinterpretation Happens:

- Many modern interpretations treat Jesus's teachings as a **replacement** for the Torah rather than a **fulfillment and clarification** of it.
- This misreading creates a false dichotomy: Torah vs. Grace, Obedience vs. Faith.

Jesus Did Not Nullify the Torah:

- Jesus didn't render the Torah obsolete—He demonstrated its spiritual depth and purpose.
- Every lesson Jesus taught carried the **weight and authority of the Torah** behind it.

Practical Example:

When Jesus says:

> *"The Sabbath was made for man, not man for the Sabbath."* (**Mark 2:27**)

He wasn't nullifying the Sabbath—He was **restoring its purpose** as a day for rest, worship, and communion with YHWH.

Submission, Not Replacement:

The Gospels do not replace the Torah and the Prophets—they **affirm, clarify, and illuminate them**.
Any teaching or interpretation of the Gospels that contradicts the Torah and Prophets is inherently flawed.

Takeaway: Jesus's words in the Gospels are not detached from the Torah—they are **inseparably connected** to it. To understand Jesus's message, we must approach it with the same reverence and submission He had for the Torah and the Prophets.

13.5 Why This Matters Today

Many modern interpretations **invert the New Testament hierarchy**, placing Paul's writings above Jesus's words.

The result:
- The Torah is dismissed as "obsolete."
- Jesus's teachings are reframed to fit Pauline theology.
- Grace is misrepresented as an escape from obedience.

Restoring the proper hierarchy brings clarity:
- The **Gospels interpret Paul—not the other way around.**
- Jesus's teachings align with the Torah, and Paul's writings must align with both.

When the Gospels are restored to their rightful place, we:
- **Hear Jesus clearly.**
- **Understand Paul accurately.**
- **See the New Testament as a cohesive whole.**

Takeaway: The Gospels are not just **one voice among many** in the New Testament—they are the **supreme voice.**

Section Takeaway:
The Gospels are the foundation of the New Testament, containing the words, actions, and teachings of Jesus Himself. They must be interpreted in alignment with the Torah and the Prophets and serve as the supreme **authority over** every other New Testament writing.

If we want clarity, we must start with Jesus and build from there.

14. Judaic Epistles: The Bridge from Jesus

Key Insight: The Judaic Epistles—including James, 1 Peter, Hebrews, and Revelation—serve as a **theological bridge** between the Gospels and the early church. These letters do not introduce new doctrines; instead, they **clarify, emphasize, and apply the teachings of Jesus** while upholding the Torah and Prophets.

14.1 The Judaic Epistles: A Bridge, Not a Break

The Judaic Epistles were primarily written by **Jewish followers of Jesus** who were deeply familiar with the Torah, the Prophets, and Hebraic tradition. These letters are not attempts to redefine faith or invent a new religion—they are **guides for practical covenantal living** under Jesus's teachings.

Key Characteristics of the Judaic Epistles:

- **Continuity, Not Innovation:** These letters operate within the theological framework of the Torah and the teachings of Jesus, rather than introducing abstract doctrines.
- **Covenantal Context:** They assume familiarity with God's commandments and build upon them as living instructions for believers.

- **Audience Awareness:** They address both **Jewish and Gentile believers**, calling them to unity under YHWH's covenant while maintaining distinct cultural and theological clarity.
- **Practical Guidance:** They emphasize **how to live out faith in a community setting**, with obedience, humility, and holiness at the forefront.

Examples of Their Role as a Bridge:

- **James:** Focuses on **faith expressed through action**—a key principle in Torah-observant life.
- **1 Peter:** Reinforces **covenant identity** and the call to live as a holy people, set apart by obedience to God.
- **Hebrews:** Frames Jesus's role as the **ultimate High Priest**, not in opposition to Torah, but as its perfect fulfillment.
- **Revelation:** Calls for **steadfast obedience** to God's commandments and faithfulness in the face of spiritual and societal pressures.

A Clear Bridge Between Two Worlds:

- **The Gospels:** The words and actions of Jesus, the Torah-fulfilling Messiah.
- **The Judaic Epistles:** Practical application of Jesus's teachings within the covenant framework by his direct disciples. Those who lived with Jesus and watched how he did everything he did to uphold and satisfy God's Law, lived out in real time.
- **The Early Church:** A diverse body called to live faithfully in light of Jesus's example and the Torah's instructions.

Takeaway: The Judaic Epistles are not a departure from the Torah or the Gospels—they are a **bridge**.

They guide believers in applying Jesus's teachings in their daily lives, reinforcing covenantal obedience and communal holiness.

14.2 They Uphold the Law, Not Alter It

Key Insight: A close reading of the Judaic Epistles reveals a **consistent commitment** to the Torah and the teachings of Jesus. These letters do not suggest the Torah's irrelevance; they uphold it as a **living guide** for covenantal obedience.

James: Faith and Works in Harmony

- *"What good is it, my brothers and sisters, if someone claims to have faith but has no deeds? Can such faith save them?"* (**James 2:14**)
- James reinforces the **inseparability of faith and obedience**—echoing the Torah's emphasis on action as a demonstration of faith.
- He describes the Torah as the **"perfect law that gives freedom"** (**James 1:25**)—a far cry from the modern misrepresentation of the Torah as a burden.
- Faith is not intellectual assent; it is **faithful action** aligned with God's commandments.

1 Peter: Holiness Through Obedience

- *"As obedient children, do not conform to the evil desires you had when you lived in ignorance. But just as he who called you is holy, so be holy in all you do; for it is written: 'Be holy, because I am holy.'"* (**1 Peter 1:14-16**)
- Peter echoes the Torah's call to holiness from **Leviticus 19:2**.
- He emphasizes the **covenantal identity** of believers: *"But you are a chosen people, a royal priesthood, a holy nation, God's special possession."* (**1 Peter 2:9**)
- Holiness is **not abstract—it's practical obedience to God's commandments**.

Hebrews: Jesus as the Ultimate High Priest

- Hebrews doesn't abolish the priesthood—it **elevates Jesus as the eternal High Priest** in the heavenly Temple.
- The sacrificial system wasn't erased—it was **upheld and perfected** in Jesus's sacrifice.

- The covenant framework remains intact; Jesus operates **within it, not outside it**.

Revelation: Obedience and Faithfulness in the End Times

- *"This calls for patient endurance on the part of the people of God who keep his commands and remain faithful to Jesus."* (**Revelation 14:12**)
- Revelation ties **obedience to God's commandments** directly with faithfulness to Jesus.
- It warns against lawlessness, compromise, and spiritual drift.

Modern Misunderstandings:

- These letters are often misread through a lens of **"faith vs. works"** or **"grace vs. law"**—false dichotomies that Jesus Himself rejected.
- The Judaic Epistles emphasize that faith is **not passive belief but active covenantal loyalty**.

Takeaway: The Judaic Epistles don't redefine or override God's commandments—they **uphold them**. They serve as a guide for faithful, Torah-aligned living in the light of Jesus's fulfillment of God's promises.

14.3 Unity with the Law, Prophets, Writings and the Gospels

Key Insight: The Judaic Epistles don't introduce a new stream of theology—they are deeply interconnected with the **Tanakh (Torah, Prophets, Writings)** and the **Gospels**. Their foundation is covenantal, their message is consistent, and their instructions are applications of the same core principles Jesus taught.

Rooted in the Torah and Prophets

The authors of the Judaic Epistles wrote with an **assumed foundation of Torah knowledge** and a deep familiarity with the Prophets and

Writings. Their letters are filled with references, allusions, and quotations from these sacred texts.

Examples of Torah and Prophetic Foundations in the Judaic Epistles:

- **James 1:25:** *"But whoever looks intently into the perfect law that gives freedom and continues in it—not forgetting what they have heard, but doing it—they will be blessed in what they do."*
    - This reference to the **"perfect law of liberty"** isn't a vague Christian principle—it directly ties back to the Torah, specifically its role in guiding righteous and covenantal living.

- **1 Peter 1:16:** *"For it is written: 'Be holy, because I am holy.'"* (Quoting **Leviticus 19:2**)
    - Peter reinforces the Torah's instruction on holiness, showing it remains central to the believer's life.

- **Hebrews 8:10:** *"This is the covenant I will establish with the people of Israel after that time, declares the Lord. I will put my laws in their minds and write them on their hearts. I will be their God, and they will be my people."* (Quoting **Jeremiah 31:33**)
    - The promise of a renewed covenant doesn't erase the Torah; it internalizes it.

The Judaic Epistles Mirror Jesus's Teachings in the Gospels:

- **Faith and Action:** James mirrors Jesus's emphasis on active faith (*"Let your light shine before others, that they may see your good deeds and glorify your Father in heaven."* - Matthew 5:16).
- **Holiness and Obedience:** Peter echoes Jesus's call to holiness (*"Be perfect, therefore, as your heavenly Father is perfect."* - Matthew 5:48).
- **Endurance and Faithfulness:** Revelation mirrors Jesus's warning to endure trials (*"But the one who stands firm to the end will be saved."* - Matthew 24:13).

The Theological Continuity is Unbroken:

- The Torah lays the **foundation** of God's covenant.
- The Prophets **enforce and amplify** that covenant.
- The Writings **reflect and worship** within that covenant.
- The Gospels **fulfill and illuminate** the covenant through Jesus's life and teaching.
- The Judaic Epistles **apply and clarify** Jesus's teachings within covenantal life.

Takeaway: The Judaic Epistles reinforce the **unbroken continuity** of God's covenant and Jesus's teachings. They are not stand-alone commentary—they are practical guides for living faithfully under the Torah through the lens of Jesus's fulfillment.

14.4 Why This Matters Today

Key Insight: In modern Christianity, the Judaic Epistles are often overshadowed by the Pauline letters, creating a theological imbalance that distorts their intended role.

The Problem of Theological Imbalance:

- **James's Epistle:** Often dismissed as "works-based righteousness" rather than understood as **faith in action.**
- **Hebrews:** Misinterpreted as an argument against the Torah instead of a declaration of Jesus as the **High Priest within Torah's framework.**
- **1 Peter:** Reduced to a guide for suffering Christians instead of a call to **holiness through obedience to God's commandments.**
- **Revelation:** Read as a future-coded prophecy rather than an urgent call for **obedience and faithfulness.**

This imbalance has had far-reaching consequences:

1. **Obedience is Downplayed:** The commandments of God are seen as optional.
2. **Faith Becomes Passive:** Belief without action is celebrated as sufficient.

3. **The Gospels Are Reinterpreted:** Jesus's clear words are filtered through secondary commentary rather than standing as the supreme authority.

Restoring the Judaic Epistles to Their Rightful Place:

To read scripture faithfully, we must allow the Judaic Epistles to fulfill their intended role as a **bridge between the Gospels and the early communities of faith**.

- They emphasize the **practical outworking of faith** in obedience to God.
- They highlight **covenantal responsibility** in both personal and communal contexts.
- They remind believers of the **holiness and distinctiveness** required to live as God's people.

Why It Matters:

- When we diminish the Judaic Epistles, we lose **critical guidance on covenantal obedience**.
- When we prioritize abstract theology over practical holiness, we distort the **message of Jesus and His disciples**.
- When we overlook the bridge they provide, we risk building our faith on fragmented interpretations rather than the **unified testimony of scripture**.

Takeaway: The Judaic Epistles are **not a footnote** in Christian theology—they are **a vital bridge connecting the Gospels to the early community of faith**.

They uphold the Torah, reinforce Jesus's teachings, and call believers to **active, covenantal obedience**.

Section Takeaway:

The Judaic Epistles are **the writings of Jesus's direct disciples**—men who walked with Him, heard His words, and lived in alignment with the Torah.

- They are **not abstract theology—they are practical covenantal guidance**.
- They are **not innovations—they are applications of Jesus's teachings**.
- They are **not secondary—they are foundational commentary for living out faith in alignment with God's commandments**.

To misunderstand or diminish their importance is to risk distorting the very foundation of faith they were meant to preserve.

---

15. The Pauline Epistles:

Letters & Commentary – Not Law & Commandment

Key Insight: The Pauline Epistles are letters written to specific communities facing specific problems in the early church. They are often read out of context, misinterpreted, and elevated above their intended role. They do not carry the same authority as the teachings of Jesus or even the Judaic Epistles.

Yet, they do carry significant lessons—lessons that most readers may not yet understand but will by the end of this book. They often contravene Jesus's Gospels, and the Law & Prophets Jesus and His direct disciples told us to uphold.

15.1 Paul's Books in the Bible Are Letters Often Read Out of Context

The Pauline Epistles—letters such as *Romans, 1 Corinthians, Galatians,* and others—were situational letters. They were written to address **specific problems in specific early church communities**. These were not systematic theological dissertations or universal commandments meant to serve as the foundation of Christian doctrine.

Instead, they function as **localized correspondence**, offering insight and pastoral guidance in unique cultural and situational contexts.

The Situational Nature of Paul's Letters

Each letter of Paul was written in response to unique challenges and circumstances:

- **1 Corinthians:** Addressed internal division, sexual immorality, and chaotic worship practices disrupting community order.
- **Galatians:** Confronted misunderstandings about whether Gentile believers needed to adhere to Jewish cultural customs like circumcision to be included in God's covenant community.
- **Romans:** Presented a theological argument balancing the relationship between Jewish and Gentile believers, addressing tensions in the early church of Rome.

While these letters were meaningful and powerful for their intended audiences, they were **never meant to override the words of Jesus** or the commandments of the Torah.

Without mincing words, those parts of his letters that sought to relax the Torah Law was an exercise of authority he did not possess.

Paul was in direct violation of the Hebrew Bible and the Gospels when he told prospective gentile converts they were not obliged to uphold God's Law.

It could be argued that this did more to impede gentile conversion to the Torah-centered faith practiced by Jesus and his disciples than facilitate it.

We will delve further into this line of inquiry in Volume 3, but for now, learning who "outranks" who in scripture, and why, is essential to reading our modern bible with Jesus's scriptural lens.

When lensed properly, the truth of God's word sets people free.

Contextual Misinterpretation and Doctrinal Drift

When Paul's situational letters are lifted out of their full scriptural context, they become susceptible to **misinterpretation and misuse:**

- Advice specific to a local community becomes interpreted as **universal mandates** for all Christians across all cultures and time periods.
- Nuanced arguments, written to address unique problems, are turned into **doctrinal cornerstones**.
- Paul's subjective opinions or rhetorical arguments are elevated to the same status as Jesus's Gospels or Torah Law – a complete theological inversion.

This misunderstanding and or misuse has historically led to major doctrinal distortions, where Paul's words are weaponized to override Jesus's commandments and the eternal principles of the Torah.

When Paul's Words Contradict Jesus or the Torah

It must be stated plainly: **If Paul's words seem to contradict the Torah, the Prophets, or the direct teachings of Jesus, they must be viewed with suspicion and carefully reexamined in context.**

- Jesus explicitly stated: *"Do not think that I have come to abolish the Law or the Prophets; I have not come to abolish them but to fulfill them."* (Matthew 5:17)
- The Torah declares: *"You shall not add to the word which I command you, nor take from it, that you may keep the commandments of the Lord your God which I command you."* (Deuteronomy 4:2)

Paul was a teacher, a missionary, and a thinker grappling with the complexities of spreading the Gospel in a multicultural world. But his letters are not the foundation of faith—they are **commentary**, responses to real-world problems faced by early communities.

Takeaway: Paul's writings are situational letters, not universal commandments.

They must be read carefully, contextually, and always interpreted through the lens of **Jesus's teachings** and the eternal commandments found in the **Torah and Prophets**.

15.2 They Do Not Carry the Same Authority as the Teachings of Jesus or the Judaic Epistles

The **hierarchy of authority** in the New Testament must be clearly understood:

1. **The Gospels:** The direct teachings, actions, and words of Jesus the Messiah.
2. **The Judaic Epistles (James, Peter, Hebrews, Revelation):** Writings from Jesus's direct disciples, deeply rooted in Torah obedience and covenant faithfulness.
3. **The Pauline Epistles:** Letters offering situational advice and commentary to specific communities.

The Unique Authority of the Gospels and the Judaic Epistles

- **The Gospels:** Contain the direct teachings of Jesus, who upheld the Torah and the Prophets. His words carry **divine authority** and are the foundation of Christian faith.
- **The Judaic Epistles:** Serve as bridges between Jesus's teachings and the early faith communities, reinforcing Torah observance and covenantal loyalty.

The Place of Paul's Letters in the Hierarchy

Paul's letters have value, but they are **not foundational commandments**. They are interpretive commentary—pastoral reflections aimed at specific communities navigating cultural, social, and theological dilemmas.

- When Paul's words are elevated above Jesus's teachings, an **inversion of authority** occurs.
- When Paul is used to reinterpret or nullify the Torah, yeast begins to spread.

The Danger of Misplacing Paul's Authority

- **Paul is not Jesus:** Paul himself never claimed divine authority equal to Jesus.

- **Paul is not Moses:** He is not the giver of the Law; he is a commentator on it.
- **Paul is not Above Correction:** When his writings seem to contradict the Torah, the Prophets, or Jesus's teachings, they must be approached with humility and critical examination.

Paul's Own Admission:

Paul himself clarified his role: *"I am the least of the apostles and do not even deserve to be called an apostle, because I persecuted the church of God."* (1 Corinthians 15:9)

His letters should have never been interpreted to override the authority of the Torah, the Prophets, or the words of Jesus.

Takeaway:

Paul's writings are not equal to the words of Jesus or the instructions found in the Judaic Epistles. They serve as commentary, pastoral advice, and situational wisdom. They must always be interpreted **in submission to the words of Jesus** and the eternal authority of the **Torah and Prophets**.

Section Transition:

Paul's letters are valuable when handled with care, humility, and a commitment to context. They can teach us about faith, cultural adaptation, and community life.

But they are not the cornerstone of Christian faith—that place belongs to Jesus alone.

In the next section, we will explore how **Paul's writings still carry significant lessons—but not in the way most readers currently understand them.**

15.3 Misunderstanding Saul/Paul's Most Significant Lessons

At first glance, the Pauline Epistles might seem like theological treatises, laying out foundational Christian doctrines. But when viewed with discernment and humility, a deeper, more significant lesson emerges—one that transcends the surface-level debates about **grace vs. works** or **law vs. freedom**.

Patterns, Inconsistencies, and Lessons Hidden in Plain Sight

Paul's writings are not void of value—they contain wisdom, pastoral advice, and reflections on faith and community life. But scattered throughout his letters are recurring **patterns, contradictions, and inconsistencies** that reveal a deeper truth:

- **Saul/Paul wrestled with his own contradictions.** He would sometimes affirm the Torah (Romans 3:31) and at other times seem to undermine it (Galatians 3:10-13).
- **Saul/Paul used rhetorical ambiguity.** He would argue passionately for one side of an issue and then hedge his argument with disclaimers or contradictory conclusions.
- **Saul/Paul's charisma created dependency.** Many communities struggled with an over-reliance on Paul's authority, leading to factions and confusion.

The Mirror Effect

The sharp-eyed reader will notice something profound: Paul's letters act as a **mirror** to the dynamics of faith communities.

- They show how **charismatic authority** can overshadow clear instruction from God.
- They illustrate how **sincerity** can still lead to **confusion** if not grounded in foundational truth.
- They highlight how well-intentioned leadership can inadvertently create **theological drift**.

Paul's letters are not a map—they are a **case study**. They reveal the inner workings of early faith communities and provide cautionary lessons about the **dangers of misplaced authority** and the **fragility of doctrinal clarity**.

Distortion Enters Slowly

The yeast that Jesus warned about (Matthew 16:6) often begins subtly, with a well-meaning interpretation, a small cultural accommodation, or a theological compromise.

Paul's letters reveal how easy it is for a community to begin straying from the foundation if they elevate a charismatic teacher above the clear instructions of God.

The Reader's Responsibility

This is not about vilifying Paul—it's about **understanding him in his proper context**. The reader must approach Paul's letters:

- With **humility**, recognizing their situational nature.
- With **discernment**, always cross-referencing them with the Torah, the Prophets, and Jesus's words.
- With **awareness**, noticing where Paul's words are being used to contradict foundational commandments.

Takeaway:

The most significant lesson of the Pauline Epistles isn't about theological debates—it's about **recognizing patterns of distortion, understanding the dangers of misplaced authority, and learning how sincerity can still lead to confusion**.

By the end of this book, the sharp-eyed reader will see the **true lesson of Paul's letters**—not as law, not as universal doctrine, but as a reflective tool, a cautionary tale, and an insight into how faith communities can easily stray from their foundation.

15.4 Why This Matters Today

The misuse of Paul's writings remains **one of the largest sources of yeast in Christianity today**. For centuries, Paul's situational letters have been elevated to the status of universal law, often overshadowing the direct words of Jesus and the eternal principles of the Torah.

When Paul is Elevated Above Jesus, Problems Arise

When Paul's words are treated as the highest authority:

- The **Torah is dismissed** as outdated or irrelevant.
- **Jesus's teachings** are reinterpreted through Pauline doctrine, rather than the other way around.
- **Grace becomes license**, allowing lawlessness to masquerade as spiritual freedom.

This elevation has led to countless doctrinal debates, schisms, and theological confusion. It has created traditions and systems that are **detached from the foundation Jesus laid** and the commandments God gave.

Restoring Proper Alignment

Correcting this issue isn't about dismissing Paul or removing his letters from scripture—it's about **understanding his proper place within the biblical hierarchy**:

1. **The Gospels interpret Paul—not the other way around.** Jesus's words remain supreme, unchallenged, and unaltered.
2. **Paul must align with the Torah and the Prophets.** Any contradiction must be addressed, examined, and understood within the proper context.
3. **Paul's writings are letters, not law.** They are reflective and situational, not universal commandments.

When we approach Paul's letters with this clarity, they become valuable tools for understanding the struggles of early faith communities, the challenges of cultural adaptation, and the importance of remaining anchored in God's commandments.

A Modern Cautionary Tale

Many modern denominations and theological systems are built almost exclusively on Pauline interpretations, often cherry-picking verses out of context to support preconceived doctrines.

- Grace becomes a free pass for disobedience.
- Faith becomes intellectual assent rather than a lifestyle of covenantal obedience.
- Unity is replaced with division as different groups cling to different Pauline proof-texts.

This is not Paul's fault—it's the fault of **misuse, misinterpretation, and elevation beyond his intended role.**

Takeaway:

Paul's letters have **immense value**, but they must always be interpreted **through the lens of Jesus's teachings** and **aligned with the Torah and Prophets.** They are **not universal commandments**, nor do they replace the foundational words of Jesus or the eternal authority of God's Law.

Proper understanding restores clarity, humility, and alignment:
- The **Gospels interpret Paul**, not the reverse.
- Paul's letters serve as **commentary and reflection**, not as the foundation of faith.

The Pauline Epistles are **letters and commentary**, not universal law or divine commandments. They addressed specific communities facing specific problems and must always be interpreted through the Gospels and Torah.

Their greatest lesson isn't about theological debates—it's about recognizing **how distortions enter faith communities, how authority can be misused, and how sincerity alone isn't enough to preserve clarity and alignment with God's word.**

As Jesus warned:
> *"Be sure that nobody deceives you."* (Matthew 24:4)

16. The Hierarchy of the New Testament.

The Gospels (Matthew, Mark, Luke, John)
- These four books stand at the summit of New Testament authority because they contain the **words, actions, and teachings of Jesus Himself**.
- They provide the foundational lens through which every other New Testament text must be interpreted.

The Judaic Epistles (James, Peter, Hebrews, Revelation, etc.)
- These letters function as **bridges**, connecting the teachings of Jesus to the early communities of believers.
- They align with the Gospels and reinforce Torah principles.

The Pauline Epistles (Romans, Corinthians, Galatians, etc.)
- These are **situational letters**, written to address specific problems in specific churches.
- They serve as **commentary and community guidance**, not universal commandments or higher revelation.

16.1 The Problem with Misreading the Hierarchy

When readers assume a **chronological progression**, they subconsciously assign greater authority to Paul's letters simply because they appear later in the New Testament than the Gospels of Jesus. This creates a dangerous theological inversion:

- Teachings meant to **clarify and reinforce Jesus's words** are instead used to **override them**.
- Contextual letters addressing localized issues are mistakenly applied as universal doctrines.
- The Gospels are viewed as predicated rather than foundational.

This misunderstanding shifts the foundation from **Jesus's direct teachings** to **Paul's situational commentary**.

The Consequences of Misplaced Authority

When Paul is elevated above Jesus:

- **Doctrinal Confusion:** Complex Pauline arguments are treated as foundational doctrines rather than contextual advice.
- **Lawlessness Disguised as Faith:** Teachings on grace are distorted into license for disobedience.
- **Jesus Sidelined:** The direct commandments of Jesus are treated as secondary to Paul's rhetorical arguments.

This inversion doesn't just lead to theological drift—it creates **systemic misunderstandings of God's character and covenantal intent**.

Correcting the Perception Problem

The issue isn't Paul himself—it's how his writings are **misused and elevated** beyond their intended role.

- Paul's words must be **checked against the Gospels**—never placed above them.
- Where Paul seems to contradict Jesus or the Law and Prophets, it's not Jesus or the Hebrew Bible that must be reinterpreted—it's Paul who must be examined more carefully.

Takeaway:

Paul's placement toward the end of the New Testament creates a **perception problem, not an authority problem**.

His letters must always be understood as **secondary commentary, evaluated against the foundational teachings of Jesus and the eternal truths of the Torah and Prophets**.

16.2 The Gospels Hold Supreme Authority in the New Testament

At the pinnacle of the New Testament stand the **Gospels—Matthew, Mark, Luke, and John.** They are not equal in authority to Paul's letters—they are **superior.**

The Gospels Interpret the Rest of the New Testament

Every New Testament text must be filtered through the lens of Jesus's teachings and the Law and Prophets:

- **The Judaic Epistles** must align with and reinforce the Gospels.
- **Paul's Epistles** must be measured against the Gospels—not the reverse.

When this understanding is respected, the message of the New Testament melds with the message of the Old Testament and the entire biblical arc becomes clear and cohesive. When it's reversed, confusion, division, and lawlessness take root.

The Theological Inversion of Modern Christianity

In many modern traditions:

- Paul's words override Jesus's commands.
- The Torah is dismissed in favor of Pauline arguments.
- Jesus's teachings are reduced to quaint moral lessons.

This inversion creates a **fractured Christianity,** built on commentary rather than commandments.

The Path to Restoration

- **Start with the Gospels.** Read and understand Jesus's words first.
- **Filter everything through His teachings.** Let His commandments guide every interpretation.
- **Align with the Torah and Prophets.** Follow the foundation Jesus upheld.

Takeaway:

The Gospels are not just **first in sequence**—they are **first in authority**. Every interpretation, every doctrine, and every theological insight must align with the words of Jesus.

16.3 Why This Matters Today

The perceived **"final word"** status of Paul's writings in modern theology has become one of the most significant stumbling blocks in following the teachings of Jesus and the Law of God.

The unintended consequence of granting Paul artificial preeminence within the New Testament has been a complete inversion of scriptural authority.

This isn't merely a scholarly concern—it's a foundational issue that impacts how faith is understood, taught, and lived out today. Reversing the Inversion

When Paul's letters are treated as the primary lens through which to view Jesus's teachings, distortions emerge:

- **Grace becomes license:** Obedience is dismissed as "legalism."
- **Faith becomes passive:** Belief is emphasized over action.
- **Jesus becomes secondary:** His direct words are subtly reinterpreted or diminished.

But when the **correct hierarchy** is restored:

- **The Gospels interpret Paul—not the other way around.** Jesus's words are the supreme authority.
- **Paul must be evaluated against Jesus, not Jesus against Paul.** If Paul's words seem to contradict Jesus's teachings or the Torah, they must be carefully reexamined.
- **Scripture regains its clarity:** The Gospels provide the interpretive lens for the rest of the New Testament.

This isn't about **rejecting Paul** or dismissing his contributions—it's about **understanding his letters in their proper place and context.**

The Blueprint Restored

When this structure is respected:

- **Jesus leads the church.** His words form the bedrock of faith and practice.
- **The Torah remains foundational.** God's commandments retain their eternal weight and purpose.
- **Paul is understood as commentary, not commandment.** His writings become practical insights into specific early church issues, not universal doctrines that override Jesus's words.

The Ripple Effect of Alignment

Restoring this hierarchy doesn't just fix abstract theological problems—it impacts real lives:

- Faith becomes active, not passive.
- Grace becomes a partnership, not a loophole.
- Obedience becomes joyful alignment, not burdensome legalism.

When Jesus leads, everything else falls into place.

Takeaway: The New Testament's structure isn't accidental—it's intentional. It's not chronological—it's hierarchical. The Gospels remain supreme, regardless of their placement in the Bible.

Jesus speaks first. Jesus speaks loudest. Jesus speaks last.

Section Takeaway:

The New Testament was designed with a clear structure, placing the Gospels as the supreme foundation. Paul's letters serve as commentary, not law, and must always submit to the teachings of Jesus and the Torah. When this hierarchy is respected, the clarity and integrity of scripture are restored.

17. Conclusion: Returning to Jesus's Scriptural Lens

Key Insight: Jesus's understanding of scripture was simple, clear, and rooted in covenantal obedience. He approached the *Law, Prophets and Writings* as a unified whole, with the Torah as its foundation, and viewed God's commandments as eternal and unchanging.

17.1 Jesus as Our Model

Jesus didn't just reference scripture—He lived it. Every word He spoke, every teaching He delivered, and every action He took was steeped in alignment with the Torah, the Prophets, and the Writings.

- **The Torah as His Foundation:** Jesus consistently upheld the Torah as the unshakable bedrock of faith and practice (Matthew 5:17-19). He clarified its intent, removed legalistic distortions, and modeled perfect obedience to its commands.
- **The Prophets as Amplifiers:** Jesus often used prophetic passages to reinforce the Torah's principles, confronting hypocrisy and calling people back to God's covenant.
- **The Writings as Reflections:** Whether in prayer, parable, or wisdom teaching, Jesus drew from the Psalms and wisdom literature to illuminate the path of covenantal living.

Scriptural Examples:

- **Temptation in the Wilderness:** In Matthew 4:1-11, Jesus countered each temptation from Satan using direct quotations from the Torah, demonstrating its sufficiency and authority.
- **On the Road to Emmaus:** In Luke 24:27, Jesus revealed how the Torah, Prophets, and Psalms all pointed to Him, creating a cohesive narrative from Genesis to Malachi.
- **The Greatest Commandment:** In Matthew 22:36-40, Jesus summarized the entire Torah with two foundational commands— love God and love your neighbor—drawing directly from Deuteronomy and Leviticus.

Takeaway: Jesus is our model for engaging with scripture. His approach was not fragmented, selective, or philosophical—it was relational, covenantal, and deeply anchored in obedience to God's Word.

17.2 A Call to Return to the Foundation.

Over centuries, distortions and doctrinal inversions have crept into scriptural interpretation. Commentary has been elevated above commandment, letters have overshadowed Jesus's words, and cultural filters have obscured God's eternal instructions.

To return to Jesus's scriptural lens, we must:

1. **Restore the Torah** as the foundation of understanding scripture.
2. **Read the Prophets** as amplifiers calling us back to God's covenant.
3. **Reflect on the Writings** as responses to living within that covenant.
4. **Place the Gospels** as supreme in the New Testament hierarchy.

This return isn't about legalism or intellectual superiority—it's about humility, obedience, and clarity. It's about seeing scripture not through inherited traditions or cultural biases, but through the same lens Jesus used.

Modern Application:

- Stop reading scripture in isolation; view it as a unified testimony.
- Stop using Paul to reinterpret Jesus; let Jesus's words interpret Paul.
- Start recognizing the Torah, Prophets, and Writings as a cohesive revelation of God's will.

Inquiry 1 Takeaway:

The path back is clear—we must see scripture the way Jesus did and obey it the way He taught. Scripture must be understood hierarchically, not as fragmented pieces or as a timeline.

- **In the Hebrew Bible:** The Law of Torah is the foundation, the Prophets are the amplifiers, and the Writings are the reflections.

- **In the New Testament:** Jesus's Gospels are submissive to Law & Prophets, but supreme in New Testament. The Judaic Epistles uphold Jesus's teachings, and the Pauline Epistles must remain carefully examined, not elevated to law.

Looking forward: When we retrain ourselves to use Jesus's scriptural lens, we attain clarity, find purpose, and can truly interpret what Christian practices are compatible with God's eternal covenantal commandments, and which are not.

A Retcon Detector

Once Jesus's scriptural lens starts to come into focus, something else quietly emerges: this lens isn't just how He read scripture. It's how He saw through distortion.

The moment Torah are understood as the foundation, the moment the Prophets are understood as covenantal amplifiers, and the Writings understood as reflections on living in covenant —everything that comes after must fall *under* that structure, not stand beside it.

Anything claiming divine truth that cannot survive that scrutiny... simply doesn't belong.

The early followers of Jesus knew this.

That's why they rejected Saul of Tarsus.

That's why the Ebionite version of Matthew—one far older and more Hebraically faithful than the canonical form—contains no virgin birth, no demigod overtures, and no subtle attempts to undermine the Law.

It tells the same story, but with all the yeast stripped away.

With Jesus's scriptural lens, you can now detect inconsistencies earlier scholars couldn't—or wouldn't.

Take Matthew 2:23: *"And he went and lived in a city called Nazareth, so that what was spoken by the prophets might be fulfilled, that he would be called a Nazarene."*

There is **no** such messianic prophecy in the Hebrew Bible.

None.

Pauline Theologians, desperate to protect the verse, perform acrobatics—pointing to words that sound similar to *netzer* (sprout) in Isaiah 11:1, or claiming "Nazarene" was simply a slur that conveniently fulfills the idea of the Messiah being despised.

However, the fact remains: no Old Testament Prophet ever said this.

A verse like Matthew 2:23 shouldn't just raise eyebrows—it should glow radioactive under Jesus's scriptural lens.

Jesus didn't teach us to discard the Law and Prophets. He taught us how to **read them**, how to **prioritize them**, and most importantly, how to **test everything else against them**.

Jesus's scriptural lens is a detector of things added to and taken away.

The overarching theme of Jesus's ministry - revealed in his rebukes of the Pharisees and how they added to the Torah Law, and rebukes of the Sadducees who ignored the Nevi'im Prophets & Writings – was to **live out Hebrew scripture** in context.

Scripture added to, or taken away from, or otherwise exercised in violation of God's Will in Heaven: was **the** recurring theme in every rebuke Jesus ever gave.

Jesus's scriptural lens aids in preserving canonical and covenantal integrity exposing distortions, insertions, and retcons that masquerade as prophecy.

Like Matthew 2:23.

With Christ's lens, the whole Bible comes into contextual focus, and we can use it to finally clearly see Him in scripture, see how he saw Himself, and see how He intended His teachings to help us reconcile our relationship with God in Heaven.

To be truly Christian, the first subject in the Bible we need to look into with Christ's scriptural lens is "Jesus of Nazareth" Himself according to His own words in the Gospels and the specific standards set forth in God's Law, Prophets, & Writings.

Inquiry 2: Who was Jesus and who wasn't He?

Introduction:

Understanding who Jesus was requires dismantling centuries of Greco-Roman distortions and returning to the prophetic blueprint.

This means looking to scripture to determine the original messianic meaning, and to history to understand why variations of it emerged, aligning our understanding of the Heavenly Father's messiah.

Core Question:

Who was Jesus according to scripture, and what distortions have obscured His true identity?

In **Inquiry 1**, we examined **how Jesus viewed, taught, and lived scripture**—with the **Torah as the foundation, the Prophets as amplifiers, and the Writings as reflections.**

Now, equipped with **Jesus's scriptural lens**, we are ready to **see Him more clearly**—not through the layers of yeast added by centuries of Greco-Roman philosophy and institutional distortion, but through the **raw, unfiltered clarity of the prophetic blueprint.**

We'll ask simple but profound questions:

- **What does scripture actually say about messiah?**
- **What does it mean that Jesus fulfilled those prophecies?**
- **How did history distort his identity?**

This Inquiry isn't about **reinventing Jesus**—it's about **revealing Him as He was always meant to be seen.**

By the end of this Inquiry, the **real Jesus**—the **Hebraic Messiah, the obedient servant of YHWH, the fulfillment of prophecy**—will come into focus.

The time has come to **meet the Messiah of God**—not as religion has painted Him, but **as scripture reveals Him.**

Some of these distortions are quite well known, others fester concealed behind centuries of Greco Roman influence.

1. Yeshua: The Name That Means YHWH's Salvation

Key Insight:

Names in scripture carry prophetic weight and divine purpose. The shift from "Yeshua" to "Jesus" reflects more than just linguistic drift—it reflects cultural and theological disconnection.

1.1 The Power of a Name in Hebraic Culture

In ancient Hebraic culture, names were far more than mere identifiers; they carried deep prophetic significance, reflecting divine purpose, calling, and identity. A name often encapsulated a person's mission, destiny, or unique relationship with YHWH. To understand Yeshua's name, we must first appreciate the Hebraic tradition of names as **identity markers tied to mission and divine intent.**

Examples from Scripture:

- **Abram → Abraham:** In Genesis 17:5, God changes Abram's name ("exalted father") to Abraham ("father of many nations"), marking the covenant promise that Abraham would be the patriarch of a multitude of nations.
- **Sarai → Sarah:** Sarai ("my princess") becomes Sarah ("princess of nations"), aligning her identity with the broader promise of lineage and nations.
- **Jacob → Israel:** In Genesis 32:28, Jacob ("heel-grabber" or "supplanter") becomes Israel ("one who struggles with God") after wrestling with the angel. This name change signifies Jacob's transformation into a patriarch of God's chosen people.

- **Hoshea → Joshua:** In Numbers 13:16, Moses renames Hoshea ("salvation") to Joshua ("YHWH saves" or "YHWH is salvation"), foreshadowing his mission to lead the Israelites into the Promised Land.

Each of these transformations is not arbitrary but directly tied to their divine purpose. These aren't just name changes—they are revelations of mission.

When the angel declares to Joseph in **Matthew 1:21**:
"You are to give him the name Yeshua, because he will save his people from their sins,"
it's not just an instruction—it's a divine pronouncement of mission.

Yeshua literally means "YHWH saves" or "salvation." It's not just a name—it's a prophecy, a declaration of purpose, and a testament to YHWH's faithfulness to His covenant with humanity.

The Prophetic Weight of Yeshua's Name

In Yeshua's time, names like His were not uncommon. The name *Yeshua* derives from the root word *yeshu'ah* (יְשׁוּעָה), meaning **"YHWH's salvation" or "deliverance."** But while others may have carried the same name, only one would perfectly embody its prophetic purpose.

- **Joshua (Yehoshua):** The Old Testament figure Joshua (Yehoshua) led the Israelites into the Promised Land, fulfilling God's covenantal promise.
- **Yeshua (Jesus):** Yeshua leads humanity not into physical land, but into alignment with God's eternal covenant—a spiritual Promised Land of reconciliation and obedience.

The parallels between Joshua and Yeshua are not coincidental. In many ways, Joshua served as a **foreshadowing archetype** of Yeshua's mission:

- Joshua conquered physical enemies; Yeshua conquered spiritual enemies.
- Joshua brought the people into a land of milk and honey; Yeshua brings people into a kingdom of eternal life.
- Joshua upheld the Torah and called people to obedience; Yeshua perfectly fulfilled the Torah and taught others to live by it.

Joshua's name and mission point directly to Yeshua.

The prophetic alignment of their names and roles underscores YHWH's unbroken narrative thread woven throughout scripture. This is why understanding the name *Yeshua* in its original Hebraic context is so crucial—it anchors Him within God's prophetic plan.

Yeshua vs. Jesus: What's in a Name?

The transition from *Yeshua* to *Jesus* wasn't just a phonetic change—it marked a profound cultural and theological shift.

To the Hebraic mind, *Yeshua* wasn't merely a name; it was a mission statement. To call upon *Yeshua* was to invoke the salvation of YHWH Himself.

In contrast:

- The English name *Jesus* carries no intrinsic meaning.
- In Western cultural imagination, *Jesus* often evokes Greco-Roman artistic portrayals: a passive, long-haired, fair-skinned man in flowing robes.
- The name *Jesus* has become detached from its Hebraic prophetic roots, obscuring its significance.

This disconnect isn't just linguistic—it's theological. It subtly shifts Yeshua from a **Hebraic Messiah obedient to YHWH** to a **Greco-Roman figure distanced from His scriptural identity.**

The Shift Away from Prophetic Understanding

Names in Hebraic culture represented **divine calling**, while in Greco-Roman culture, names became more about **titles, mythology, and honorary designations**:

- Greek gods like *Zeus* or *Apollo* had legends with mythological connotations, and great power, but they lacked the covenantal intimacy seen in the Hebrew relationship with their God and Heavenly Father.
- This cultural lens altered how early Gentile Christians understood *Yeshua's* name.

Over time, Yeshua became:

- *Iēsous* in Greek.
- *Iesus* in Latin.
- *Jesus* in English.

While these translations were not malicious, they carried unintended consequences:

- The prophetic weight of *Yeshua* was diluted.
- The cultural context of His mission was obscured.
- Western Christianity grew distant from its Hebraic foundation.

Why It Matters Today

When we call Him *Yeshua*, we aren't just using a historically accurate name—we are invoking His mission. We are reminding ourselves of:

- The prophetic significance of His coming.
- The intimate connection between His name and YHWH's salvation.
- The Hebraic roots of our faith, unbroken and unaltered.

When we reduce Him to *Jesus* without understanding His original identity, we risk:

- Viewing Him through Western mythological or theological distortions.

- Missing the covenantal weight embedded in His name.
- Detaching His mission from the larger narrative of YHWH's salvation plan.

Takeaway:

The name *Yeshua* isn't just a label—it's a **prophetic declaration of His mission and role in God's plan**. The loss of His original name represents more than just a linguistic change—it reflects a **disconnect from the Hebraic understanding of the Messiah**.

To call Him *Yeshua* is to remember:

- His name means **"YHWH saves."**
- His mission was foretold, specific, and covenantal.
- His identity is inseparable from His role as the Messiah of YHWH.

Understanding and honoring *Yeshua's* name isn't just about semantics—it's about restoring clarity, faithfulness, and alignment with the scriptural blueprint.

1.2 From Yeshua to Jesus: Greco-Roman Linguistic Drift

Key Insight:

The evolution from *Yeshua → Iēsous → Jesus* wasn't just a matter of translation—it was a cultural shift that subtly detached Yeshua from His Hebraic roots and identity. This transition mirrored broader theological and cultural distortions, altering how subsequent generations understood messiah's mission and identity.

The Challenge of Translating Yeshua into Greek and Latin

At the heart of the shift from *Yeshua* to *Jesus* lies the unavoidable reality of **linguistic limitations**.

Hebrew and Greek, though both ancient languages, operate with fundamentally different phonetic systems, grammatical structures, and cultural emphases.

1. **Hebrew Phonetics vs. Greek Phonetics:**
   - The Hebrew name *Yeshua* (יֵשׁוּעַ) contains the **/sh/ sound** (as in *shoe*), represented by the letter *shin* (שׁ).
   - Greek, however, lacks an equivalent /sh/ sound. The closest approximation was **/s/** represented by the Greek letter *sigma* (Σ).
   - Similarly, the Hebrew letter *yodh* (יְ) with its /y/ sound had no phonetic equal in Greek, the corresponding Greek letter "ι" has an /i/ sound as in the Greek word "ιώτα" and the English loan-word "iota."
   - Additionally, Yeshua ends with a soft /a/ sound, understood as feminine in Greek, while Greek male names frequently end in an /s/ sound (usually -*os* or -*us*), so it was altered to comply with Greek grammatical gendering convention.
2. **Transformation into Iēsous (Ἰησοῦς):**
   - The name *Yeshua* became *Iēsous* in Greek because it followed Greek naming conventions.
   - The **/y/** sound was replaced with an **/i/** pronunciation.
   - The **/sh/** pronunciation was replaced with a simple **/s/** sound.
   - The final **/a/** sound was replaced with **/ous/** for grammatical consistency in Greek.
   - While this was not malicious, it nonetheless stripped the name of its original Hebraic phonetic and cultural richness.
3. **Transition into Latin (Iesus):**
   - When the New Testament was translated into Latin, *Iēsous* became *Iesus*.
   - The Greek diphthong **/ou/** became the Latin vowel **/u/**.

- While this version retained some similarity to the Greek pronunciation, it was already a step removed from the original *Yeshua*.

4. **Final Evolution into English (Jesus):**
   - In early English translations, the Latin *Iesus* became *Jesus*.
   - The letter "J" (which didn't exist in early Greek or Hebrew alphabets) emerged in the Middle Ages as a stylistic variation of the letter "I".
   - By the time of the King James Bible (1611), "*Jesus*" had become the standard rendering in English.

Every linguistic step—*Yeshua* → *Iēsous* → *Iesus* → *Jesus*—was a natural byproduct of phonetic and grammatical constraints, but each step also took the name further away from its Hebraic prophetic meaning.

Theological Consequences of Linguistic Drift

The Loss of the Prophetic Connection to God's Salvation.

- The name *Yeshua* means **"YHWH saves"**—a declaration of divine purpose and prophetic mission.
- In Hebrew, every mention of *Yeshua* invokes the foundational truth of God's salvation.
- The Greek name *Iēsous* and the Latin *Iesus* obscure this direct prophetic connection. By the time we arrive at *Jesus*, the name no longer inherently conveys the idea of salvation through YHWH, it started to take on another concept of savior.

Cultural Disconnect from Hebraic Roots

- As Christianity spread westward into Greek and Roman territories, it increasingly distanced itself from its Hebraic origins.
- For Gentile converts, the Hebraic meaning of *Yeshua* was often overlooked or misunderstood.
- Instead of viewing Yeshua as the **Hebraic Messiah obedient to YHWH**, He began to be perceived through the lens of **Greco-Roman cultural paradigms**—as a divine figure akin to Hercules or Achilles.

Rise of a Hellenized Jesus

- Greek and Roman mythology frequently depicted hybrid celestial-human figures (*demigods*) with supernatural powers and grandiose destinies.
- As the Greco-Roman church absorbed these cultural frameworks, they began to project these mythological tropes onto Jesus.
- The result was a gradual transformation of the **Hebraic Yeshua into a Greco-Roman Jesus**—a cosmic figure stripped of His original prophetic identity.

Alienation from Jewish Believers

- Early Jewish followers of Yeshua remained deeply connected to His Hebraic identity and prophetic role.
- As the Greek and Latin linguistic forms gained dominance, Jewish believers felt increasingly alienated from Gentile Christian expressions of faith.
- The name *Yeshua*, which resonated deeply with Jewish prophetic expectations, was replaced by a foreign-sounding *Iēsous* and later *Jesus*.

This alienation was not just cultural—it had profound theological implications. The Messiah who was foretold in the Torah, Prophets, and Writings began to feel less like a fulfillment of Jewish prophecy and more like a foreign figure introduced from outside their tradition.

Resistance to the Linguistic Shift

Not everyone accepted the shift from *Yeshua* to *Iēsous* without concern. Historical records show that:

- **Jewish Believers in the First Century:** Many early Jewish followers continued using the name *Yeshua* in their communities. They saw no need to adopt Greek or Latin renderings.
- **Early Ebionites and Nazarene Communities:** These sects resisted the Hellenization of Yeshua's identity and teachings.
- **Rabbinic Pushback:** As Christianity increasingly became identified with Gentile expressions, rabbinic leaders distanced themselves

from anything associated with *Iēsous*. This name carried connotations of foreign domination and cultural erasure.

These tensions underscore that the shift was not universally accepted but was instead part of a larger cultural drift away from the original Hebraic roots of the faith.

Was This Malicious?

No. The evolution from *Yeshua* to *Jesus* was not part of a deliberate conspiracy to erase Yeshua's Hebraic identity.

It was primarily a **byproduct of language barriers, cultural transmission, and the natural evolution of names across linguistic boundaries**.

However:

- **Unintended Consequences:** Each step in the linguistic journey obscured part of Yeshua's prophetic significance.
- **Theological Drift:** The loss of connection to the name's meaning paralleled a broader theological shift away from YHWH-centered worship and into Greco-Roman mythological paradigms.
- **Cultural Reinterpretation:** The cultural dominance of the Greco-Roman church meant that their interpretation of *Jesus* became the dominant lens through which the Messiah was understood.

This wasn't an act of rebellion, but it was still a distortion. And distortions, even unintentional ones, have consequences.

Why This Matters

- **Names Carry Meaning:** In Hebraic culture, names were prophetic declarations of mission and purpose. The name *Yeshua* connects directly to salvation and God's covenant.
- **Cultural Drift Distorts Theology:** As the name transitioned through Greek, Latin, and English, its prophetic weight and cultural identity were lost.

- **Restoring the Name Restores the Mission:** Recognizing Yeshua by His Hebraic name isn't about pedantic accuracy—it's about reclaiming the prophetic meaning behind His identity.

Takeaway:

While the linguistic shift from *Yeshua* to *Jesus* wasn't malicious, it obscured the prophetic weight and cultural identity tied to His original name. In English, *Yeshua* aligns most closely with *Joshua*, emphasizing His prophetic mission as a servant tasked with guiding people towards God's provision and salvation.

Understanding and using *"Yeshua"* rather than *"Jesus"* helps us:

- Reconnect with his purpose.
- Restore the prophetic clarity of His name.
- Align ourselves more closely with the scriptural portrayal of the Messiah.

This is not a minor detail—it's a critical step in seeing the Messiah not through Greco-Roman distortion, but as the Hebraic Servant of YHWH, perfectly fulfilling His divine mission.

1.3 Jesus of Nazareth vs. Yeshua of Bethlehem

Key Insight:

Prophecy points to Bethlehem, not Nazareth, as the Messiah's defining birthplace (*Micah 5:2*). Yet, history gave us "Jesus of Nazareth"—a title shaped more by cultural shorthand than prophetic identity.

The Prophetic Blueprint: Bethlehem Foretold

The Hebrew Scriptures were explicit about the Messiah's birthplace:

Micah 5:2 – "But you, Bethlehem Ephrathah, though you are small among the clans of Judah, out of you will come for me one who will be ruler over Israel, whose origins are from of old, from ancient times."

2 Samuel 7:12-16 – God promises David that his lineage will produce an eternal ruler, establishing the significance of Bethlehem, David's hometown.

Bethlehem was not just a poetic detail—it was a divine marker of messianic legitimacy. Any figure claiming to fulfill the Messianic prophecies had to align with this birthplace.

Bethlehem: A Forgotten Keystone

The Messiah's birthplace was not incidental—it was central to His identity.
- Bethlehem ties Yeshua directly to David's lineage.
- Bethlehem fulfills specific prophecies pointing to the Messiah.
- Bethlehem validates His divine appointment and mission.

Yet, the shorthand of Nazareth replaced this prophetic cornerstone with a more accessible cultural marker.

This is not just a historical footnote—it's a theological fault line.

Why This Matters

1. **Prophecy Matters:**
   - Micah 5:2 isn't a casual prediction—it's a cornerstone of Messianic prophecy.
   - Ignoring Bethlehem diminishes the prophetic credibility of Yeshua's identity.
2. **Precision Matters:**
   - Titles and identifiers shape perception.
   - "Jesus of Nazareth" emphasizes His earthly upbringing; "Yeshua of Bethlehem" emphasizes His prophetic fulfillment.
3. **Cultural Drift Distorts Scripture:**
   - As Christianity moved westward, cultural convenience often overshadowed scriptural precision.
   - This shift, while unintentional, altered how billions of people understand the Messiah's identity.

Takeaway:

The label *"Jesus of Nazareth"* reflects a **cultural misunderstanding**, not a prophetic truth. While Nazareth was where Yeshua grew up, **His true identity is rooted in Bethlehem**, the prophesied birthplace of the Messiah.

Understanding and restoring the emphasis on Bethlehem isn't about pedantic accuracy—it's about prophetic alignment.

- **Bethlehem validates Yeshua's Messianic identity.**
- **Nazareth explains His upbringing, but not His purpose.**

When we remember *Yeshua of Bethlehem*, we honor the prophetic blueprint given in scripture and realign ourselves with God's intended revelation.

1.4 The Prophetic Identity Obscured:

Key Insight:

Yeshua's birthplace in Bethlehem was not universally known by those he preached to.

The confusion surrounding Yeshua's birthplace was not a misunderstanding invented by later generations—it was an issue **during His earthly ministry.**

The tension between prophetic expectation and apparent reality caused many to stumble over Yeshua's identity as the Messiah, even as they watched him perform miracles in YHWH's name, uphold the Law and Prophetic call to covenantal alignment, in both letter and spirit. This stumbling block remains a persistent force today.

> *"He went into his own, and they received him not"* John 1:11

This verse, while referring to Yeshua, reflects a recurring theme in the Hebrew Bible concerning the relationship between YHWH and the people of Israel.

Several passages in the Law, Prophets, and Writings depict instances where God's chosen people, Israel, failed to recognize, obey, or remain faithful to him, despite being in a covenant relationship with Him.

- **Deuteronomy 32:19-21:** This passage highlights how Israel's actions provoked YHWH's anger, leading to rejection and consequences.

- **Judges 2:12-14:** This describes how the Israelites forsook YHWH and worshipped other gods, leading to His anger and them being delivered into the hands of enemies.

- **Isaiah 1:4:** This verse describes Israel as a sinful nation laden with iniquity, who have forsaken and provoked the Holy One of Israel.

- **Jeremiah 5:23:** This speaks of Israel having a defiant and rebellious heart, revolting and departing from God.

- **Psalm 78:40-42:** This recounts how often Israel provoked YHWH in the wilderness and limited the Holy One of Israel by not remembering His power.

These examples from the Hebrew Bible illustrate the same pattern of rejection by God's chosen people as described in John 1:11.

They show a consistent pattern of Israel failing to recognize and obey YHWH, His messiahs, even after all the blessings and guidance provided by God, and clear call to covenantal alignment by Yeshua.

The Prophetic Expectation: Bethlehem, City of David

"But you, Bethlehem Ephrathah, though you are small among the clans of Judah, out of you will come for me one who will be ruler over Israel, whose origins are from of old, from ancient times." (Micah 5:2)

This prophecy wasn't vague; it specifically identified Bethlehem as the birthplace of the Messiah, directly tying Him to King David's lineage. The Messiah was expected to emerge from David's ancestral home, not from an obscure town in Galilee.

For many in Yeshua's time, this expectation was crystal clear. Yet His upbringing in Nazareth created a **disconnect between expectation and observation.**

The Confusion Documented in Scripture

John 7:41-42 — Open Debate in the Crowd

"Others said, 'He is the Messiah.' Still others asked, 'How can the Messiah come from Galilee? Does not Scripture say that the Messiah will come from David's descendants and from Bethlehem, the town where David lived?'"

Even among those who witnessed Yeshua's miracles and teachings, Bethlehem's prophetic importance was a stumbling block.

The crowd's reasoning was sound—they knew Micah's prophecy—but they made a **surface-level judgment** based on Yeshua's Galilean upbringing.

John 1:11 — Rejection by His Own People

"He came to His own, and His own did not receive Him."

Part of this rejection was rooted in unmet expectations about His geographic origins. The people of Israel had a clear framework for identifying the Messiah, and Yeshua seemed to deviate from it.

Mark 6:4 — A Prophet Without Honor in His Hometown

"A prophet is not without honor except in his own town, among his relatives and in his own home."

In Nazareth, Yeshua was simply *"the carpenter's son"* (Matthew 13:55). His local identity obscured His prophetic significance to those who had known Him as a boy.

These accounts highlight a recurring theme: **familiarity breeds dismissal.** Many judged Yeshua not by His actions, teachings, or fulfillment of prophecy but by their assumptions about His origins.

Cultural and Societal Expectations of the Messiah

At the time of Yeshua's ministry, **Messianic expectations were intense and multifaceted**:

A Political Savior:
- Many expected the Messiah to be a **warrior-king like David**, who would overthrow Roman oppression and restore Israel's sovereignty.
- This expectation blinded many to Yeshua's mission as the **suffering servant of Isaiah 53.**

A Geographic Marker:
- The expectation of a Davidic Messiah from Bethlehem was so ingrained that any deviation seemed irreconcilable.
- People didn't anticipate a Messiah who would spend His youth in Nazareth and minister in Galilee.

Signs and Wonders:
- While Yeshua's miracles demonstrated divine authority, they weren't always enough to override people's assumptions.
- The belief in Bethlehem's prophetic importance overshadowed even miraculous acts for some.

Competing Messianic Figures

Yeshua wasn't the only person in His time to be considered a potential Messiah. Other figures claimed (or were believed) to fulfill the

Messianic role, and many of them aligned more closely with prevailing expectations.

Judas of Galilee (6 AD):
- Led a tax revolt against Roman authorities.
- Seen by some as a Messianic figure because of his militant approach.

Simon Bar Kokhba (132–135 AD):
- Declared Messiah by Rabbi Akiva.
- Led a rebellion against Rome but ultimately failed.

Theudas (44 AD):
- Claimed to be a prophet and Messiah.
- Gathered followers with promises of deliverance but was executed by the Romans.

Each of these figures aligned, in some way, with the political and military expectations of the Messiah.

Yeshua's mission—focused on spiritual reconciliation, humility, and covenant fulfillment—stood in stark contrast.

While these figures often had strong political or geographical alignment with Messianic expectations, they lacked the prophetic depth and spiritual mission demonstrated by Yeshua.

Human Assumptions and Cultural Biases

The confusion about Bethlehem versus Nazareth wasn't just a misunderstanding—it stemmed from deeply ingrained cultural biases:

Surface-Level Judgments:

- People judged Yeshua by His upbringing in Nazareth, failing to investigate His actual birthplace.
- His miraculous birth in Bethlehem wasn't widely known or emphasized during His ministry.

Rigid Expectations:
- Many people clung tightly to their preconceived notions of what the Messiah *should* look like.
- Yeshua's humble appearance and Galilean ministry didn't match the grandeur they expected from a Davidic ruler.

Resistance to Spiritual Fulfillment:
- The focus on a physical Messiah—one who would restore an earthly kingdom—blinded people to the spiritual depth of Yeshua's mission.

The Significance of Looking Deeper

Despite the confusion and misconceptions, those who **looked beyond surface details recognized the truth**:

- The shepherds at Yeshua's birth understood Bethlehem's prophetic importance (*Luke 2:8-20*).
- The Magi traveled from the East specifically to worship the King foretold to be born in Bethlehem (*Matthew 2:1-12*).
- Simeon and Anna in the temple recognized Yeshua's identity despite His humble presentation (*Luke 2:25-38*).

These examples remind us that **Yeshua's prophetic identity was never hidden—it was always there for those willing to see.**

Takeaway:

The confusion surrounding Bethlehem versus Nazareth wasn't unique to later generations—it was an issue **during Yeshua's lifetime.** His prophetic identity was clear to those who looked deeper but hidden from those who judged by surface details.

- **Bethlehem validated His prophetic mission.**
- **Nazareth obscured it for those easily dismissive, or unwilling to see beyond appearances.**

This tension reminds us that **God's plans often defy human expectations, but they are always clear to those who seek Him with humility and faith.**

Human Assumptions vs. Divine Fulfillment

Many people in Yeshua's time, despite knowing the prophecies, missed their fulfillment because they were distracted by appearances.

- They saw a carpenter's son from Nazareth.
- They missed the divine thread running through His birthplace, lineage, and mission.

Luke 2:4-7 – The Fulfillment

The Gospel of Luke provides an account of **how this prophecy was fulfilled with divine precision**:

> *"So Joseph also went up from the town of Nazareth in Galilee to Judea, to Bethlehem the town of David, because he belonged to the house and line of David. He went there to register with Mary, who was pledged to be married to him and was expecting a child. While they were there, the time came for the baby to be born, and she gave birth to her firstborn, a son."*

The Divine Mechanism of the Census:

- The Roman census wasn't coincidental—it was a divine tool ensuring Joseph and Mary would travel to Bethlehem.
- What seemed like a bureaucratic order was, in reality, **God's orchestration of prophecy fulfillment.**

A Lineage Anchored in David:

- Joseph's descent from the house of David validated Yeshua's Davidic lineage.
- This genealogical connection was essential for fulfilling 2 *Samuel* 7:12-16.

Purposeful, Preordained, Precise:

- Yeshua's birth in Bethlehem was not happenstance—it was **preordained and carefully orchestrated by divine providence.**

Bethlehem wasn't just a backdrop to a nativity scene—it was the **theological bedrock** of Yeshua's Messianic legitimacy.

Takeaway:

Yeshua's birth in Bethlehem wasn't incidental—it was **divinely orchestrated to fulfill Micah 5:2.**

- The circumstances surrounding His birth were not random but purposeful.
- Bethlehem wasn't just a historical detail—it was a prophetic credential.

Understanding the importance of Bethlehem anchors Yeshua's identity firmly within **God's covenantal promises** and validates His role as the **long-anticipated Messiah foretold by the prophets.**

1.5 Why Nazareth Stuck

Key Insight:

Despite Bethlehem's prophetic significance, the title *"Jesus of Nazareth"* became the dominant identifier. This shift wasn't prophetically accurate—it was the result of **early church missteps, cultural convenience, and limited scriptural literacy among Gentile converts.**

Early Church Missteps

The early church's identity was shaped in a transitional period where Hebraic roots began to fade under the growing influence of **Gentile converts** and **Greco-Roman culture.**

Limited Knowledge of Hebrew Prophecy:
- The earliest followers of Yeshua were primarily Jewish, and Bethlehem's significance was well understood through *Micah 5:2* and the Davidic covenant.
- However, as the Gospel spread beyond Judea into Gentile-dominated regions (Greece, Rome, and North Africa), many new converts had **no background in the Hebrew Bible**.
- For Gentile audiences, Bethlehem carried little theological weight—it was an obscure town in a foreign land.

Evangelistic Practicality:
- In missionary contexts, Nazareth became a **practical reference point**.
- Yeshua spent most of His life and ministry in Nazareth; this fact was immediate, verifiable, and familiar to both Jewish and Gentile audiences.
- Early church leaders often prioritized **accessibility over accuracy**, emphasizing Nazareth as a relatable identifier.

Failure to Reinforce Prophetic Markers:
- As Gentile influence grew, many church leaders failed to emphasize Bethlehem as a prophetic credential.
- Instead, the narrative of "Jesus" as the "man from Nazareth" overshadowed the deeper scriptural context of Yeshua's Davidic lineage and Bethlehem origin.

This wasn't an act of malice—it was a failure of **discernment and scriptural literacy**. Over time, this cultural shorthand became a **theological cornerstone**, eclipsing the prophetic clarity of Bethlehem, especially to Jewish listeners trying to discern his legitimacy in light of scriptural understanding of Law and Prophets.

Convenience Over Accuracy

For Greco-Roman society, practical and memorable identifiers often took precedence over prophetic nuance.

Geographic Shorthand:
- In Roman administrative systems, people were typically identified by their **place of residence**, not their birthplace.
- Referring to someone as "of Nazareth" was administratively consistent and culturally understandable.

Narrative Simplicity:
- Greco-Roman storytelling favored clear, streamlined narratives.
- Nazareth became the default geographic marker in the Gospel accounts because it was **where Yeshua grew up, where He ministered, and where He was known.**
- Bethlehem, though critically important, was less familiar to Gentile audiences and required more context to explain its significance.

Cultural Memory:
- As Christianity spread through the Roman Empire, familiarity with Nazareth outpaced theological emphasis on Bethlehem.
- Over generations, the prophetic significance of Bethlehem faded, while the shorthand of Nazareth solidified into church tradition, art, and liturgy.

This **geographic convenience slowly overshadowed prophetic precision**, distorting the Messianic identity of Yeshua in subtle but profound ways.

Lack of Scriptural Literacy

The shift wasn't merely cultural—it was also theological, driven by a **lack of access to the Hebrew Scriptures** among early Gentile believers.

Dependence on Oral Teachings:
- Early Gentile converts often lacked direct access to the Tanakh.
- They relied on **oral teachings from church leaders**, many of whom prioritized Yeshua's ministry over His prophetic roots.
- Subtle details—like the prophetic importance of Bethlehem—were either overlooked or deemphasized.

Misplaced Emphasis:
- Bethlehem carried **deep Messianic weight** in Jewish tradition but was lost on Gentile audiences.
- Nazareth, by contrast, became a practical and tangible identifier for Yeshua.

Institutional Drift:
- As Christianity became increasingly institutionalized in the Roman Empire, Bethlehem's significance continued to fade.
- Art, literature, and church teachings perpetuated "Jesus of Nazareth" as the dominant cultural title, further burying the prophetic significance of Bethlehem.

This lack of scriptural literacy wasn't merely ignorance—it was a **systemic failure to preserve prophetic accuracy in favor of cultural familiarity**.

Theological Consequences of Prioritizing Nazareth Over Bethlehem

Obscuring the Davidic Covenant:
- By centering Yeshua's identity on Nazareth, the connection to David's lineage through Bethlehem was **weakened in theological perception**.
- The fulfillment of *Micah* 5:2 became a secondary detail rather than a primary prophetic credential.

Shifting Focus from Prophecy to Geography:
- Prophetic markers are central to validating Yeshua's role as the Messiah.
- When geography (Nazareth) replaced prophecy (Bethlehem) as the dominant identifier, **the theological emphasis shifted from divine fulfillment to cultural familiarity**.

A Pattern of Distortion:
- The Nazareth-over-Bethlehem shift became a **template for future theological distortions**.
- Convenience and cultural adaptation began to outpace scriptural alignment, creating gaps in understanding that persist to this day.

Why This Matters

Prophecy Validates the Messiah:
- Yeshua's legitimacy as the Messiah is built on prophetic fulfillment, not cultural labels.
- Every fulfilled prophecy serves as **evidence of divine orchestration and YHWH's faithfulness.**

Theological Accuracy Over Cultural Convenience:
- Christianity's historical drift away from its Hebraic roots began with subtle shifts like this one.
- Restoring the emphasis on Bethlehem isn't about semantics—it's about **alignment with scripture.**

Understanding the True Messianic Identity:
- The Messiah wasn't just a teacher from Nazareth—He was the **Davidic ruler born in Bethlehem, fulfilling Micah 5:2.**
- Prophecy gives context, authority, and validation to Yeshua's mission.

Takeaway:

The label *"Jesus of Nazareth"* became dominant not because of prophetic accuracy, but because of:

- **Early church missteps**
- **Cultural convenience**
- **Limited scriptural literacy among Gentile converts**

Geography was prioritized over prophecy—a **pattern of distortion** that would repeat itself in later theological errors.

Understanding "Jesus of Nazareth" more accurately as *"Yeshua of Bethlehem"* reclaims:

- The **prophetic foundation of His identity**
- The **theological weight of His Davidic lineage**
- The **truth of his role in God's plan for humanity**

This isn't a minor correction of perception—it's a necessary realignment with **God's covenant and Yeshua's teachings**.

Transition to Section 2:

Understanding Yeshua's prophetic birthplace is only one part of the larger revelation. Just as His birth was foretold and divinely orchestrated, so too was **His life, mission, and sacrifice.**

- How did cultural distortions affect our understanding of Him?
- What does scripture reveal about the true nature of the Messiah?

In the next section, we'll uncover how the **Hebraic understanding of Messiah** reveals a profound progression of truths about Yeshua's identity.

---

2. Clarifying the Hebraic Messiah:

Key Insight:

Hebraic Messiah are **covenantal, obedient to God's Law, and are anointed by Him for a divine mission**.

2.1 Mashiach: Anointed One

The term **"Messiah" (Mashiach)** carries a profound and precise meaning in Hebrew—it means **"anointed one."** It does not imply deity, celestial origins, or hybrid divinity. Instead, it speaks of **divine appointment, empowerment, and approval** for a sacred task **by God within the framework of His covenant.**

Within modern Pauline Christianity, believers are taught that Jesus is their messiah. When the actual definition of messiah is applied, another inversion is revealed, they believe that Jesus is *"their"* anointed one.

This inverted perception of procession runs in reverse to everything Yeshua, his direct disciples, and all the patriarchs of Judaism knew.

Messiah are anointed by God, not man.

This reveals a deeper truth regarding Yeshua: **he is God's messiah (anointed), not ours**. That is the proper flow of procession.

Yeshua knew full well what his own name meant: "YHWH-Saves".

Who humanity's "Savior" is was of no question to any of God's anointed.

Only God Saves.

The Significance of Anointing in Ancient Israel

In ancient Israel, **anointing with oil was a sacred ritual** used to mark someone as set apart for a divine purpose. This was not a casual ceremony—it was a **holy act, rich in symbolism and prophetic weight**.

The Act of Anointing:
- Sacred oil, often a fragrant mixture including olive oil and spices (*Exodus 30:22–25*), was poured over the head of the chosen individual.
- This ritual symbolized **God's Spirit resting upon the anointed person**, empowering them for their divine mission.
- The anointing wasn't about the oil itself—it was about **God's favor, presence, and appointment**.

Who Was Anointed?
- **Kings:** To lead and protect God's people (*1 Samuel 16:13* — David anointed by Samuel).
- **Prophets:** To declare God's word and call people to repentance (*1 Kings 19:16* — Elisha anointed as a prophet).

- **Priests:** To mediate between God and humanity, offering sacrifices and interceding on behalf of the people (*Leviticus 8:12* — Aaron anointed as high priest).

Each role carried unique responsibilities, but none implied divinity. Anointing was about **alignment with God's purpose and empowerment by His Spirit**, not about becoming a godlike figure.

Yeshua as the Fulfillment of King, Prophet, and Priest

Yeshua uniquely fulfills **all three anointed roles simultaneously**, weaving them together in perfect harmony:

Yeshua the King:
- Yeshua is referred to as the **"Son of David"**, the rightful heir to David's throne (*Matthew 1:1; Luke 1:32-33*).
- Unlike earthly kings, Yeshua's kingship isn't about political conquest but **spiritual leadership and covenantal restoration** (*John 18:36* — "My kingdom is not of this world").

Yeshua the Prophet:
- Yeshua spoke the words of YHWH with authority (*John 12:49* — "For I did not speak on my own, but the Father who sent me commanded me to say all that I have spoken").
- Like the prophets before Him, He called people to **repentance, covenantal faithfulness, and alignment with YHWH's will** (*Matthew 4:17*).

Yeshua the Priest:
- Yeshua mediated between humanity and YHWH, offering Himself as a sacrifice in perfect obedience (*Hebrews 9:11-12*).
- He functioned as both **priest and offering**, fulfilling the sacrificial requirements outlined in the Torah (*Leviticus 17:11*).

No other figure in scripture seamlessly embodies all three roles. **Yeshua's anointing transcends individual office—it encompasses the fullness of God's mission for His anointed one.**

The Messiah's Role is Covenantal, Not Celestial

The Hebrew scriptures consistently present the Messiah as a **covenantal servant**, not a celestial being descending in radiant power. His mission was to **fulfill YHWH's covenant promises**, not to replace or overshadow YHWH Himself.

Isaiah 42:1:
"Here is my servant, whom I uphold, my chosen one in whom I delight; I will put my Spirit on him, and he will bring justice to the nations."
- This passage emphasizes the Messiah's **servanthood and divine appointment**.
- The Messiah's authority comes not from celestial status but from **YHWH's Spirit resting upon Him**.

Psalm 2:7:
"You are my son; today I have become your father."
- The term *"son"* here signifies **divine favor and appointment**, not biological or celestial divinity.
- In Hebraic understanding, the term emphasizes **a covenant relationship, not celestial hybridity**.

Deuteronomy 18:18:
"I will raise up for them a prophet like you from among their fellow Israelites, and I will put my words in his mouth."
- The Messiah was expected to arise from among the people—a human figure, divinely appointed and empowered.
- This passage directly counters the Greco-Roman idea of demigods or celestial hybrids.

The Power of Obedience, Not Celestial Essence

Obedience as the Core of the Messiah's Mission:
- Yeshua's authority stemmed from His **perfect obedience to YHWH's will** (*John 5:30* — "I seek not to please myself but him who sent me").

- Unlike earthly kings who often succumbed to pride and rebellion, Yeshua remained **aligned with YHWH in every word, action, and sacrifice.**

Not Replacing, but Fulfilling:
- Yeshua didn't come to replace YHWH or to demand worship for Himself.
- His mission was to **fulfill the covenant, restore alignment, and call humanity back to YHWH's instruction** (*Matthew 5:17*).

Greco-Roman Distortions:
- In Greco-Roman mythology, celestial/terrestrial hybrid heroes often occupied a **demigod status**, blending celestial and earthly natures.
- Early Gentile converts projected these mythological templates onto Yeshua, distorting the Hebraic vision of the Messiah.
- The result was a theological drift away from the **obedient servant role described in the Hebrew scriptures.**

Why This Matters

Distorting the Messiah Distorts the Mission:
- Redefining Yeshua as a celestial or hybrid being undermines the significance of His **human obedience and sacrifice.**
- If Yeshua were not fully human, His obedience would not carry the weight of a representative sacrifice.

Obedience is the Key:
- Yeshua's power didn't come from his own essence—it came from **perfect, unyielding obedience to YHWH's instruction.**

The Covenant Remains Central:
- The Messiah's mission was to fulfill, not overwrite, the covenant between YHWH and humanity.
- Recognizing Yeshua as the **anointed servant** aligns us with the covenantal framework established by YHWH.

Takeaway:

The title "messiah" means "anointed one," not "divine one."

- Kings, prophets, and priests were anointed for sacred missions, but they were never deified.
- Yeshua's role is **covenantal, not celestial**, and His authority comes from **perfect obedience, not celestial hybridity.**

Understanding Yeshua as the **anointed servant of YHWH** restores clarity to His mission and aligns us with the **prophetic vision of the Messiah described in the Hebrew Scriptures.**

Transition to Section 2.2

The Hebraic understanding of messiah is not monolithic—it was **layered and multifaceted.** The prophets described **archetypal roles** for messiah: two of these are **Messiah Ben-Joseph (Suffering Servants)** and **Messiah Ben-David (Conquering Kings).**

These archetypes aren't always contradictory—they represent **a two-phase mission** that Yeshua is still in the process of fulfilling.

In the next section, we'll uncover how these **two Messianic archetypes reveal Yeshua's mission in profound ways,** tying together prophecy, fulfillment, and future expectation.

2.2 Messianic Archetypes: Ben-Joseph and Messiah Ben-David
Key Insight:

Yeshua's mission wasn't just about fulfilling one role—it was about **fulfilling multiple prophetic archetypes.**

- How do the roles of **Messiah Ben-Joseph** and **Messiah Ben-David** deepen our understanding of Yeshua's identity?
- Why did He fulfill the Joseph archetype first, and what does that mean for the Davidic fulfillment still to come?

Messiah Ben-Joseph: The Suffering Servant

The archetype of **Messiah Ben-Joseph** is rooted in **prophetic imagery, sacrificial symbolism, and the life of Joseph, the son of Jacob.** This Messianic role emphasizes **suffering, humility, rejection, and ultimate redemption.**

The Origins of the Messiah Ben-Joseph Archetype

The foundation of **Messiah Ben-Joseph** lies in two primary sources:

The Life of Joseph (Genesis 37–50)
- Joseph, son of Jacob, was **beloved by his father but rejected by his brothers** (*Genesis 37:4*).
- He was **betrayed and sold into slavery** by his own people (*Genesis 37:28*).
- Through immense **suffering and humiliation**, Joseph eventually rose to a position of **salvation and deliverance** for his family and the surrounding nations (*Genesis 41:41–44*).
- His suffering had **redemptive significance**, saving countless lives during the famine.

The Prophecy of the Suffering Servant (Isaiah 53)
- Isaiah paints a striking portrait of a **suffering servant** who would bear the iniquities of others.
- He would be **rejected, despised, and crushed** for the sake of bringing healing and reconciliation.
- This figure would act as a **substitutionary sacrifice**, willingly taking upon Himself the sins of others to restore covenantal harmony with YHWH.

These two sources—**Joseph's life story** and **Isaiah's prophecy**—merged into the archetype of **Messiah Ben-Joseph**, the one who would **suffer on behalf of the people.**

Yeshua as Messiah Ben-Joseph

Yeshua's earthly ministry and sacrifice align precisely with the archetype of **Messiah Ben-Joseph:**

Rejected by His Own People:
- Just as Joseph was rejected by his brothers, Yeshua was rejected by His people.
- *John 1:11 — "He came to that which was his own, but his own did not receive him."*
- Yeshua was seen as an outlier, a threat to the established religious power structure, and was ultimately handed over to Roman authorities.

A Man of Sorrows, Acquainted with Grief:
- *Isaiah 53:3 — "He was despised and rejected by mankind, a man of suffering, and familiar with pain."*
- Yeshua experienced hunger, thirst, exhaustion, betrayal, and the agony of crucifixion.
- His suffering was not incidental—it was **integral to His mission.**

Bearing the Iniquities of Others:
- *Isaiah 53:5 — "But he was pierced for our transgressions, he was crushed for our iniquities; the punishment that brought us peace was on him, and by his wounds we are healed."*
- Yeshua's crucifixion wasn't just an act of political execution—it was a **sacrificial offering.**
- He willingly bore the collective guilt and consequences of humanity's failure to uphold the covenant with YHWH.

The Willing Sacrifice:
- Unlike earthly kings who use power to avoid suffering, Yeshua **embraced suffering** as part of His divine mission.
- *John 10:18 — "No one takes it from me, but I lay it down of my own accord."*
- This willingness set Yeshua apart from any earthly ruler or revolutionary.

Prophetic Layers: Yeshua's Fulfillment in Light of Isaiah 53

Isaiah 53 serves as the **cornerstone prophecy** for Messiah Ben-Joseph. Let's examine its key elements and their fulfillment in Yeshua:

He Was Rejected:
- *Isaiah 53:3* — *"He was despised and rejected by mankind."*
- Fulfilled in *Luke 4:28-30*, when Yeshua was rejected in His hometown.

He Bore Our Sins:
- *Isaiah 53:6* — *"The Lord has laid on him the iniquity of us all."*
- Fulfilled in *1 Peter 2:24* — *"He himself bore our sins in his body on the cross."*

He Remained Silent Before His Accusers:
- *Isaiah 53:7* — *"He was oppressed and afflicted, yet he did not open his mouth."*
- Fulfilled in *Matthew 27:12-14*, when Yeshua stood silent before Pilate.

His Death Brought Redemption:
- *Isaiah 53:10* — *"It was the Lord's will to crush him and cause him to suffer."*
- Fulfilled in *Luke 22:42*, when Yeshua prayed, *"Not my will, but yours be done."*

These fulfillments are not isolated coincidences—they are **divine markers** pointing unmistakably to Yeshua as **Messiah Ben-Joseph**.

Why This Matters

The Mission Was Always Covenantal:
- The role of Messiah Ben-Joseph was not about **earthly power or conquest**.
- It was about **restoring the covenantal relationship between humanity and YHWH**.

Obedience, Not Strength, Was Central:
- Yeshua's mission as Messiah Ben-Joseph was defined by **obedience, humility, and sacrifice**, not celestial power.

This Archetype Explains the Cross:
- Without understanding the archetype of Messiah Ben-Joseph, the crucifixion appears as a tragic accident or defeat.
- But through this lens, the cross becomes **the ultimate fulfillment of YHWH's plan for redemption**.

The Two-Phase Mission:
- Messiah Ben-Joseph was only the **first phase** of Yeshua's mission.
- The suffering servant had to come before the conquering king.

Takeaway:

The archetype of **Messiah Ben-Joseph** reveals Yeshua's mission as **the Suffering Servant prophesied in Isaiah 53**.

- He was **rejected, pierced, and crushed** for our iniquities.
- His authority came not from celestial power but from **perfect obedience and self-sacrifice**.
- This archetype sets the stage for the next phase of His mission—as **Messiah Ben-David, the Conquering King**.

Understanding **Messiah Ben-Joseph** aligns us with the **prophetic expectation of YHWH's plan** and prepares us for the **coming fulfillment of Messiah Ben-David**.

Transition to Section 2.3:

If Messiah Ben-Joseph represents **sacrifice and redemption**, then Messiah Ben-David represents **victory, restoration, and eternal kingship**.

- Why is the Davidic archetype essential to Yeshua's identity?
- How do the scriptures describe the Messiah's future role as King?
- What does this mean for humanity's covenantal future?

In the next section, we will explore how **Yeshua will fulfill the archetype of Messiah Ben-David**—the ruler who will **establish God's kingdom and reign with justice and righteousness.**

2.3 Messiah Ben-David: The Conquering King

Key Insight:

Messiah Ben-David represents the **second phase of Yeshua's mission**—a role not yet fulfilled but deeply rooted in Hebraic prophecy. Where Messiah Ben-Joseph embodied **humility, sacrifice, and suffering**, Messiah Ben-David embodies **authority, kingship, and eternal justice.**

The Prophetic Foundation of Messiah Ben-David

The archetype of **Messiah Ben-David** emerges directly from **God's covenant with King David** and the prophetic promises given through figures like **Isaiah, Jeremiah, and Ezekiel.**

The Davidic Covenant (2 Samuel 7:12-16)
- *"Your house and your kingdom will endure forever before me; your throne will be established forever."*
- God promises David an **eternal dynasty**, culminating in a ruler who will reign **forever in justice and righteousness.**
- This covenant establishes the **Messiah as a Davidic king**—a ruler in both lineage and mission.

The Prophecy of Isaiah 9:6-7
- *"For to us a child is born, to us a son is given, and the government will be on his shoulders... He will reign on David's throne and over his kingdom, establishing and upholding it with justice and righteousness from that time on and forever."*
- This passage presents Messiah Ben-David as:
  - **A Mighty Ruler** with God-granted authority.
  - **A Prince of Peace** bringing lasting shalom.
  - **An Eternal King** whose reign will never end.

The Messianic Kingdom (Jeremiah 23:5-6)

- *"I will raise up for David a righteous Branch, a King who will reign wisely and do what is just and right in the land."*
- This prophecy emphasizes the Messiah's **righteous leadership**, **wisdom**, and **justice**—qualities often absent from earthly rulers.

The Messiah Ben-David archetype doesn't replace the Messiah Ben-Joseph archetype—it **completes it**. Yeshua first came to suffer and redeem; He will return to **reign and restore**.

Understanding the Dual Archetypes in "Second Temple" Judaism

In Yeshua's time, Jewish communities had a **nuanced understanding** of the dual Messianic archetypes.

Messiah Ben-Joseph and Messiah Ben-David Were Expected:

- Rabbinic traditions, such as those recorded in the *Talmud* and *Midrash*, reflect an expectation of **two Messianic figures**.
- Messiah Ben-Joseph would **suffer, struggle, and prepare the way.**
- Messiah Ben-David would **conquer, establish the kingdom, and reign eternally.**

Rabbinic Commentary on Messiah Ben-David:

- **Talmud (Sanhedrin 98a):** The Messiah is referred to as the **"Son of David,"** who will arise to deliver Israel.
- **Midrash Tehillim on Psalm 2:** The Messiah is described as a **kingly ruler** who will crush the enemies of God and bring peace to the world.
- **Targum Jonathan on Isaiah 11:** The Davidic Messiah is seen as a leader empowered by the Spirit of God to rule with wisdom and justice.

Misunderstanding During Yeshua's Ministry:

- Many Jewish people in Yeshua's time expected the Messiah to fulfill the **Ben-David archetype immediately**—a conquering king who would overthrow Roman rule.
- When Yeshua instead fulfilled the **Ben-Joseph archetype (suffering servant)**, many rejected Him as the Messiah because He didn't fit their immediate expectations.

- This disconnect wasn't a failure of prophecy—it was a failure of **interpretation and timing.**

Yeshua as the Future Messiah Ben-David

While Yeshua fulfilled the role of **Messiah Ben-Joseph** during His earthly ministry, the full of his **Messiah Ben-David phase remains unfulfilled.**

The Promise of His Return:
- In Acts 1:11, the angels declare: *"This same Jesus, who has been taken from you into heaven, will come back in the same way you have seen him go into heaven."*
- His return will not be as the suffering servant but as the **eternal king and judge.**

The Revelation of His Kingship:
- *Revelation 19:16 — "On his robe and on his thigh he has this name written: KING OF KINGS AND LORD OF LORDS."*
- The image of Yeshua returning as a conquering king aligns perfectly with the **Messiah Ben-David archetype.**

Restoring Justice and Righteousness:
- Yeshua will fulfill Isaiah 9:6-7, ruling with **justice, wisdom, and everlasting peace.**
- Unlike earthly kings, His reign will not be corrupted by power, greed, or violence.

The Final Restoration of Israel:
- The Davidic Messiah is prophesied to **restore Israel fully** and establish God's kingdom on earth (*Ezekiel 37:24-25*).
- Yeshua will **unite all nations** under His righteous rule, bringing eternal harmony and reconciliation.

How the Greco-Roman Church Misunderstood These Archetypes

As Christianity transitioned from its **Hebraic roots to a Greco-Roman cultural context**, the nuanced dual-archetype understanding of the Messiah was **largely abandoned or distorted.**

Emphasis on the Divine Christ:
- The Greco-Roman church often emphasized Yeshua's **divinity over His humanity**, creating a hybrid celestial figure.
- This emphasis overshadowed the **two-phase prophetic mission** described in scripture.

Obscuring the Two Roles:

- Instead of seeing Yeshua as **both the Suffering Servant and the Conquering King**, many Gentile converts viewed Him primarily through **Hellenistic theological lenses.**
- The sacrificial aspect (Ben-Joseph) was exaggerated, while the kingly fulfillment (Ben-David) was minimized or spiritualized.

Spiritualizing the Davidic Kingdom:

- Instead of anticipating a **physical reign of Messiah Ben-David**, many early church leaders spiritualized His kingship into **a metaphorical rule over hearts and minds.**
- This undermined the prophetic expectation of a **literal Messianic kingdom on earth.**

Loss of Jewish Context:

- Without a firm grasp of Jewish prophetic frameworks, Gentile church leaders lost sight of how **Messiah Ben-Joseph leads into Messiah Ben-David.**

Why This Matters

The Two-Phase Mission Provides Clarity:

- Without understanding **Messiah Ben-Joseph and Messiah Ben-David**, Yeshua's mission seems incomplete or contradictory.

Prophecy Remains Unfulfilled:

- Recognizing Yeshua as **Messiah Ben-David** reminds us that **His mission is ongoing** and that His return is central to God's plan.

Restoring Theological Accuracy:

- Abandoning or spiritualizing the Davidic archetype distorts the prophetic narrative.
- Restoring it aligns us with **the covenant promises made to David.**

Takeaway: Messiah Ben-David represents the **culmination of Yeshua's mission**—the phase where He will:

- **Reign on David's eternal throne.**
- **Establish justice and righteousness forever.**
- **Restore God's kingdom on earth.**

Understanding this archetype aligns us with the **prophetic vision of the Messiah** and reminds us that Yeshua's mission is **not yet complete—it is still unfolding.**

If Messiah Ben-Joseph was about **suffering and redemption,** and Messiah Ben-David is about **kingship and restoration,** how do these two phases fit together in YHWH's plan?

In the next section, we will explore **how these archetypes form a cohesive, two-phase fulfillment** of God's Messianic promises.

2.4 The Two-Phase Fulfillment

Key Insight:

The Messiah's mission, as prophesied in scripture, was never meant to be a **single, one-time event.** It was—and is—a **two-phase fulfillment** encompassing the dual archetypes of **Messiah Ben-Joseph (the Suffering Servant)** and **Messiah Ben-David (the Conquering King).**

These roles are not contradictory—they are **complementary**, completing the prophetic picture of YHWH's redemptive plan.

The Expectation vs. The Reality

In Yeshua's time, many people struggled to reconcile the dual archetype of the Messiah. Their expectations were shaped by **centuries of suffering under foreign powers, political oppression, and unfulfilled prophecies.**

A King, Not a Servant:
- The Jewish people longed for **Messiah Ben-David**—a **conquering king who would overthrow Roman oppression** and establish an eternal kingdom.
- They expected immediate **justice, power, and visible victory,** not suffering and crucifixion.

Prophecies in Conflict?
- Passages like *Isaiah 53* (Suffering Servant) and *Isaiah 9:6-7* (Conquering King) seemed contradictory on the surface.
- Some rabbis speculated that **two separate Messiahs** would come— one to suffer and one to rule.
- Yeshua's mission reveals these are **not two Messiahs but two phases of one Messiah's mission.**

The Disciples' Struggle:
- Even Yeshua's closest disciples had difficulty understanding the two-phase mission.
- *Luke 24:21* — *"But we had hoped that he was the one who was going to redeem Israel."*
- They didn't grasp that the **redemption of Israel would come through sacrifice before sovereignty.**

The problem wasn't with the prophecies—it was with **human impatience and misunderstanding of God's timeline.**

Phase One: Messiah Ben-Joseph Fulfilled

Yeshua's first coming aligned perfectly with the **Messiah Ben-Joseph archetype:**

The Suffering Servant:
- Yeshua willingly suffered rejection, humiliation, and death (*Isaiah 53:3-7*).
- **The Redemptive Sacrifice:**
  - He bore humanity's iniquities on the cross, fulfilling the sacrificial archetype (*Isaiah 53:5*).
- **The Role of Obedience:**
  - Yeshua demonstrated perfect submission to YHWH's will (*John 5:30*).
- **Spiritual Restoration:**
  - Through His sacrifice, He opened the path for spiritual reconciliation between humanity and YHWH.

Yeshua's death and resurrection were not signs of **defeat**, but of **victory**—a fulfillment of the Messiah Ben-Joseph mission.

However, the story does not end there.

Phase Two: Messiah Ben-David Yet to Come

The second phase of Yeshua's mission aligns with the **Messiah Ben-David archetype:**

The Conquering King:
- Yeshua will return to rule as a **righteous and eternal king.** (*Isaiah 9:6-7*).

Justice and Restoration:
- He will establish **justice, peace, and righteousness** across all nations (*Jeremiah 23:5-6*).

The Davidic Throne:
- He will sit on the **throne of David** and reign forever (*2 Samuel 7:16*).

The End of Oppression:
- All earthly powers and spiritual forces opposed to YHWH will be crushed (*Revelation 19:11-16*).

While Yeshua's first coming addressed **humanity's spiritual condition**, His return will address the **structural, political, and cosmic dimensions of God's kingdom.**

The Two Roles Are Complementary, Not Contradictory

The archetypes of **Messiah Ben-Joseph and Messiah Ben-David** work together in perfect harmony.

Messiah Ben-Joseph (The First Phase):
- Focus: **Redemption and Atonement**
- Role: **Suffering Servant**
- Purpose: To **heal the spiritual wound** caused by humanity's disobedience.

Messiah Ben-David (The Second Phase):
- Focus: **Restoration and Rule**
- Role: **Conquering King**
- Purpose: To **establish God's kingdom** with justice and eternal peace.

These are not two separate missions but two **connected movements** in God's divine plan.

Why This Matters

Understanding Prophetic Fulfillment:
- Misunderstanding these archetypes creates **theological confusion** about Yeshua's mission.
- Recognizing the two-phase mission aligns our expectations with **scriptural prophecy.**

A Lens for Scripture:

- The dual archetypes provide a **coherent framework** for understanding the Messiah's mission across the Old and New Testaments.
- Apparent contradictions vanish when seen through this lens.

The Importance of the Return:

- Without the **second phase (Messiah Ben-David)**, Yeshua's mission remains incomplete.
- His return is not optional—it is **essential to fulfilling the covenant promises** made to David and Israel.

Hope for the Future:

- Understanding the **Messiah Ben-David archetype** anchors us in **hope and expectation**.
- Yeshua's first coming guarantees His return; His sacrifice assures His reign.

Takeaway:

Yeshua's mission is not a single event—it is a **two-phase fulfillment** of God's Messianic plan:

- **First, as Messiah Ben-Joseph:** The **Suffering Servant** who bore humanity's sin through sacrifice and obedience.
- **Second, as Messiah Ben-David:** The **Conquering King** who will establish eternal justice, peace, and restoration.

These two archetypes do not **compete**—they **complete** the prophetic picture of the Messiah.

Understanding this dual role:

- **Clarifies prophetic expectations.**
- **Reconciles apparent contradictions.**
- **Underscores the necessity of Yeshua's return.**

YHWH's plan is still unfolding. The story isn't over yet.

3. The Nephilim Controversy: YHWH Doesn't Do Demigods

Key Insight:

The Hebrew Scriptures make one thing abundantly clear: **YHWH does not tolerate celestial-human hybrids.**

The Nephilim in *Genesis 6:1-4* were an abomination, and God wiped them out in the flood.

If Yeshua had been a **demigod—a celestial-human hybrid—He would not have been exalted as the Messiah.** Instead, He would have been rejected and destroyed.

3.1 Genesis 6:1-4 — The Nephilim and God's Rejection

> *"When human beings began to increase in number on the earth and daughters were born to them, the sons of God saw that the daughters of humans were beautiful, and they married any of them they chose... The Nephilim were on the earth in those days—and also afterward—when the sons of God went to the daughters of humans and had children by them. They were the heroes of old, men of renown." (Genesis 6:1-4)*

This brief but weighty passage sets a precedent in scripture about **YHWH's stance on celestial-human unions and their offspring.**

The Nature of the Nephilim

- The term *Nephilim* is often interpreted as **"fallen ones"** or **"giants."**
- They were the offspring of the **"sons of God"** (*b'nei Elohim*) and **"daughters of men."**
- These unions were **unnatural, unauthorized, and corrupting** to YHWH's created order.

The Corruption of Creation

- The Nephilim are described as **"heroes of old, men of renown"** — implying great power and influence.
- Yet, despite their fame and might, they represented a **perversion of God's creation.**
- These beings weren't part of YHWH's intended design for humanity. They were **a distortion, an abomination, and a threat to the covenantal order.**

God's Judgment on the Nephilim

- The flood narrative in *Genesis 6–9* reveals YHWH's response to the corruption brought about by the Nephilim.
- The flood was not just about general human wickedness — it was about **purging the earth of unnatural corruption and preserving the integrity of humanity as YHWH created it.**
- *Genesis 6:5-7 — "The Lord saw how great the wickedness of the human race had become on the earth, and that every inclination of the thoughts of the human heart was only evil all the time."*
- YHWH didn't redeem the Nephilim. He **destroyed them** along with the rest of the corrupted earth.

A Clear Precedent

- The destruction of the Nephilim establishes a firm theological principle:
  YHWH does not create, tolerate, or exalt celestial-human hybrids.
- If YHWH wiped out the Nephilim, it makes no theological sense that He would later intentionally create a celestial-human hybrid Messiah.
- The Messiah, by necessity, had to be fully human — anointed, obedient, and aligned with God's covenantal design.

Theological Consequences of a Hybrid Messiah

The idea of Yeshua being a celestial-human hybrid—a demigod—stands in direct opposition to the foundational principles of scripture.

A Hybrid Messiah Would Contradict God's Nature:

- YHWH is a **God of order, justice, and consistency** (*Malachi 3:6 — "I the Lord do not change."*).
- To send a hybrid Messiah would contradict YHWH's established patterns in Genesis.

The Messiah's Obedience Requires Humanity:

- The power of Yeshua's sacrifice lies in His **obedience as a fully human being** (Hebrews 4:15 — "For we do not have a high priest who is unable to empathize with our weaknesses, but we have one who has been tempted in every way, just as we are—yet he did not sin.").
- A demigod Messiah would lack the capacity to fully represent humanity before YHWH.

Distortion of Prophecy:

- The Hebrew scriptures consistently describe the Messiah as "one like us" (*Deuteronomy 18:18*).
- There is no room in Hebraic prophecy for a celestial, mythological hybrid ruler.

3.2 A Side-by-Side Comparison: Mythological Demigods vs. Yeshua

Characteristic	Mythological Demigods	Yeshua
Origin	Born of gods and humans	Born of a woman, anointed by YHWH
Purpose	Glory, power, conquest	Redemption, obedience, covenantal restoration
Moral Character	Often arrogant and self-serving	Perfectly humble and obedient to YHWH
Alignment with God	Capricious, morally ambiguous	Fully aligned with YHWH's will
Relationship to Humanity	Superior, distant	Identifies fully with humanity
End Result	Often tragic or morally tainted	Exalted, fulfilling YHWH's eternal covenant

This comparison highlights the stark difference between mythological demigods and the Hebraic Messiah.

Yeshua's humanity was not a flaw—it was essential to His role.

The Influence of Greco-Roman Mythology

A World Saturated in Demigod Narratives:

- The Greco-Roman world was steeped in myths of **demigods like Hercules, Perseus, and Achilles.**
- These figures were often portrayed as **powerful but morally flawed,** occupying a liminal space between gods and humans.

Cultural Projection onto Yeshua:
- As Christianity spread into Greco-Roman culture, mythological paradigms were subtly projected onto Yeshua.
- Yeshua began to be interpreted **through the lens of Hercules or Achilles** rather than the suffering servant of Isaiah.

Distorting the Messiah:
- These distortions stripped Yeshua of His **covenantal humanity** and replaced it with **mythological celestial qualities.**
- Over time, the Greco-Roman portrayal of Jesus overshadowed the **Hebraic Messianic archetype.**

Why This Matters

YHWH's Consistency:
- YHWH does not change His standards. The destruction of the Nephilim proves that **celestial-human hybrids are outside His design.**

The Power of Obedience:
- Yeshua's mission required **full humanity**, not celestial hybridity.
- His obedience carries power precisely because He was **fully human.**

Rejecting Mythological Distortions:
- The blending of Greco-Roman demigod imagery with Yeshua's identity obscures the **clear, consistent message of scripture.**
- Restoring the **Hebraic understanding of the Messiah** is essential for clarity and alignment with YHWH's word.

Takeaway:
YHWH does not create, tolerate, or exalt celestial-human hybrids.
- The Nephilim were an abomination, destroyed in the flood.
- Yeshua was fully human, fully obedient, and perfectly aligned with YHWH's will.
- Viewing Him as a demigod introduces a distortion that undermines the core message of scripture and His mission.

Hebrew messiahs , YHWH's anointed, are not Greco Roman demigods like Hercules or Perseus—they are anointed servants chosen to fulfill prophecy, return people to God's Covenant and Calendar.

Transition to Section 3.3:

The mythological distortions we've discussed didn't emerge in a vacuum. They were part of a **broader cultural obsession with demigods and hybrid figures in Greco-Roman society.**

- How did this obsession influence early Christianity?
- What theological damage resulted from blending these paradigms with the identity of Yeshua?

In the next section, we'll uncover the **Greco-Roman obsession with demigods** and how it shaped—and distorted—the early church's understanding of the Messiah.

3.3 The Greco-Roman Obsession with Demigods

Key Insight:

In **Greco-Roman mythology**, demigods were revered as **heroes, saviors, and hybrid figures**—beings who bridged the gap between gods and humans. Figures like **Hercules, Perseus, and Achilles** were celebrated for their superhuman strength, godly favor, and heroic exploits.

When Christianity spread into the **Greco-Roman world**, these mythological paradigms seeped into **Christian theology**, distorting the identity of Yeshua. Instead of being understood as the **fully human, fully obedient Messiah foretold in Hebrew prophecy**, Yeshua began to be interpreted through the lens of **pagan hero archetypes.**

But here's the issue: **YHWH does not operate like Zeus or Poseidon.** The Hebrew Scriptures **reject hybrid beings entirely**—they are **corruptions of creation, not part of God's order.** Presenting Yeshua as a celestial-human hybrid is not just **inaccurate**—it is **offensive to the entire scriptural narrative.**

The Greco-Roman Demigod Paradigm

In the Greco-Roman world, **demigods were central to mythological storytelling and religious devotion.** They served as cultural heroes and objects of worship, embodying an aspirational blend of **inherited power and human relatability.**

Famous Demigods in Greco-Roman Mythology:

Hercules (Heracles in Greek):
- Son of **Zeus and Alcmene,** a mortal woman.
- Known for his **incredible strength and heroic feats,** including the Twelve Labors.
- Despite his power, Hercules was often **flawed, reckless, and morally ambiguous**—traits inconsistent with the Hebrew Messianic archetype.

Perseus:
- Born of **Zeus and Danaë,** a mortal princess.
- Famous for **slaying the Gorgon Medusa** and rescuing Andromeda.
- Perseus was portrayed as a hero, but his story emphasized **individual heroism and Olympian favor, not obedience to a higher moral authority.**

Achilles:
- The son of the **goddess Thetis and mortal Peleus.**
- Known for his **invincibility (except his heel) and martial prowess.**
- His story ends in **tragedy and moral ambiguity,** revealing the **unstable moral foundation of demigod archetypes.**

Theological Implications of Demigod Worship:

- **Demigods were worshipped because of their power, not their moral obedience.**

- Their exploits often included **violence, vengeance, and self-serving actions.**
- These figures operated **outside moral law**, acting as intermediaries between gods and humans.

In short, demigods in Greco-Roman mythology were **heroic, powerful, and deeply flawed**—a far cry from the **obedient, covenantally faithful Messiah described in Hebrew prophecy.**

The Influence on Early Christianity

When Christianity spread into the **Greco-Roman world**, it encountered a population **steeped in mythological thinking.**

Mythological Frameworks Were Familiar:
- Pagan converts were accustomed to **hybrid heroes and demigods** as religious archetypes.
- The idea of a **"celestial-human savior"** fit neatly into their worldview.

Yeshua Recast as a Demigod:
- For many Gentile converts, it was easier to view Yeshua as a **"hybrid hero" like Hercules** rather than the **obedient servant prophesied in Isaiah 53.**
- This distortion introduced theological problems, shifting the focus away from **obedience and covenantal fulfillment** to **supernatural power and celestial spectacle.**

Art and Literature Reinforced the Distortion:
- Early Christian art often depicted Yeshua in **Greco-Roman heroic poses**, resembling figures like Apollo or Zeus.
- Titles like *"Son of God"* were interpreted **through mythological frameworks** rather than Hebraic prophecy.

Theological Drift:

- As the church became **less Hebraic and more Greco-Roman**, the focus on Yeshua's **obedience and humanity diminished**.
- Emphasis shifted toward **celestial authority, cosmic spectacle, and mythological grandeur**.

This cultural overlay didn't just add poetic flourish—it **distorted the fundamental understanding of Yeshua's role as the Messiah**.

The Scriptural Messiah: Fully Human, Fully Obedient

The Hebrew Scriptures make it abundantly clear: **The Messiah was to be fully human, not a celestial-human hybrid.**

Isaiah 53: The Suffering Servant

- *"He was despised and rejected by mankind, a man of suffering, and familiar with pain... But he was pierced for our transgressions, he was crushed for our iniquities."* (Isaiah 53:3,5)
- The Messiah is portrayed as **a man**, not a celestial hybrid.
- His power comes not from **superhuman strength**, but from **obedience to YHWH**.

Deuteronomy 18:18 — A Prophet Like Moses

- *"I will raise up for them a prophet like you from among their fellow Israelites, and I will put my words in his mouth."*
- The Messiah would be **a human prophet, raised up from among His people**.
- He would not descend as a celestial demigod figure.

Luke 2:52 — Yeshua Grew in Wisdom and Stature

- *"And Jesus grew in wisdom and stature, and in favor with God and man."*
- Growth is a **human characteristic**, not a celestial one.
- Yeshua's development as a person underscores His **full humanity**.

These verses align perfectly with the **Hebraic understanding of the Messiah**, but they stand in sharp contrast to **Greco-Roman demigod myths**.

Why This Matters

A Theological Distortion:
- Recasting Yeshua as a **demigod** undermines the **scriptural foundation of His role as Messiah.**
- It prioritizes **mythological power dynamics** over **obedience, covenant faithfulness, and sacrifice.**

Obedience Over Spectacle:
- Yeshua was not exalted because of supernatural strength or celestial origins.
- He was exalted because of **His perfect obedience and alignment with YHWH's will.**

A Pattern of Mythological Drift:
- Recognizing how Greco-Roman paradigms influenced early Christianity helps us **uncover and correct distortions** that persist to this day.

Takeaway:

If Yeshua were a **celestial-human hybrid,** He would have been **rejected, not exalted.**

- The God of Israel does not create or tolerate demigods—He **destroys them** (*Genesis 6:1-4*).
- Yeshua fulfilled the role of Messiah as a **fully human, perfectly obedient servant of YHWH,** not as a celestial hybrid.

The difference is not academic—it's foundational.

- **Yeshua is not Hercules.**
- **Yeshua is not Perseus.**

- Yeshua is YHWH's anointed Messiah, fully human, fully obedient, and perfectly aligned with God's covenantal plan.

Transition to Section 3.4:

The Nephilim narrative doesn't stop at Genesis. The **Ethiopian Apocrypha**, particularly *1 Enoch*, provides additional context about these celestial-human hybrids.

- What do these ancient texts reveal about the Nephilim?
- How do they reinforce YHWH's stance against hybrid beings?
- What warnings do they offer for our understanding of the Messiah?

In the next section, we'll delve into the **Apocryphal Context for the Nephilim**, exploring insights preserved in the **Ethiopian Apocrypha**.

3.4 Apocryphal Context for Nephilim – Ethiopian Apocrypha

Key Insight:

While Apocryphal texts are not considered canonical scripture, they were widely known, respected, and referenced in Jewish thought before and during Yeshua's time.

These texts offer valuable historical, cultural, and theological context for understanding key biblical events—including the Nephilim controversy in *Genesis 6:1-4*.

The Ethiopian Icebox: A Preserved Legacy

The **Ethiopian Orthodox Tewahedo Church** is one of the **oldest Christian traditions**, tracing its roots to the **4th century AD**.

Unlike Western Christianity, the Ethiopian Church preserved texts that were **lost, dismissed, or suppressed in** Roman and Byzantine traditions.

A Haven from Censorship

- While Europe endured periods of **inquisitorial purges, crusades, and doctrinal centralization**, Ethiopia remained largely insulated from these forces.
- The Ethiopian Church became an **"icebox" of ancient knowledge**, preserving texts like the **Book of Enoch** and the **Book of Jubilees** in their entirety.
- These texts survived not as fringe manuscripts but as **respected theological resources**.

An Alternate Tradition

- Ethiopian Christianity followed a trajectory **independent of Roman and Byzantine influences**.
- They preserved a **Judeo-Christian cultural continuity** that kept many early texts in circulation.
- The **Book of Enoch** and **Jubilees** were maintained not as curiosities, but as **meaningful theological sources**.

This unique preservation grants us access to first-century thought patterns, Messianic expectations, and cultural understandings that were largely lost or distorted in Western Christianity.

Apocrypha: Informative, Not Authoritative

While Apocryphal texts are not considered canonical scripture, they serve an informative purpose, shedding light on ancient beliefs, traditions, and theological perspectives.

Cited in Canonical Scripture

- Many readers are unaware that canonical scripture directly references non-canonical texts.

- **Jude 1:14-15 quotes the Book of Enoch:**
  "Enoch, the seventh from Adam, prophesied about them: 'See, the Lord is coming with thousands upon thousands of his holy ones to judge everyone...'"
- This direct reference validates that such texts were respected and familiar to first-century Jewish audiences, including Yeshua and His disciples.
- The fact that canonical scripture quotes non-canonical texts is a hidden bombshell—revealing that the Apocrypha were part of the cultural and theological fabric of Yeshua's time.

Cultural Familiarity in Yeshua's Time
- Texts like the **Book of Enoch** and **Jubilees** were widely known and respected among Jewish communities.
- They were not viewed as **scriptural equals to the Torah**, but as **significant theological commentaries and expansions** on key narratives.
- Yeshua and His disciples would have been **familiar with these texts**, and their theological landscape was shaped, in part, by the ideas presented in them.

The Apocrypha provides **contextual clarity**, especially for passages that are otherwise sparse in detail—like the **Nephilim narrative in Genesis 6.**

The **Book of Enoch** offers a **rich, detailed expansion** of the brief account in *Genesis 6:1-4.*

The Watchers: Angelic Rebellion
- According to Enoch, the "sons of God" are identified as Watchers—angelic beings tasked with overseeing humanity.
- These angels rebelled against YHWH's order and descended to earth, taking human women as wives.
- This rebellion wasn't an accident—it was intentional and catastrophic, corrupting humanity both spiritually and physically.

The Birth of the Nephilim

- The unions between the Watchers and human women produced the Nephilim—giants and beings of immense power and corruption.
- These offspring became tyrants, devourers of human life, and agents of chaos.
- Their influence led to violence, idolatry, and widespread wickedness, necessitating divine intervention.

In the Book of Enoch, YHWH responds with severe judgment:

- The Watchers are **imprisoned in the abyss** until the final judgment.
- The Nephilim and their corrupted offspring are **wiped from the face of the earth through the flood.**
- The flood was not just about general human wickedness—it was about eradicating a cosmic corruption of God's creation.

This narrative emphasizes a clear theological principle: YHWH does not tolerate celestial-human hybrids.

The Book of Jubilees: A Parallel Witness

Sometimes referred to as the **"Little Genesis"**, the **Book of Jubilees** offers additional insight into the **Nephilim controversy.**

The Corruption of Humanity

- The Book of Jubilees emphasizes the moral and spiritual decay caused by the Nephilim.
- It describes the rampant violence, idolatry, and corruption they brought upon the earth.

Echoing Enoch's Themes

- Like Enoch, Jubilees confirms that the unions between the Watchers and human women were an abomination.
- It underscores the necessity of divine intervention through the flood to preserve humanity.

God's Immutable Standards

- Jubilees reiterates a critical point: **God's standards do not change.**

- If YHWH rejected and destroyed celestial-human hybrids in Noah's day, He would not later **create a Messiah in that same mold.**

These texts align with the **Genesis account**, reinforcing the theological principle that **YHWH rejects hybrid beings** as corruptions of His Heavenly order.

Why These Texts Matter

They Provide Contextual Clarity:
- The sparse account of the Nephilim in *Genesis 6:1-4* is greatly expanded and explained in these texts.
- They reveal the **spiritual and moral dimensions** of the Nephilim controversy.

They Align with the Scriptural Narrative:
- Both Enoch and Jubilees reinforce YHWH's rejection of celestial-human hybrids and the importance of covenantal alignment.

They Were Known in Yeshua's Time:
- These texts were part of the **cultural and theological landscape** of "Second Temple" Judaism.
- Understanding them allows us to **see Yeshua's teachings and actions in their proper context.**

Takeaway:

The **Book of Enoch** and **Book of Jubilees** provide critical context for understanding the **Nephilim controversy** in *Genesis 6:1-4*.

- **They reinforce the principle that YHWH rejects celestial-human hybrids.**
- **They clarify the moral and spiritual corruption that necessitated the flood.**
- **They remind us that Yeshua's humanity was essential—He was not a demigod, not a hybrid, but a fully human servant obedient to YHWH.**

These texts, while not canonical, offer valuable insight into ancient thought patterns and theological expectations, bridging gaps in our understanding of God's consistency and covenantal faithfulness.

Transition to Section 3.5

With the weight of both scripture and Apocryphal insight behind us, we can now ask: Why does all of this matter?

- How do these insights affect our understanding of Yeshua's mission?
- Why is rejecting the demigod distortion essential for a true Messianic framework?

In the next section, we'll tie these threads together to understand why this matters deeply for theology, prophecy, and our relationship with YHWH.

3.5 Why This Matters

Key Insight:

The Nephilim narrative isn't a fringe discussion—it was **significant, widely understood, and deeply embedded in Jewish culture** during Yeshua's time. The Apocryphal texts, particularly the *Book of Enoch* and *Jubilees*, were part of the **theological atmosphere** in which Yeshua and His followers operated. Their insights clarify **how ancient Jewish communities understood Genesis 6:1-4** and reinforce an essential truth: **YHWH rejects celestial-human hybrids.**

The Nephilim Narrative Was Not Obscure

In modern theological discussions, the Nephilim are often treated as a **curious side note**—a vague mystery in Genesis. However:

- In "Second Temple" Judaism, the Nephilim were a **central topic of discussion and concern.**
- Texts like the **Book of Enoch** and **Jubilees** reveal that the **Nephilim controversy was not marginal—it was mainstream.**

- These narratives were seen as **critical for understanding divine justice, human corruption, and the purpose of the flood.**
- The corrupting nature of the Nephilim was known to continue in the form of possession by the disembodied spirits that remained after their bodies died in the flood.

The Cultural Context of Yeshua and His Followers

- Yeshua and His disciples would have been **familiar with the stories from Enoch and Jubilees.**
- These texts shaped the cultural and theological expectations of **purity, covenantal obedience, and the nature of the Messiah.**
- When Yeshua spoke about the **"days of Noah"** (*Matthew* 24:37), His audience would have immediately understood the reference to **divine judgment on a corrupted world**—a world corrupted by the Nephilim, whose disembodied spirits plagued Israel's soul – leading many to corruption.

The Canonical Connection

- The fact that the **Book of Enoch is directly quoted in Jude 1:14-15** demonstrates the **interconnectedness of canonical and non-canonical texts.**
- Ancient audiences didn't compartmentalize these texts—they viewed them as **interwoven threads within a shared theological tapestry.**
- Modern readers often miss this interconnectedness, stripping scripture of valuable context.

The Nephilim controversy wasn't **obscure** or **trivial**—it was **a theological linchpin** that shaped ancient understandings of **purity, corruption, and divine justice.**

The Apocryphal Context Adds Layers of Understanding

While **Apocryphal texts are not authoritative scripture,** they are:

- **Windows into Ancient Thought:** They allow us to see how ancient Jewish communities interpreted and understood Genesis 6:1-4.

- **Clarifiers of Ambiguous Texts:** They provide narrative expansions that help clarify **why God's response to the Nephilim was so severe.**
- **Messianic Contextualizers:** They reveal the **expectations of the Messiah** within a cultural framework that rejected celestial-human hybrids.

The Weight of the Flood Narrative

The flood was not just about human wickedness—it was about **cosmic corruption.**

- The Nephilim represented a **perversion of God's created order**—a hybridization that polluted humanity.
- If such corruption warranted total destruction, it is **unthinkable that YHWH would later use a hybrid to fulfill His covenant.**

Reinforcing God's Consistency

- YHWH does not **change His standards** (*Malachi 3:6*).
- If celestial-human hybrids were rejected in Genesis, they would also be rejected in the Messianic plan.

The Apocrypha serves as a **witness**—not equal to scripture, but **aligned with scripture**—providing clarity on God's standards and expectations.

The Broader Takeaway

The Nephilim controversy isn't just an academic debate—it has **profound theological implications:**

Messianic Identity Must Align with Prophecy:
- The Messiah could not—and would not—be a **celestial-human hybrid.**
- If He were, He would have been **rejected like the Nephilim, not exalted as the fulfillment of prophecy.**

Humanity Is Central to the Messiah's Role:

- The Messiah had to be **fully human** to represent and redeem humanity.
- His qualification came from **obedience, not celestial origins or mythological grandeur.**

The Dangers of Greco-Roman Influence:

- The cultural obsession with **demigods and celestial hybrids** in the Greco-Roman world distorted the **Hebraic vision of the Messiah.**
- Recognizing and rejecting these distortions restores clarity to the **true prophetic mission of Yeshua.**

A Question That Must Be Asked

If YHWH utterly rejected the Nephilim, then:
How could a celestial-human hybrid Messiah align with God's will?

This question exposes the **theological impossibility** of a hybrid Messiah within the context of **YHWH's consistent standards.**

Takeaway:

The **Apocryphal texts**, while not canonical, are **invaluable historical and theological resources.**

- They **reveal the deep interconnectedness** between canonical scripture and cultural understanding.
- They **underscore the seriousness of the Nephilim controversy** and clarify why **YHWH rejects celestial-human hybrids.**
- They show us that **Yeshua's humanity was not incidental—it was essential.**

Understanding this reality helps us avoid **Greco-Roman distortions** and re-align our understanding of Yeshua with the **prophetic framework of scripture.**

The Nephilim narrative isn't just ancient history—it's **a theological precedent with profound implications for how we understand the Messiah.**

3.6 Did Yeshua ever claim equality with YHWH?

No, Yeshua did not claim equality with God. However, there are verses, such as the short line in John 10:30, that have been seized upon by Pauline traditions as a proof-text for co-divinity.

"I and the Father are one."

Yet when read with a Hebraic understanding and Yeshua's scriptural lens, it is neither a claim to demigod status nor an ontological merger with YHWH.

Instead, it reflects the ancient covenantal language of unity in purpose and obedience.

- The Greek word ἕν (hen) is neuter — "one thing," not masculine "one person."

In other words, Yeshua was not claiming, "I am the same being as the Father." He was declaring, "The Father and I share the same mission."

This concept of "oneness" resonates with the Hebrew echad — the word at the very heart of the Shema: "YHWH is one"(Deuteronomy 6:4).

- The Hebrew, echad conveys unity, exclusivity, and covenant loyalty, not metaphysical fusion.

The Hebrew Bible is full of these covenantal uses of echad:

- "The two shall become one flesh" (Genesis 2:24) — two persons bound in covenant, not collapsed into a single body.
- "All the people rose as one man" (Judges 20:8) — many voices acting with one resolve.
- "The dread of YHWH fell upon the people so they came out as one" (1 Samuel 11:7).

- "I will give them one heart and one way" (Jeremiah 32:39).
- "The hand of God was on Judah to give them one heart" (2 Chronicles. 30:12).
- Even in Numbers 13:23, one cluster of grapes (echad eshkol) contains many grapes joined together.

To Hebraic minds, "oneness" is always about alignment under YHWH's will — never a blending of essences.

Yeshua's words were no different.

Yeshua, just seven chapters later prayed that His disciples "may be one, as we are one" (John 17:21-23).

Did He mean His followers would dissolve into His being?

Of course not. He meant that they would share the same Spirit, mission, and obedience.

YHWH does not "do" demigods. To suggest that Yeshua claimed equality with God is to miss the point of His life entirely.

His whole ministry pointed away from himself and upward to the Father. He showed us what perfect obedience looks like. He was one with the Father not because He shared YHWH's essence, but because He bent His entire will into alignment with YHWH's will.

Takeaway:

Yeshua never claimed to be equal with YHWH. His claim of oneness reflects Hebraic covenantal unity, not Greco-Roman celestial hybridity or co-divinity.

- Yeshua embodied the Torah Law by living it perfectly, not by being a "second god."

Other Misunderstood Verses

"He who has seen me has seen the Father" (John 14:9)

Pauline interpreters often read this as Yeshua claiming identity with YHWH. Yet within the covenant world of Israel, this language is nothing more—or less—than the ancient principle of shaliaḥ. A shaliaḥ is a sent one, an authorized agent. "A person's agent is as himself," the sages would say.

Yeshua is not collapsing Himself into the Father. He is pointing out that His words and works are the Father's own, perfectly embodied. When you saw Yeshua heal, forgive, or rebuke, you were seeing YHWH's will in action.

- A Torah judge does not become YHWH when he renders a verdict, yet in that moment he bears God's justice. The verdict belongs to the Judge of heaven; the human judge is His shaliaḥ.

"Before Abraham was, I am" (John 8:58)

This verse has launched many sermons equating Yeshua with the burning bush of Exodus 3:14. However, the Greek phrase egō eimi ("I am") in John is most often recognition language: "I am he," the one promised, the one appointed.

Isaiah's servant oracles echo the same: "I am he; before me no god was formed" (Isaiah 43:10).

The dispute here is about Abraham's faith. Yeshua declares Himself the one anticipated by Abraham's hope—the servant for this hour. Not a rival to YHWH, but the Abrahamic heir.

When asked, "Are you the one to come?" Yeshua could simply say, "I am." This is covenant recognition, not ontological identity.

"All authority in heaven and on earth has been given to me" (Matthew 28:18)

This text ends the debate if we allow the words to stand.

- Authority given is not authority intrinsic.
- Yeshua did not seize divinity, nor claim it as His own nature.
- The King of the universe entrusted Him with power to carry out the mission.

This verse prepares the way for what we will later discuss regarding the "Seat of Glory vs. Throne of Heaven" distinction.

YHWH never abdicates His throne. But He does seat His anointed one at His right hand, conferring delegated authority for covenant purposes.

A king may give his signet ring to a trusted servant. Every order stamped bears royal weight, yet the ring does not make the servant king.

"My Lord and my God!" (John 20:28)

Thomas's cry has been treated as the final nail: proof of Yeshua's divinity. But Semitic language often layers confessions. "My lord" fits Yeshua, risen before Thomas's eyes. "My God!" fits YHWH, who raised Him from the grave.

Even if both titles are read toward Yeshua, the shaliaḥ principle still governs.

In Torah, human judges were called elohim when rendering YHWH's judgments (Exodus 22:8–9). Their function, not their essence, bore God's name.

When Moses confronted Pharaoh, he was told, "I have made you as God to Pharaoh" (Exodus 7:1).

No one mistook Moses for YHWH; he was His vessel.

"In the beginning was the Word..." (John 1:1–14)

Finally, the prologue of John. For centuries this poetry has been flattened into proof of a co-eternal Jesus. But Jewish ears hear something else. The Word (dabar, logos) was always Torah, Wisdom, God's revealed will.

The poetry celebrates that Word taking on flesh in Yeshua. He did not preexist as a rival deity. He embodied Torah so completely that God's wisdom could be touched and heard.

Even the opening of John's Gospel becomes clear when read through this lens. "In the beginning was the Word, and the Word was with God, and the Word was God." To Jewish ears, the Word (Logos, Dabar) always meant Torah — God's law, His revealed will, His living covenant.

To say Yeshua was the Word made flesh is to say that he embodied the Torah completely — living it, teaching it, and showing us its perfect fulfillment.

It does not mean Yeshua was a second co-eternal deity beside YHWH.

Yeshua was not the Lawgiver; He was the obedient servant who carried the Law in every fiber of his physical being.

To say "the Word became flesh" is like saying "justice walked into the room" when a righteous judge enters.

What you encounter is God's will alive before you, not a new god.

Takeaway:
The so-called "proof-texts" of Yeshua's co-divinity all collapse under His own Hebraic lens.

- Seeing Him was seeing the Father's will in action.
- Hearing Him was hearing the echo of Abraham's faith and Isaiah's servant songs.
- Obeying Him was obeying the Father who gave Him authority.

None of this makes Yeshua a co-equal deity. It makes Him the perfect Son, Servant, and messenger of YHWH. To read these verses otherwise is to impose foreign categories onto Hebrew lives and words.

3.7 Conclusion

Key Insight:

Misunderstanding Yeshua as a **celestial-human hybrid** doesn't just distort His identity—it **undermines the foundational covenant between YHWH and humanity.**

Why Yeshua's Humanity Matters

- The Messiah was prophesied to be **fully human, perfectly obedient, and aligned with YHWH's commandments.**
- *Isaiah 42:1 — "Here is my servant, whom I uphold, my chosen one in whom I delight."*
- *Isaiah 53:3 — "He was despised and rejected by mankind, a man of suffering, and familiar with pain."*
- These prophecies leave **no room for celestial hybridity or mythological interpretations.**

A Different Kind of Qualification

- Yeshua's humanity wasn't a **limitation—it was His qualification.**
- He was **one of us, yet without sin** (*Hebrews 4:15*).
- His sacrifice was meaningful because He was a **fully human representative** acting in perfect obedience.

The Weight of This Truth

- Yeshua was not **exalted because of celestial power.**
- He was **exalted because of His obedience, sacrifice, and covenantal faithfulness.**
- The **Greco-Roman fascination with demigods** distorted this truth, creating an attractive yet **unscriptural image of the Messiah.**

Takeaway:

Yeshua's humanity wasn't a **limitation—it was His qualification.**

- He wasn't a celestial-human hybrid.
- He wasn't exalted because of celestial power.
- He was **anointed, obedient, and faithful—the perfect servant of YHWH.**

Understanding this truth isn't just theological—it's **transformative.** It re-centers Yeshua within the **covenantal framework of prophecy** and elevates His mission to its **rightful place in YHWH's plan.**

Walking toward YHWH

Key Insight: The Exodus is often reduced by Pauline Christianity to a one-time event when God's people escaped from Egypt.

This differs from the Jewish understanding of the Exodus as a forty-year journey whereby former slaves of Pharaoh learned how to become people of YHWH.

Slavery under a Pharaoh defined:

- **Pharaohs in Egypt were man-god -kings.** They were viewed as absolute monarchs: administratively, militarily, and religiously.
- Unlike Greek and later Roman demigod traditions based on legend and lore: Egyptian Pharaohs were human rulers who expected to be worshipped as gods.

More than anything else, what YHWH sent Moses to free his people from was slavery under a system built around the belief a man could be a god.

A basic understanding of YHWH worship holds that celestial-human hybrids, Nephilim, and man-god-kings , Pharaohs, are antithetical to YHWH's plan for humanity.

Transition to Section 4:

If Yeshua was not a **celestial-human hybrid**, and if His qualification was rooted in **obedience and humanity**, then what did He say about Himself?

- How did Yeshua describe His own role and purpose?

In the next section, we'll examine **Yeshua's own words** to understand **how He presented Himself—and how that aligns with prophecy and scripture.**

4. Yeshua's Own Words: Not God, Not Equal to God

Key Insight:

Throughout His ministry, Yeshua consistently rejected divine worship and pointed all glory to YHWH. The doctrine of Trinitarianism violates core commandments, twisting Yeshua's clear words and actions into something He never claimed nor intended.

Yeshua's own words, especially His prayers, provide a direct window into His understanding of His identity, mission, and relationship with YHWH. In every instance, Yeshua directs worship upward, not inward, firmly aligning with Hebraic prophetic tradition and rejecting any notion of self-deification.

4.1 Yeshua's Prayers: Third-Party Worship, Never Self-Directed

Key Insight:

Every recorded prayer of Yeshua demonstrates third-party upward worship—always directed to YHWH, never to Himself.

If Yeshua ever believed He was God, His prayers would look drastically different. Instead, they reflect humility, obedience, and alignment with YHWH's will.

Let's examine these prayers closely.

The Lord's Prayer (*Matthew 6:9-13*)

"Our Father who art in heaven, hallowed be Thy name. Thy kingdom come, Thy will be done, on earth as it is in heaven."

Observation:
- Yeshua instructs His disciples to pray **directly to YHWH**, referring to Him as **"Our Father."**
- The prayer gives **glory, authority, and reverence to YHWH alone.**

Upward Worship:

- Yeshua models a pattern of prayer that **points upward, never inward.**
- He doesn't ask for His own name to be hallowed—He asks for **YHWH's name to be glorified.**

Takeaway:

- This foundational prayer would be **absurd** if Yeshua considered Himself God.
- Instead, He demonstrates **absolute deference and submission to YHWH.**

The Garden of Gethsemane (*Matthew 26:39*)

"My Father, if it is possible, let this cup pass from me; yet not as I will, but as You will."

Observation:

- Yeshua submits His will entirely to **YHWH's will.**
- He does not assert divine authority to bypass suffering.

Upward Worship:

- Yeshua's words display total humility and obedience.
- His prayer is not an assertion of divine power but an appeal for divine guidance and alignment.

Takeaway:

- A being who claims **divine equality** would not need to **submit their will** to another.
- Yeshua's humanity and servant role are unmistakable in this moment.

On the Cross: Forgiveness (*Luke 23:34*)

"Father, forgive them, for they do not know what they are doing."

Observation:

- Yeshua asks YHWH to forgive His executioners.
- He does not declare forgiveness on His own authority.

Upward Worship:
- Even in unimaginable suffering, Yeshua turns **upward to YHWH.**
- Forgiveness is not claimed from Himself but **sought from YHWH.**

Takeaway:
- Yeshua reinforces that forgiveness comes from YHWH, not Himself.
- This prayer contradicts any claim of self-sufficient divine authority.

On the Cross: Abandonment (*Matthew* 27:46)

"My God, my God, why have You forsaken me?"

Observation:
- Yeshua addresses **YHWH directly,** expressing profound human anguish.
- He does not address Himself or appeal to His own supposed divine nature.
- This cry of anguish was not an invention of Yeshua, it was him quoting King David in Psalms 22. As in his life and ministry, Yeshua's final moments were a living upholding of scripture. As he hovered between life and death, Yeshua used the Writings of the Hebrew Bible as a guide to maintain covenantal obedience.

Upward Worship:
- This cry is a direct appeal to YHWH.
- It reflects Yeshua's humanity and His alignment with God.

Takeaway:
- Yeshua's cry shows dependence on the Word of YHWH, not self-reliance.
- A deity would not cry out to another deity in this manner.

Before Raising Lazarus (*John 11:41-42*)

"Father, I thank You that You have heard me. I knew that You always hear me, but I said this for the benefit of the people standing here, that they may believe that You sent me."

Observation:
- Yeshua explicitly thanks YHWH for hearing His prayer.
- He emphasizes that He was sent by YHWH—not self-appointed.

Upward Worship:
- Yeshua's authority is derived from **YHWH, not Himself.**
- His words demonstrate **deference and gratitude to YHWH.**

Takeaway:
- Yeshua's clear articulation of His **role as a messenger sent by YHWH** dismantles claims of divine self-identity.

Before His Arrest (*John 17:1-5*)

"Father, the hour has come. Glorify Your Son, that Your Son may glorify You."

Observation:
- Yeshua seeks glorification from YHWH, not self-glorification.
- His mission is to glorify YHWH, not Himself.

Upward Worship:
- The relationship is one of obedience and alignment, not equality.
- Yeshua operates as a servant carrying out YHWH's will.

Takeaway:
- Yeshua's prayer reinforces His submissive role under YHWH's authority.

At His Baptism (*Matthew 3:17*)

"This is my Son, whom I love; with him I am well pleased."

Observation:
- This voice comes from YHWH, not Yeshua Himself.
- Yeshua does not declare His own identity—YHWH declares it.

Upward Worship:
- The focus remains on YHWH's affirmation and authority.

Takeaway:
- If Yeshua were claiming divine self-identity, this moment would make no sense.

In Public Prayer (*John 12:28*)

"Father, glorify Your name!"

Observation:
- Yeshua's priority is **YHWH's glorification.**
- He does not ask for **self-glorification.**

Upward Worship:
- Yeshua's consistent focus remains on **YHWH's name and authority.**

Takeaway:
- The pattern of upward worship remains unbroken and consistent.

Why This Matters

A Pattern, Not an Exception:
- Every prayer of Yeshua demonstrates third-party, upward-directed worship.

Alignment with Prophetic Tradition:
- Yeshua's prayers mirror the prayers of **Moses, David, and Elijah**—all prophetic servants of YHWH.

Contradiction to Trinitarian Claims:

- If Yeshua were God, His prayers would have been **radically different.**
- Instead, His prayers confirm **a servant relationship with YHWH.**

Takeaway:

In every recorded prayer, Yeshua prays to YHWH—not to Himself, not in third-person self-reference, and never as a self-elevated deity.

- His alignment with **Hebraic prophetic tradition** is consistent.
- His humanity and **obedience to YHWH's will** are central to His role as the Messiah.

Thought Experiment for the Reader

Take a moment to **reimagine these prayers** if Jesus had been praying **to Himself.** Picture each scenario and ask:

- Would these prayers still make sense?
- Would they still carry the same emotional weight and relational depth?

If the answer is **"No"**, then the conclusion is clear:

- **Jesus never prayed to Himself. He directed all worship, all obedience, and all submission to YHWH—the One True God.**

Why This Matters

Prayer is an act of humility, dependence, and worship.
- Jesus prayed **to YHWH, not as YHWH.**

His prayers model the **relationship between humanity and God**, not **equality with God.**

- If Jesus intended to **claim divinity**, why did He consistently **defer authority, glory, and worship to YHWH?**

4.2 A Violation of the Greatest Commandments

Key Insight:

The commandments in Exodus 20:3 and Deuteronomy 6:4 are crystal clear: YHWH alone is God, and no other gods are to be placed before Him.

Worshiping Yeshua as equal to YHWH directly violates these foundational laws, distorting the very essence of the covenant between God and His people.

"You shall have no other gods before me." (Exodus 20:3)

The First and Foundational Commandment

- This commandment is not just one among many—it is the cornerstone of covenantal faithfulness.
- It establishes YHWH's absolute and undivided authority over all creation.
- No being—whether celestial, angelic, or human—can share divine status with YHWH.

The Messiah Is Not an Exception

- The Hebrew scriptures make no allowances for exceptions to this commandment.
- The Messiah, by prophetic description, is an anointed human servant, not a divine counterpart.
- Elevating Yeshua to equal status with YHWH violates the fundamental boundary set in this commandment.

The Theological Distortion of Trinitarian Worship

- The doctrine of the Trinity artificially creates an illusion of shared divinity, placing Yeshua on equal footing with YHWH.
- This doctrine directly conflicts with Exodus 20:3, as it attempts to shoe-horn an additional figure into the space reserved solely for YHWH.
- Worshiping Yeshua as equal to God is, by definition, heretical, under the terms of the first commandment.

Deuteronomy 6:4 – "The LORD is One"

"Hear, O Israel: The LORD our God, the LORD is one." (Deuteronomy 6:4)

The Shema: The Core of Israelite Faith

- The Shema is the declaration of monotheism and the spiritual cornerstone of the Hebrew faith.
- It affirms YHWH's indivisible singularity, making it impossible for Him to be divided into multiple persons or entities.

Yeshua's Affirmation of the Shema

- In Mark 12:29, Yeshua directly reaffirms the heart of the Shema: **"The most important one," answered Jesus quoting Deuteronomy 6:5, "Love _the_ Lord your God with all of your heart, soul, and mind."**

The Third Temptation of Jesus

As you will recall from Inquiry 1, when Satan shows Jesus all the kingdoms of the world, and offers to give them to him if Jesus will worship him. Jesus responds by quoting Deuteronomy 6:13.

"...for it is written, 'You shall worship the Lord your God, and him only shall you serve',".

If Yeshua considered Himself part of a "Trinity," either of these instances would have been the moment to clarify such a belief—but He didn't, he **always** pointed all glory and submission to **YHWH, our Heavenly Father.**

The Distortion of Divine Unity
- The Trinity violates the clarity of the Shema by multiplying divine persons and diluting YHWH's absolute oneness.
- Instead of YHWH being undivided and singular, He becomes a fragmented figurehead shared among three distinct "persons."
- This not only contradicts Deuteronomy 6:4, but it undermines the covenantal identity of YHWH.

Yeshua's Affirmation of These Commandments

Yeshua repeatedly upholds these commandments, emphasizing the supremacy and singularity of YHWH.

The Rich Young Man (Matthew 19:16-17)

> *"And behold, a man came up to him, saying, "Teacher, what good deed must I do to have eternal life?" And he said to him, "Why do you ask me about what is good? There is only **One** who is good. If you would enter life, keep the commandments."*

- Yeshua insists that the title of "good" belongs only to YHWH.
- He identifies covenantal obedience — keeping the commandments — as the path to eternal life.
- Yeshua points seekers to faithfulness in God's law.
- This directly refutes Pauline claims that law is abolished or secondary to belief.

This passage reveals Yeshua's consistent role: a teacher pointing Israel back to YHWH and His commandments, not redirecting devotion toward Himself.

The Greatest Commandment (Matthew 22:37-38)

> *"'Love the Lord your God with all your heart and with all your soul and with all your mind.' This is the first and greatest commandment."*

- Yeshua identifies the greatest commandment as total, undivided love and devotion to YHWH.

- He does not include Himself in this commandment.
- Yeshua points all worship, love, and devotion upward to YHWH—not inward to Himself.

No Claims of Divine Equality

- Nowhere in the Gospels does Yeshua claim equality with YHWH.
- When confronted with worship, He redirects it to YHWH

Theological Breach: Trinitarian Worship

The Trinity as a Theological Innovation

- The doctrine of the Trinity was not present in Yeshua's teachings or in early Hebraic Messianic expectations.
- It arose centuries later as an attempt to reconcile Greek philosophical ideas with Christian theology.

Worshiping Jesus as God Distorts His Role

- The Messianic mission of Yeshua was about obedience, covenantal faithfulness, and serving YHWH.
- Worshiping Yeshua as a divine equal distorts His purpose and misrepresents His identity as the anointed servant of YHWH.

Historical Evidence of Early Debate

- Early Church Councils, such as Nicaea (325 AD) and Chalcedon (451 AD), were convened specifically because of deep divisions over Yeshua's nature.
- Many early followers of Yeshua, particularly Jewish believers, rejected the Trinitarian formulation as inconsistent with the Shema and Torah.

Practical Examples of Modern Distortions

- In modern Christianity, worship songs, prayers, and doctrinal creeds often elevate Yeshua to divine status.

- This emphasis overshadows YHWH and creates a functional polytheism rather than Hebraic monotheism.

Why This Matters

Violating the First Commandment Is No Small Error:

- This isn't a minor theological disagreement—it's a violation of the foundational covenantal law.
- Worshiping Yeshua as God is idolatry, no matter how well-intentioned.

The Integrity of the Shema Is at Stake:

- The Shema isn't just a theological statement—it's a binding declaration of YHWH's absolute oneness.
- Diluting it with Trinitarian distortions breaks the core foundation of faith.

Yeshua Modeled Covenant Faithfulness:

- Yeshua upheld the commandments, directing all worship, love, and glory to YHWH.
- To reinterpret His role as divine or co-equal undermines His obedience and humility.

Takeaway:
The commandments in Exodus 20:3 and Deuteronomy 6:4 are non-negotiable foundations of faith.

- YHWH alone is God—undivided, unshared, and absolute.
- Worshiping Yeshua as equal to YHWH violates these commandments and introduces a theological breach that distorts both Yeshua's role and YHWH's oneness.
- Yeshua affirmed these commandments throughout His ministry, always pointing glory, worship, and authority upward to YHWH.

Understanding this isn't just theological—it's foundational to living in alignment with YHWH's will and covenant.

Transition to Section 4.3: Jesus's Hierarchical Language

If Yeshua isn't equal to YHWH, how did He describe Himself?

- Did His own words reveal a **clear hierarchy** in His relationship with YHWH?
- How did Yeshua frame His role as Messiah and servant?

In the next section, we'll explore how Yeshua carefully described His **role, authority, and relationship with YHWH.**

4.3 Yeshua's Hierarchical Language

Key Insight:

Yeshua's own words consistently establish a clear hierarchy between Himself and YHWH.

He never claimed equality with God—instead, He emphasized His submission, dependence, and distinction from the Father.

Every statement Yeshua made about His relationship with YHWH reinforces this hierarchical structure, aligning perfectly with Hebraic monotheism and covenantal faithfulness.

"The Father is Greater Than I" (John 14:28)

"You heard me say, 'I am going away and I am coming back to you.' If you loved me, you would be glad that I am going to the Father, for the Father is greater than I."

Clear Hierarchy

- Yeshua explicitly states that "the Father is greater than I."
- This is not metaphorical or abstract—it's a straightforward declaration of subordination and distinction.

Hierarchy Incompatible with Equality

- Equality does not allow for one being to be "greater" than the other.
- If Yeshua were co-equal with YHWH, such a distinction would be impossible.

A Direct Refutation of Trinitarian Claims

- Trinitarian theology attempts to explain this verse with philosophical abstractions about Jesus's "earthly limitations."
- However, Yeshua does not qualify or add context to His statement—He simply says "the Father is greater."
- This reflects an unambiguous relationship of authority and distinction.

Takeaway:

Yeshua's words in *John 14:28* dismantle the notion of divine equality. He identifies YHWH as supreme, placing Himself under the Father's authority and greatness.

"I Can Do Nothing by Myself" (*John 5:30*)

"By myself I can do nothing; I judge only as I hear, and my judgment is just, for I seek not to please myself but Him who sent me."

Dependence and Submission

- Yeshua openly admits that He can do nothing by Himself.
- His actions, authority, and judgments are entirely dependent on YHWH's will.

Alignment with YHWH's Will

- Yeshua does not act autonomously or make decisions independently.
- His purpose is singular: to fulfill the will of the One who sent Him.

Not the Language of a Co-Equal Deity

- A co-equal deity would not need to defer authority, seek alignment, or disclaim autonomy.
- These words reflect the language of a servant, not an equal.

Takeaway:

Yeshua's dependence on YHWH in *John 5:30* highlights a clear relationship of submission and obedience, not equality or divine co-sovereignty.

"Only the Father Knows the Hour...Not the Son" (*Matthew 24:36*)

"But about that day or hour no one knows, not even the angels in heaven, nor the Son, but only the Father."

Reserved Divine Knowledge

- Yeshua openly declares that there is knowledge He does not possess.
- Specifically, knowledge of the timing of the end of days is reserved exclusively for YHWH.

The Implications of Limited Knowledge

- A co-equal divine being would have equal access to divine knowledge.
- The fact that Yeshua does not know this information underscores a clear distinction between Yeshua and YHWH.

Defying Trinitarian Doctrine

- Trinitarian theology attempts to explain this by claiming Yeshua's "earthly humanity" limited His knowledge.
- However, there's no indication in the text that Yeshua is speaking from a "limited human perspective."
- He makes a clear and universal statement: Only the Father knows.

Takeaway:
Yeshua's words in *Matthew 24:36* dismantle any notion of divine omniscience on His part. This hierarchical distinction is unavoidable and undeniable.

Additional Examples of Yeshua's Hierarchical Language

"My Teaching is Not My Own" (John 7:16)

"Jesus answered, 'My teaching is not my own. It comes from the one who sent me.'"

- Yeshua does not claim independent authority over His teachings.
- He attributes His message directly to YHWH.

"The Son Can Do Nothing by Himself" (*John 5:19*)

"The Son can do nothing by Himself; He can do only what He sees His Father doing."

- Yeshua states, again, that His actions are entirely dependent on YHWH.
- He is not self-directed or autonomous.

"Why Do You Call Me Good?" (*Mark 10:18*)

"Why do you call me good? No one is good—except God alone."
- Yeshua redirects the title "good" away from Himself and toward YHWH.
- If He were co-equal with YHWH, this redirection would be unnecessary and confusing.

"Not My Will, But Yours Be Done" (*Luke 22:42*)

"Father, if you are willing, take this cup from me; yet not my will, but yours be done."
- Yeshua demonstrates total submission to YHWH's will.
- His desires are secondary to YHWH's plan.

Takeaway:

In every instance, Yeshua's language emphasizes:
- **Dependence on YHWH**
- **Submission to YHWH's will**
- **Clear distinction from YHWH's supreme authority**

How These Words Were Reinterpreted by Early Church Councils

The Influence of Greco-Roman Thought

- Greek philosophy introduced concepts like "divine substance" and "co-equality."
- These ideas were foreign to Hebraic monotheism but became central to church councils.

Reinterpretation of Hierarchical Statements

- Verses where Yeshua emphasizes dependence, submission, or distinction were reframed as temporary limitations tied to His humanity.
- Councils like Nicaea (325 AD) ignored the plain reading of Yeshua's hierarchical language in favor of philosophical abstraction.

Consequences of Theological Drift

- The shift from Hebraic understanding to Greco-Roman theology resulted in widespread misunderstanding of Yeshua's role.
- Instead of being viewed as YHWH's anointed servant, Yeshua became a Greco-Roman styled demigod.

Takeaway:

Yeshua's own words leave no ambiguity:
- He speaks as a servant, not an equal.
- He acknowledges YHWH's superiority, authority, and knowledge.
- His hierarchical language aligns with Hebraic prophecy and the Shema.

Any attempt to redefine Yeshua's words through philosophical or doctrinal lenses distorts His identity and contradicts the clear meaning of His teachings.

Transition to next section:

Yeshua's own words consistently emphasize hierarchy, dependence, and submission, why does this matter?

- How does this understanding affect worship and theological alignment?
- What are the consequences of misunderstanding this hierarchy?

4.4 Why This Matters

Key Insight:

The verses we've explored are not isolated anomalies—they form a **consistent, unbroken pattern throughout Yeshua's teachings.** Every time Yeshua discusses His relationship with the Father, He emphasizes **hierarchy, obedience, and distinction.**

These are not the words of someone claiming **divine equality.** They are the words of a **faithful servant, anointed Messiah, and obedient Son.**

Any theological interpretation that **elevates Yeshua to co-equality with YHWH** directly contradicts **His own words and actions.**

A Consistent Pattern, Not Outliers

- Yeshua consistently identifies the **Father as supreme** (*John 14:28 —* *"The Father is greater than I"*).
- He acknowledges His **dependence on YHWH's authority and will** (*John 5:30 — "I can do nothing by myself"*).
- He openly admits **limitations in knowledge** (*Matthew 24:36 —* *"Only the Father knows the hour"*).

This is not a scattered collection of ambiguous verses—it's a **recurring theme woven through Yeshua's words and actions.**

Alignment with the Shema and Torah

- These teachings **align perfectly** with the Shema (*Deuteronomy 6:4*): *"YHWH is One."*
- They uphold the **first commandment** (*Exodus 20:3*): *"You shall have no other gods before me."*

If Yeshua were claiming **equality with YHWH**, His teachings would **contradict the very commandments He upheld** and referred to as the **greatest commandments.**

Why This Misunderstanding Matters

- **Idolatry:** Worshiping Yeshua as equal to YHWH violates the **first commandment** and distorts monotheism into **functional polytheism.**
- **Theological Drift:** Misinterpreting Yeshua's words introduces **doctrinal confusion** and leads to **worship practices that Yeshua Himself would reject.**
- **Obscuring the Messiah's Mission:** Yeshua's role as **Messiah, Servant, and Anointed One** becomes clouded by layers of **philosophical abstraction.**

Takeaway:

Yeshua **never claimed co-equality with YHWH.**

- His words and actions consistently reinforce a **hierarchical relationship** where **YHWH is supreme, and Yeshua operates in obedience to Him.**
- Recognizing and honoring this distinction isn't just a matter of theological accuracy—it's about **faithfulness to the commandments YHWH gave and Yeshua upheld.**

The clarity of this truth aligns us with **God's covenant, prophetic expectations, and the true identity of the Messiah.**

Transition to Section 5:

With Yeshua's words reinforcing **hierarchy and obedience**, the question arises:

- **What about heavenly authority?**
- **Who sits on the throne, and what is Yeshua's role in that divine structure?**
- Is Yeshua the King, or is He something more nuanced—perhaps akin to a **divine consigliere?**

In the next section, we'll explore the **heavenly positions** described in scripture and the distinction between **YHWH's ultimate authority and Yeshua's delegated responsibility.**

---

5. The Throne of Heaven Belongs to our Heavenly Father.

Key Insight:

The **Throne of YHWH** is the **singular seat of absolute divine authority, power, and sovereignty.** It is not shared, borrowed, or occupied by any being—not angels, not prophets, not kings, and **not even the Messiah.** The throne represents the **exclusive dominion of YHWH over all creation**, and this exclusivity is not subject to compromise, reinterpretation, or dilution.

5.1 Isaiah 42:8 – A Declaration of Exclusivity

"I am the LORD; that is my name! I will not yield my glory to another or my praise to idols." (Isaiah 42:8)

A Non-Negotiable Declaration

- This verse is not metaphorical or open to flexible interpretation—it is an **absolute declaration** of divine exclusivity.
- YHWH will not **share His glory, authority, or throne** with any being.

The Throne Is Not Communal

- The throne is not a **cooperative seat** nor a **joint authority**.
- It is **the singular epicenter of divine rule and justice.**

Theological Ramifications

- Any suggestion that someone—**even the Messiah—shares this throne** conflicts with **Isaiah 42:8.**
- This declaration forms a **boundary line** that cannot be crossed without **theological error and blasphemy.**

Takeaway:

YHWH's throne is **His alone**, and any claim suggesting co-occupancy or shared rulership violates the **clear, unyielding boundaries of Isaiah 42:8.**

5.2 Heavenly Imagery of the Throne

Isaiah's Vision of the Throne (*Isaiah 6:1-4*)

"I saw the Lord, high and exalted, seated on a throne; and the train of his robe filled the temple."

Key Observations:

- **Absolute Authority:** YHWH is **"high and exalted"** above all.
- **Divine Majesty:** The imagery reflects **unapproachable holiness and sovereign power.**
- **Singular Rule:** The throne is occupied **solely by YHWH.**

John's Vision of the Throne (*Revelation 4:2-11*)

"At once I was in the Spirit, and there before me was a throne in heaven with someone sitting on it... The twenty-four elders fall down before him who sits on the throne and worship him who lives forever and ever."

Key Observations:

- The throne is **surrounded by unceasing worship.**
- There is **one figure on the throne**, and all worship is directed **toward Him alone.**
- The throne represents **uncontested, supreme authority.**

No Rival, No Equal

- *Psalm 47:8: "God reigns over the nations; God is seated on His holy throne."*
- *Psalm 103:19: "The LORD has established His throne in the heavens, and His kingdom rules over All."*

Key Takeaways from These Passages:

1. The throne is **established, immovable, and eternal.**
2. YHWH's authority cannot be **shared, diminished, or challenged.**
3. Any suggestion that **another being occupies or shares this throne** is **not just misguided—it's blasphemous.**

5.3 The Throne Is the Ultimate Symbol of Divine Authority

More Than a Physical Location

- The throne is not just a **literal chair in heaven**—it is the **eternal representation of YHWH's dominion over all creation.**
- It symbolizes **absolute authority, justice, and divine power.**

Misunderstanding the Throne Distorts Theology

- To place **Yeshua on YHWH's throne** is to **elevate Him to a position YHWH explicitly reserves for Himself.**
- It **blurs the hierarchical structure** presented consistently in scripture.

Even the Messiah Is Not Exempt

- Yeshua's exaltation does not grant Him **co-ownership of the throne.**
- His place at the **right hand of YHWH** is a position of **reward and authority, not equality.**

Why This Matters

Worship Alignment

- Misunderstanding the **Throne of God** distorts worship practices, shifting **glory and focus away from YHWH.**
- True worship must center on **YHWH alone, who sits on the throne.**

Theological Integrity

- The distinction between the **Throne of God** and the **right hand** preserves the **integrity of Hebraic monotheism.**
- Erasing this distinction introduces **theological confusion and idolatry.**

Faithful Representation of Yeshua's Role

- Recognizing Yeshua's position at the **right hand of YHWH** honors **His obedience, exaltation, and Messianic mission.**
- Misrepresenting His role diminishes **His humanity, obedience, and prophetic fulfillment.**

Takeaway:

The **Throne of God** is the **singular, immovable seat of YHWH's divine authority, sovereignty, and holiness.**

- It is **not shared, borrowed, or occupied by anyone—not prophets, not angels, and not even Yeshua.**
- Yeshua's exaltation to the **right hand of the throne** does not imply **co-ownership or equality.**
- This distinction safeguards **YHWH's supreme authority** and preserves **Yeshua's true identity as Messiah and Servant.**

Understanding this truth is **essential for aligning worship, theology, and faith practices** with **scriptural integrity.**

Yeshua and the Throne: A Clear Distinction

Hebrews 1:3 – At the Right Hand of the Throne

"After He had provided purification for sins, He sat down at the right hand of the Majesty in heaven."

Key Observations:

- Yeshua is **at the right hand of the throne,** not **on the throne itself.**
- This distinction is **deliberate, consistent, and theologically essential.**
- The **right hand** is a position of **honor, delegated authority, and favor—not equality.**

The Right Hand vs. The Throne

- The **throne** represents **ultimate and unshared sovereignty.**
- The **right hand** represents **delegated authority and reward.**
- Sitting at the **right hand** emphasizes **obedience and exaltation, not co-sovereignty.**

Prophetic Expectations of the Messiah

- Nowhere in Hebraic prophecy is the Messiah described as **sitting on YHWH's throne.**
- Instead, the Messiah is described as being **seated at the right hand, acting as YHWH's agent and representative.**

Takeaway:

The distinction between the **throne of YHWH** and the **right hand of YHWH** is not a trivial detail—it is a **theological boundary marker** that preserves YHWH's singular sovereignty while honoring Yeshua's obedience and role.

Transition to next section:

If the **Throne of YHWH** represents **absolute, unshared divine authority**, then what does the **Seat of Glory** represent?

- What is the **significance of Yeshua's position at the right hand of YHWH?**
- How does this position honor Yeshua's obedience without violating YHWH's singular authority?

5.4 The Seat of Glory: A Reward for Obedience

Key Insight:

The **Seat of Glory at YHWH's right hand** is not the **Throne of God**. It represents a **position of honor, divine authority, and fulfillment of covenantal justice**—earned through perfect obedience and faithful submission. While the **Throne of God** signifies **ultimate divine sovereignty**, the **Seat of Glory** symbolizes a **reward for obedience** and a **delegated role within YHWH's sovereign plan.**

Hebrews 1:3 – A Clear Distinction

"After He had provided purification for sins, He sat down at the right hand of the Majesty in heaven." (Hebrews 1:3)

The Phrasing Is Deliberate

- The verse explicitly states **"at the right hand"**, not **"on the throne."**
- This distinction isn't just **semantic or stylistic—it's foundational to understanding Yeshua's exaltation.**
- The **Seat of Glory** is a **rewarded position**, not a **co-rulership on YHWH's throne.**

Acts 7:54-56: Stephen sees Yeshua at the Right Hand of God

> *"When the council members heard Stephen's speech, they were angry and furious. But Stephen was filled with the Holy Spirit. He looked toward heaven, where he saw our glorious God and Jesus standing at his right side. Then Stephen said, "I see heaven open and the Son of Man standing at the right side of God!"*

The result:

> *"The council members shouted and covered their ears. At once they all attacked Stephen and dragged him out of the city. Then they started throwing stones at him. The men who had brought charges against him put their coats at the feet of a young man named Saul."* Acts 7:57-58

A Position of Honor, Not Equality

- Sitting **at the right hand** carries a **symbolic and functional difference** from sitting on the **Throne of God.**
- The **right hand** denotes **delegated authority—a role of acting on behalf of YHWH, not alongside Him as an equal.**

Theological Significance

- This distinction safeguards **YHWH's absolute sovereignty** while simultaneously **honoring Yeshua's obedience and fulfillment of His mission.**
- Any attempt to **merge these two positions** distorts **YHWH's exclusive authority** and **Yeshua's Messianic role.**

Takeaway:

The **Seat of Glory** at YHWH's right hand is a **position of exalted honor and authority, earned through obedience.** It is **not the throne itself** and does not signify **co-equality with YHWH.**

Why This Distinction Matters

Scriptural Integrity

- The distinction between the **Throne of God** and the **right hand** appears consistently in both **Hebrew Scripture** and the **New Testament.**
- *Hebrews 1:3* and *Psalm 110:1* align perfectly in depicting **Yeshua's role as honored servant and agent of YHWH's will.**

Worship Alignment

- Recognizing this distinction prevents **misdirected worship** that would blur the lines between **YHWH's sovereign authority and Yeshua's rewarded position.**
- Worship directed to the **Seat of Glory** risks **idolizing the role of the Messiah** instead of honoring **YHWH alone as supreme.**

Preserving YHWH's Sovereignty

- The **Throne of God** represents **absolute, non-transferable sovereignty.**
- The **right hand** represents **delegated power and honor under YHWH's supreme rule.**

Takeaway:

Understanding the difference between the **Throne of God** and the **Seat of Glory** preserves **theological integrity, scriptural consistency, and proper worship alignment.**

Context Within Hebraic Understanding
Prophetic Expectation

- The **Hebrew prophets** never described the Messiah as sitting **on YHWH's throne.**
- Instead, they consistently portrayed the Messiah as **an exalted servant and trusted representative.**
- *Psalm 110:1* reinforces this: The Messiah sits **at YHWH's right hand,** not on YHWH's throne.

Patterns of Delegated Authority in Scripture

The imagery of **sitting at the right hand** appears repeatedly in biblical history:

Joseph in Egypt (*Genesis 41:40*)
- Joseph was placed **at Pharaoh's right hand**—second in command, yet never equal to Pharaoh.

King Solomon's mother (*1 Kings 2:19*)
- She sat **at Solomon's right hand** as a position of honor, but not on the throne itself.

Yeshua in the Pattern of Honor

- Yeshua's exaltation **follows the same pattern**—an elevated seat of honor and authority, but **not a position of co-equality.**
- The **right hand represents proximity, favor, and trust,** not **shared sovereignty.**

The **Seat of Glory aligns with consistent biblical patterns** of delegated authority. It reflects **honor, trust, and reward**—not equality or shared dominion.

Final Takeaway for 5.4:

The **Seat of Glory at YHWH's right hand** represents delegated **authority to execute YHWH's will** (*Psalm 110:1*).

- A position of trust and fulfillment of prophetic expectation.

It is **not the Throne of God** and does not grant **co-equality or co-sovereignty: .**

5.5 Not a Seat of Co-Divinity

Key Insight:

The **Seat of Glory** does not alter the **divine hierarchy.** YHWH remains **supreme, singular, and unchallenged on the throne.** The Messiah, seated at YHWH's right hand, serves a **specific role of authority, representation, and intercession.** Any interpretation that equates the **Seat of Glory with YHWH's throne** distorts the structure outlined in scripture.

Timothy 2:5 – Distinct Roles

"For there is one God and one mediator between God and mankind, the man Christ Jesus."

YHWH as Sovereign King

- YHWH remains the **singular, sovereign authority** on the throne.
- His throne represents **unshared divine dominion, power, and absolute sovereignty.**

Yeshua as Mediator and Honored Servant

Yeshua's role is defined as **mediator, intercessor, and servant of YHWH's will.**

- Yeshua's role is as a prophet pointing people back to covenantal alignment, as an embodiment of the bin Joseph, suffering servant messianic archetype and as the exalted intercessor, all center on **"the Will of our Father who is in Heaven"**.
- His seat at the **right hand** signifies **delegated authority**—not **shared divinity**.

The Right Hand: A Seat of Delegated Authority

- The **right hand** of YHWH symbolizes **honor, trust, and delegated authority**.
- It is not synonymous with the **Throne of God**.
- The Messiah acts **on behalf of YHWH**, not **as a co-sovereign or rival**.

Scriptural Precedents for the Right Hand

- **Joseph in Egypt (Genesis 41:40):** Delegated authority while Pharaoh retained supreme power.
- **King Solomon's mother (1 Kings 2:19):** Seated at the right hand as an **honored advisor, not a co-ruler**.

Yeshua at the Right Hand

- Yeshua operates **within the divine hierarchy** set by YHWH.
- His position is **that of honored and trusted subordinate**, not of **co-sovereignty**.

Avoiding Theological Drift

- Misinterpreting the **Seat of Glory** as a **co-equal throne** creates **doctrinal inversion**.
- It risks **misdirecting worship** toward Yeshua instead of **YHWH alone**.
- Proper understanding ensures that **worship remains centered where it belongs**.

The **Seat of Glory does not alter the divine hierarchy.**

Our Heavenly Father YHWH remains on the **throne as the sovereign King,** and Yeshua serves as the **honored mediator and servant.**

The distinction between the **throne and the right-hand** preserves both **YHWH's absolute authority** and Yeshua's honored role.

Why These Distinctions Are Vital

Preserving Scriptural Integrity:
- Upholding these roles aligns with **biblical patterns of authority and delegation.**

Proper Worship Alignment:
- Worship must remain directed **solely toward YHWH.**

Protecting Theological Foundations:
- Misunderstanding these roles risks **idolizing the Messiah** instead of **honoring YHWH, forcing Yeshua** to tell you **on that day:**

    "I never knew you" and "depart from me you worker of lawlessness."

Conclusion:
The **Seat of Glory** is a **subordinate position** that reflects **obedience, humility, and desire to uphold YHWH's will.** It does not signify **co-divinity or shared sovereignty.**

- YHWH remains the **Sovereign King on the throne.**
- Yeshua remains the **honored mediator, servant, and agent of God's authority.**

Final Reflection:
- The **Throne of God** represents **absolute, singular sovereignty.**
- The **Seat of Glory** represents **delegated authority, earned honor, and faithful service.**
- Confusing these two undermines **YHWH's divine authority** and **Yeshua's Messianic role.**

Core Takeaway:

The **Seat of Glory** is not about **Yeshua sharing YHWH's throne.**

It's about **YHWH honoring Yeshua's obedience and empowering Him to act on His behalf.**

6: Catastrophic Penalties of Misdirected Worship

If **Yeshua's exaltation is misunderstood**, what are the **consequences for worship, faith, and theology?**

The Danger of Misplaced Worship cannot be understated.

Misdirected worship distorts both YHWH's authority and Yeshua's role.

Neither YHWH nor Yeshua will tolerate such relational violations – both view idolatry as spiritual adultery.

6.1 Violating the Covenantal Commandments

Key Insight:

The **first commandment** and the **Shema** form the **spiritual and theological foundation** of the covenant between YHWH and humanity.

Misplacing worship—however well-intentioned—violates these foundational principles, distorts YHWH's sovereignty, and undermines Yeshua's faithful obedience.

The First Commandment: No Other Gods Before Me

"You shall have no other gods before Me." (*Exodus 20:3*)

The Weight of the First Commandment

- This commandment is **not just one among ten—it's the foundation upon which all others stand.**
- It establishes the **exclusive worship and devotion** that YHWH demands from His people.
- YHWH declares Himself **unrivaled, undivided, and unchallenged** in His divine authority.

The Heart of the Commandment

- Worship directed to **anyone or anything other than YHWH**—even with sincere intentions—constitutes **idolatry.**
- The commandment isn't merely about **avoiding pagan gods**; it's about recognizing that **no intermediary, no prophet, no Messiah is to be worshiped as God.**
- **Sincerity does not sanctify idolatry.** Even with pure motives, misdirected worship violates divine law.

Jesus Affirmed the First Commandment

Yeshua Himself upheld this commandment during His ministry:
- **Matthew 4:10:** *"Worship the Lord your God, and serve Him only."*
- **John 4:23-24:** *"True worshipers will worship the Father in spirit and truth, for they are the kind of worshipers the Father seeks."*

At no point did Yeshua **direct worship to Himself** or claim a right to the worship that belongs to YHWH.

The **first commandment is non-negotiable.** Any worship directed toward Yeshua as though He occupies YHWH's throne is not an act of reverence—it's **spiritual idolatry.**

The Shema: YHWH is One

"Hear and Obey, O Israel: The LORD our God, the LORD is one."
(Deuteronomy 6:4)

The Core Declaration of Faith

- The **Shema** is more than a prayer—it's the **creedal foundation of Hebraic faith.**
- It declares YHWH's **absolute oneness**, leaving no room for **division, duplication, or co-equality.**
- The word "one" (echad) signifies **unity, singularity, and indivisibility.**

Yeshua Affirmed the Shema

In **Mark 12:29**, Yeshua reaffirms the Shema without hesitation:

- *His command: "And thou shalt love the LORD thy God with all thy heart, and with all thy soul, and with all thy mind."* aligns perfectly with the Shema. The Shema is Deuteronomy 6:4, Jesus's "greatest commandment" is Deuteronomy 6:5.
- *That* **God is one, and He is to be loved completely and exclusively are inseparable.**

Theological Implications of the Shema

- Any doctrine suggesting **co-equality or division within God's identity** fundamentally contradicts the Shema.
- Trinitarian interpretations **subtly undermine the Shema,** portraying God as **divided into multiple persons.**
- YHWH's oneness is **not metaphorical—it's literal, eternal, and absolute.**

The **Shema is clear and uncompromising.** Elevating Yeshua to divine equality with YHWH is not a misunderstanding—it's a **theological breach** of the most sacred declaration in Hebraic faith.

Trinitarianism: A Violation of Commandments

The Core Issue with Trinitarianism

- The **doctrine of the Trinity** suggests a **co-equal, triune God** composed of **three distinct persons:** Father, Son, and Holy Spirit.

- An unscriptural conclusion that **explicitly introduces division** into YHWH's absolute singularity.
- Trinitarianism **misdirects worship** to Yeshua as if He were equal to YHWH.

Worship Distorted by Misunderstanding

- Worship directed toward **Yeshua as God** violates the **first commandment** and the **Shema**.
- **Revelation 5:13** often gets misinterpreted as Yeshua sharing worship with YHWH, yet the distinction is clear: **YHWH remains on the throne while Yeshua is honored at the right hand.**

Yeshua's Own Words Contradict Trinitarian Claims

- **John 14:28:** *"The Father is greater than I."*
- **John 5:30:** *"I can do nothing on my own. I judge only as I hear, and my judgment is just, because I do not seek my own will but the will of Him who sent me."*
- Yeshua consistently places Himself **below and in service to YHWH.**

The **Trinitarian framework** creates a significant theological distortion. It misrepresents Yeshua's role and violates both the **first commandment** and the **Shema**.

Worship: Reserved for YHWH Alone

Scripture Leaves No Wiggle Room

- **Exodus 20:3** and **Deuteronomy 6:4** are **clear, consistent, and unchanging.**
- Worship belongs to **YHWH alone**, and no amount of theological reasoning can override this foundational truth.

The Gravity of Idolatry

- Worshiping Yeshua as God, even with sincere intentions, **crosses a sacred boundary.**
- Idolatry isn't just about golden calves or carved statues—it's about **misdirected worship.**

The Warning of Yeshua

- Yeshua consistently **redirected worship to YHWH.**
- Yeshua prayed to YHWH, obeyed YHWH, and honored YHWH as the **supreme authority.**

Yeshua gave an explicit warning to those who will seek his intercession without upholding the will of our Heavenly Father.

I Never Knew You

> *"Not everyone who says to me, 'Lord, Lord,' will enter the kingdom of heaven, but the one who does the will of my Father who is in heaven.*
>
> *On that day many will say to me, 'Lord, Lord, did we not prophesy in your name, and cast out demons in your name, and do many mighty works in your name? And then will I declare to them, 'I never knew you; depart from me, you workers of lawlessness.'" (Matthew 7:21-23)*

Yeshua's heavenly **position as intercessor carries very specific terms and qualifications.**

- He does not offer **a "free pass"** to those who ignore the Covenantal Commandments of YHWH, no matter what they do in his name — either as "Jesus" or "Yeshua".
- Messiah's stated purpose is not protecting corrupt lawlessness: it is upholding the Will of our Heavenly Father, YHWH.

Yeshua is God's messiah: not ours. He reports to YHWH, not humanity.

Yeshua promises to intercede for us when that day comes: but under an extremely specific qualifier.

This qualifier is based not upon what his followers do in his name, but what is they do to uphold the will of God in Heaven.

No matter what wonders or miracles you did in "Jesus's name", Yeshua only cares about the glorification of God's name: YHWH.

When worship is directed at Yeshua **as though He shares YHWH's throne**, it's not an act of reverence—it's an act of idolatry **Yeshua** would not intercede over.

Section Reflection

- The **first commandment** and the **Shema** are the **cornerstones of faith.**
- Yeshua's role as Messiah was to **fulfill God's will, not to replace YHWH as an object of worship.**
- Misplacing worship, no matter how sincere, is **spiritually catastrophic.**

Core Takeaway:

Worship belongs to **YHWH alone.** Misplacing it, even toward Yeshua, **violates the commandments, distorts YHWH's sovereignty, and dishonors the Messiah's obedience.**

Transition to Section 6.2

If Yeshua's role wasn't to **share YHWH's throne or divine worship,** then **what was the role of the Messiah according to scripture?**

In the next section, we'll uncover how the **messianic role aligns with YHWH's purpose and covenant.**

6.2 Misunderstanding Messiahship

Key Insight:

Yeshua did not come to **replace YHWH, share His throne, or receive divine worship.** His mission was **restorative, prophetic, and covenantal**—a divine appointment to **reconcile humanity with YHWH** and demonstrate **perfect obedience to God's will.**

Yeshua's Own Words Define His Role

John 17:3 – The One True God and His Sent Servant

"Now this is eternal life: that they know You, the only true God, and Jesus Christ, whom You have sent." (John 17:3)

Yeshua Identifies YHWH as the One True God

- Yeshua leaves **no ambiguity** here: YHWH is the one true God.
- He does not include Himself in the **singular divinity of YHWH**.
- This declaration aligns perfectly with **Exodus 20:3** and **Deuteronomy 6:4.**

Yeshua Identifies Himself as Sent by God

- Yeshua defines His role as **"the one whom YHWH has sent."**
- His identity is **mission-centered, not power-centered.**
- He is a **servant and messenger of YHWH's will.**

John 5:30 – Dependence on YHWH's Will

"By myself I can do nothing; I judge only as I hear, and my judgment is just, for I seek not to please myself but Him who sent me."

- Yeshua declares **total dependence on YHWH.**
- He doesn't claim **independent divine authority** but instead **aligns His will with YHWH's will.**

Yeshua's own words dismantle the notion of **shared divinity or co-equality with YHWH.** He identifies as **YHWH's servant, messenger, and mediator—not as His equal.**

The Prophetic Mission of Messiah

Messiah was sent to fulfill not just Prophecy – but exemplify the Prophetic purpose itself: turning people back to YHWH's Law & Covenantal alignment.

- Yeshua's mission was **foretold by the prophets** and **anchored in covenantal expectations.**

- **Isaiah 42:1:** *"Here is my servant, whom I uphold, my chosen one in whom I delight; I will put my Spirit on him, and he will bring justice to the nations."*
- The Messiah was to be a **servant, not a rival deity.**

Walking in Submission to God's will

- Yeshua's earthly ministry was marked by **obedience and humility.**
- His authority comes from **his perfect upholding of God's Law, not his own innate divinity.**
- Submission to YHWH was the source of all power and authority Yeshua exercised.

Restoring Humanity to YHWH

- The Messiah's purpose was **reconciliation, not self-exaltation.**
- Yeshua served as a **bridge back to YHWH, not as a replacement deity.**

The **anointed role** is always one of **service to God's Law.**

Yeshua came to **fulfill prophecy and guide humanity back to YHWH,** not to **claim divine worship or sovereignty** for himself.

Worship as a Misguided Response

- Yeshua's exaltation to the **Seat of Glory** was a **reward for obedience,** not an invitation for divine worship.
- Directing worship to Yeshua as if He occupies **YHWH's throne** is a **misreading of His role and purpose.**

Ritualism vs. Obedience

- When worship focuses on **Yeshua as a divine equal,** it often shifts away from **obedience to YHWH.**
- Rituals and ceremonies meant to honor Yeshua can **distract from following YHWH's commandments.**
- This creates a **spiritual shortcut**—reverence replaces **action, faithfulness, and covenant alignment.**

Worship According to Yeshua's Own Example

Yeshua never **sought worship for Himself.**
He consistently **pointed worship upward to YHWH:**

- **John 4:23:** *"True worshipers will worship the Father in spirit and truth."*
- **Matthew 4:10:** *"Worship the Lord your God, and serve Him only."*

When worship is **misdirected toward Yeshua as a divine equal,** it undermines **His mission** and **violates the commandments Yeshua upheld.**

Faithfulness means **following Yeshua's example of worshiping YHWH alone.**

The Significance of Getting Messiahship Right

Theological Integrity

- Misunderstanding Yeshua's role creates **doctrinal confusion** and **spiritual disorder.**
- Theology becomes centered on **a distorted Messiah** rather than **YHWH's sovereign plan.**
- **YHWH's Covenantal Plan does not operate through demigod archetypes.**

"Demigods" as heroes is a Greco-Roman construct.

- Hebraic theology does not recognize celestial-terrestrial hybrids as *demigod saviors*, it views them as *Nephilim destroyers*.

- Hebraic Messiahs are faithful human servants anointed by YHWH for specific purpose related to his Covenantal plans and promises.

Honoring Yeshua Properly

- Honoring Yeshua means **recognizing and respecting the role He fulfilled.**
- His exaltation is a **reward for obedience,** not a **license for worship.**

Realigning Faith and Worship

- Getting Yeshua's role right **realigns worship to YHWH.**
- It ensures **faithful obedience** to the first and greatest commandments.

Understanding Yeshua's **true Messianic role** safeguards **theological clarity, faithful worship, and proper covenantal alignment.**

Final Reflection

- Yeshua did not come to **replace YHWH, demand worship, or share the throne of God.**
- His mission was one of **obedience, humility, and reconciliation.**
- Worship directed at Yeshua as **a divine equal to YHWH** undermines both **YHWH's authority** and **Yeshua's faithfulness.**

Core Takeaway:

Yeshua's mission was to **point humanity back to YHWH**, fulfill prophecy, and demonstrate **perfect obedience.** Getting Yeshua right means **getting worship right.**

Transition to Section 7: Conclusion

If Yeshua is **not co-equal with YHWH** and **does not share YHWH's throne**, then **how should we view and honor Him appropriately?**

7. Messiah's True Face

Key Insight:

Yeshua's life, identity, and mission stand unshaken when viewed through the lens of prophecy, scripture, and his own words. He wasn't a celestial hybrid, nor a rival deity vying for YHWH's throne. He was— and remains—the **Messiah**, the **Servant of YHWH**, born in Bethlehem as foretold, fulfilling every prophetic expectation, and ultimately seated at the **Seat of Glory** as a reward for perfect obedience.

7.1 Back to Bethlehem: Prophecy Fulfilled, Misunderstanding Corrected

"But you, Bethlehem Ephrathah, though you are small among the clans of Judah, out of you will come for me one who will be ruler over Israel, whose origins are from of old, from ancient times." — **Micah 5:2**

Bethlehem was no incidental birthplace; it was a **divine appointment etched into prophecy** centuries before Yeshua's arrival. It wasn't just where He was born—it was a **symbolic anchor** of His legitimacy as the prophesied Messiah.

- **Prophecy Fulfilled:** Yeshua's birth in Bethlehem fulfilled Micah's words, aligning Him with Davidic lineage and prophetic expectation.
- **Nazareth's Misunderstanding:** While Nazareth became a convenient label, it diluted the prophetic weight of Bethlehem, subtly misdirecting focus from His true Messianic identity.
- **Identity Restored:** Recognizing Yeshua as **Yeshua of Bethlehem**, not simply "Jesus of Nazareth," realigns Him with His prophesied purpose.

Takeaway:
Bethlehem wasn't just a setting—it was a **scriptural seal**. To misunderstand or overlook this detail is to miss one of the clearest signposts pointing to Yeshua's Messianic legitimacy.

7.2 The True Role of the Messiah: Servant, Mediator, and Exemplar

"Now this is eternal life: that they know You, the only true God, and Jesus Christ, whom You have sent." — **John 17:3**

Yeshua's mission wasn't about self-exaltation—it was about **obedience, fulfillment, and pointing humanity back to YHWH.**

- **Restoring Covenant Alignment:** Yeshua came to fulfill the role of the Messiah, walking in perfect obedience to YHWH's commands.
- **Obedience Unto Death:** His mission was sealed in humility and sacrifice, culminating at the cross.

- **Mediator, Not Rival:** As **1 Timothy 2:5** clarifies, Yeshua serves as the **one mediator between God and mankind.**

Misunderstood Messiahship:

- Worship directed at Yeshua **as though He shares YHWH's throne** distorts His role.
- Yeshua didn't come to **demand divine worship** but to **model perfect obedience** and **redirect all worship upward to YHWH.**

Takeaway:
Understanding Yeshua as **the Messiah** means embracing His role as **servant, mediator, and obedient son—not as a co-equal deity.**

7.3 Worship Aligned: Honoring YHWH and Yeshua Correctly

"You shall have no other gods before Me." — **Exodus 20:3**
"Hear, O Israel: The LORD our God, the LORD is one." — **Deuteronomy 6:4**

Worship isn't a casual detail—it's the **core expression of spiritual alignment.**

- **Worship Belongs to YHWH Alone:** Both the **First Commandment** and the **Shema** leave no ambiguity—YHWH alone is God, and He alone is worthy of worship.
- **Yeshua's Example:** At every moment, Yeshua pointed worship away from Himself and directed it upward to YHWH.
- **Theological Drift:** Misplacing worship toward Yeshua as a co-equal deity distorts the covenantal framework YHWH established with humanity.

The Simplicity of Alignment:

- YHWH is God alone.
- Yeshua is the Messiah, the obedient servant exalted to the Seat of Glory.
- Our worship must follow Yeshua's example: directed exclusively to YHWH.

Takeaway:
True worship aligns with Yeshua's own words and actions: **worship YHWH alone and honor Yeshua for His obedience, not as a rival deity.**

7.4 The Greco-Roman Distortions: Recognizing the Fault Lines

Centuries of theological drift have introduced **subtle yet catastrophic distortions** into how Yeshua is understood:

- **Bethlehem Overlooked:** The prophetic importance of Bethlehem was eclipsed by cultural shorthand emphasizing Nazareth.
- **The Throne vs. The Seat:** The Seat of Glory was confused with YHWH's Throne, creating a false narrative of co-divinity.
- **Misplaced Worship:** Ritualistic worship of Yeshua as a divine equal replaced His true role as mediator and servant.

Each distortion, while seemingly small in isolation, has compounded over time, leading to a **fundamental misalignment of worship and theology.**

Takeaway:
Restoring clarity requires peeling away centuries of distortion, returning to **scripture's prophetic blueprint**, and realigning our understanding of Yeshua's role.

7.5 Final Reflection: A Path Restored

This Inquiry has shown how from **Bethlehem** to the **Seat of Glory**, Yeshua's mission was covenantal, prophetically aligned, and completely submissive to the Will and Word of our Heavenly Father. It has clarified Yeshua's identity and mission with scriptural precision.

- **Yeshua was born in Bethlehem, fulfilling prophecy.**
- **He lived in perfect obedience to YHWH's will.**
- **He earned the Seat of Glory—not the Throne of God—as a reward for His faithfulness.**
- **He directed all worship upward, never toward Himself.**

To misunderstand these truths is to miss the **clarity and simplicity** of the covenant YHWH established with humanity.

The Path Forward:

- **Worship YHWH alone.**
- **Honor Yeshua as one of God's anointed, a perfectly obedient servant exalted by YHWH.**
- **Follow Yeshua's example of humility, obedience, and faithfulness to the Covenant and Calendar of our Heavenly Father.**

Final Takeaway:
Yeshua of Bethlehem wasn't a hybrid god or a celestial rival.

He was a prophet, one of God's anointed **messiahs**, an **obedient servant of YHWH**, seated at God's right hand in continuing service as a reward for His obedience.

He is **not sharing the Throne of God**, but instead sits at the **Seat of Glory**, pointing humanity upward to the **One True God.**

In this clarity, worship becomes pure, faith becomes aligned, and the path back to YHWH is restored.

Looking Ahead to Inquiry 3

The first step in this journey was **understanding how Yeshua interpreted and taught scripture.** We learned that scripture follows a **strict hierarchy—the Law is supreme, the Prophets call people back to it, and the Writings reflect upon it.**

The second step was asking **who Yeshua truly was—and who he wasn't.**

Using Christ's **own scriptural lens**, we examined the biblical messiah through **His words in the Gospels and His role as defined by the Law & Prophets.**

This realization brings us to our next inquiry—**if Messiah Himself upheld the Law and the Prophets**, then **How do we best interpret the Prophets?**

Inquiry 3: How Do We Best Interpret The Prophets?

Introduction

Before we can answer the question of how to best interpret the prophets, we must first address the inherited confusion surrounding the term "prophet."

Across millennia, this word has taken on different meanings depending on cultural, religious, and historical contexts.

To refine our understanding, we must distinguish between differing concepts surrounding prophets, as well as those surrounding martyrs and zealots—as each embodies vastly different spiritual and behavioral characteristics.

1. Opening Question: "What is a Prophet?"

Depends on who you ask, and when.
The concept of a prophet varies dramatically depending on whether one views the term through the lens of Pauline Christianity, Rabbinic Judaism, or Yeshua's teachings.

To answer the question "What is a prophet?" we must first explore these divergent perspectives and their theological implications.

Varying interpretations have shaped how both modern Pauline Christians and Rabbinical Jews view "prophets" and "prophecy" and how these views contrast with the understanding of Yeshua, the Jerusalem Church, and late "Second Temple" Jews.

1.1 Pauline Traditions: The Mystical Foretellers

The word *prophet* (Greek: *prophētēs*) found its way to English with layers of inherited Greco-Roman linguistic overtones that distort the relational context of the original Hebraic understanding. In common speech today, a "prophet" is imagined as a mystical oracle — a fortune-teller, seer, or predictor of far-off events. This conceptual conflation arises from accumulated linguistic convergences that have diminished the original context.

In English, much of the confusion regarding the word "prophet" arises from other related words prophecy and prophesy. These related words are similar in both spelling and sound. The word "prophecy", with a *c*, is a noun: the word "prophesy", with an *s*, is a verb.

Only one letter separates them, the similar spelling and sound present the impression that the role of a "prophet" is defined by predicting the future.

Tracing the translational history of prophet: Hebrew → Greek → Latin → French → English, reveals how the understood meaning became so convoluted.

- *Prophecy* (noun) appears in English before 1200, borrowed from Old French (*prophetie*), which itself came from Late Latin and Greek.
- To *prophesy* (verb) emerges in English by 1350, also through Old French.
- Both words pointed back to the Greek root *prophētēs* — literally, "one who speaks forth."

In Hebraic understanding, the word for prophet is *navi* — one called to be the spokesperson of God.

A *navi* is not a fortune-teller, they are covenantal messengers. The main tasking of a Hebrew Prophet was not to astound audiences with actions expected in a far-off-future; the mission of a Hebrew Prophet was to call people back to alignment with God's Commandments with actions expected in the here-and-now.

- Through multiple translations over thousands of years, the Hebraic understanding was overshadowed by Greco-Roman understandings.

When the Greco-Roman understanding dominates, "prophet" is often reduced to mysticism and future-telling. When the foundational Hebraic understanding is restored, the prophets are revealed as covenant messengers.

Recognizing the translational history and linguistic drift of the terms prophet, prophecy and prophesy, helps restore Hebraic context. A prophet in Hebraic thought is not primarily a predictor but a messenger — a living mouthpiece of God's Covenantal Law.

- This matters because the meaning of "prophet" is best understood in biblical context..
- How one defines a prophet shapes how one hears Isaiah or Jeremiah, and even how one understands Yeshua Himself.

Later Christian traditions, divided by history and creed, absorbed these linguistic ambiguities in different ways. Catholics, Eastern and Oriental Orthodox, and Protestant traditions all carry slightly different assumptions about what "prophet" means.

Pauline Christianity's Definition of Prophets

Pauline traditions, rooted in the writings of Paul, view prophets as spiritual figures gifted with divine revelations, often for the edification and guidance of the church. Paul's epistles, particularly **1 Corinthians 12-14**, emphasize prophecy as a central gift of the Holy Spirit, highlighting its practical purpose of building up the Christian community.

In Modern Pauline theology:

- **Old Testament Prophets** are often reduced to being forerunners or foretellers of Yeshua.
- **Modern Prophecy** is seen less as predictive (foretelling future events) and more as instructive (bringing divine insight into present circumstances).
- **Modern Prophesy** often includes elements like inspired preaching, exhortation, and encouragement, which serve to strengthen faith and align the community.

This broad definition paved the way for different interpretations across Christian denominations, leading to conflated understandings of the role of a prophet and what it means to prophesy a prophecy.

Catholic Tradition: Modern Prophets as Mystics and Saints

Mystical Foretellers: The Catholic Church, influenced by Pauline thought, often associates prophets with **mystics**—individuals who experience direct divine encounters or revelations.

Figures like **St. Francis of Assisi, St. Catherine of Siena**, and **St. Teresa of Ávila** are celebrated for their visionary experiences and divine messages.

- **Prophets and Saints Overlap**: Catholicism frequently links prophecy with sainthood, emphasizing the suffering and martyrdom of prophets as evidence of their divine favor. Saints like **Joan of Arc**, who claimed divine guidance, are elevated as both prophets and martyrs.

- **Church Authority Over Prophecy**: The Catholic Church maintains strict oversight of prophecy, requiring visions or revelations to align with established doctrine. This institutional control ensures that prophetic claims support church unity rather than challenge it.

- **Miracles and Prophetic Legitimacy**: Prophets in Catholic tradition often exhibit mystical signs (e.g., stigmata, healings) as confirmation of their divine mission, echoing Pauline emphasis on miraculous gifts.

Eastern Orthodox Tradition: Modern Prophets as Spiritual Guides

Focus on Holiness and Wisdom: In the Eastern Orthodox Church, prophets are not primarily seen as future-predictors but as **spiritual guides** who embody holiness and offer wisdom rooted in divine revelation.

Figures like **St. Seraphim of Sarov** and **St. Gregory Palamas** are revered for their ascetic lives and theological insights, which are considered prophetic in their alignment with God's will.

- **Continuity with the Early Church**: Orthodox theology emphasizes the **continuity of prophecy** from the early church through monastic tradition. Prophets are often monks or elders (known as "starets") who guide communities with spiritual discernment.
- **Prophecy and Mysticism**: Like Catholicism, Orthodoxy values mystical experiences, but it places greater emphasis on the **inner transformation** of the prophet through prayer and asceticism.
- **Prophecy as a Communal Gift**: Prophetic gifts are viewed less as individualistic and more as serving the community, reflecting the Pauline ideal of prophecy as edifying the body of Christ.

Oriental Orthodox Tradition: Modern Prophets as Custodians of Tradition

- **Historical and Liturgical Emphasis**: The Oriental Orthodox Churches (e.g., Coptic, Armenian) view prophets as custodians of tradition who safeguard the faith amidst persecution and external pressures.

Prophets are often tied to historical continuity, such as **St. Moses the Black** or **St. Shenouda the Archimandrite**, whose actions preserved doctrinal purity.

- **Martyrdom and Prophecy**: Prophets are closely associated with martyrs in Oriental Orthodox thought, reflecting the Pauline emphasis on suffering as a marker of divine calling.
- **Lesser Emphasis on Mysticism**: While mystical experiences are respected, the Oriental Orthodox focus more on the **prophet's role in preserving orthodoxy** and their ability to inspire faithfulness under duress.

Protestant Tradition: Modern Prophets as Reformers and Preachers

Prophetic Role as Teacher and Reformer: In many Protestant denominations, prophets are equated with **reformers**, such as **Martin Luther** or **John Calvin**, who challenged institutional corruption and pointed the church back to scripture. Prophets are often seen as

preachers who boldly proclaim God's Word, emphasizing sola scriptura (scripture alone) as the source of their authority.

Cessationist vs. Continuationist Views: Some Protestant groups (e.g., Presbyterians) adopt a **cessationist** view, believing that prophecy ceased with the apostolic age. Others (e.g., Pentecostals) hold a **continuationist** view, embracing prophecy as an ongoing spiritual gift. Prophets in these traditions often claim charismatic gifts like speaking in tongues, healing, or receiving visions.

Prophecy and Evangelism: Protestant prophets are known for using their perceived divine insight to inspire conversions and spiritual revival (e.g., **Charles Spurgeon, John Wesley**).

Decentralized Prophecy: Protestantism lacks centralization, so prophecy is validated by individual denominations or congregations.

Comparison of Denominational Views on Prophets

Tradition	Role of Prophets	Markers of Prophetic Legitimacy	Key Figures
Catholic	Mystics, saints, and visionaries	Miracles, suffering, alignment with doctrine	St. Francis, Joan of Arc
Orthodox	Spiritual guides and holy ascetics	Holiness, wisdom, alignment with tradition	St. Seraphim, St. Gregory
Oriental Orthodox	Custodians of tradition, martyrs	Faithfulness under persecution	St. Moses, St. Shenouda
Protestant	Reformers, charismatic preachers	Biblical alignment, evangelistic impact	Martin Luther, John Wesley

Takeaway:

While Pauline theology emphasizes the spiritual gifts and mystical elements of prophecy, denominational interpretations diverge significantly:

- **Catholics** focus on miraculous and mystical experiences, linking prophecy with sainthood.
- **Orthodox Churches** emphasize spiritual wisdom and communal guidance.
- **Oriental Orthodox Churches** prioritize the preservation of orthodoxy and faithfulness amidst persecution.
- **Protestants** often see prophets as reformers or charismatic leaders, with varying degrees of emphasis on ongoing prophecy.

This diversity reflects how modern Pauline concepts of prophecy have been adapted to fit different theological frameworks, sometimes at the expense of the original Hebraic understanding of prophets as those who primarily point people back to God's law and covenant.

1.2 What Is Meant by "Prophets" in Modern Rabbinical Traditions?

In modern Rabbinical traditions, the concept of a "prophet" is often tied to the classical understanding of the Navi'im—the major and minor figures from the Hebrew Bible who served as God's spokespeople.

However, the Rabbinical lens views prophecy as a phenomenon of the past, something that ceased with the destruction of the First Temple or shortly thereafter. While these traditions hold the prophets in high esteem, they often emphasize their roles as teachers of moral and legal principles rather than purely as forecasters of the future.

This perspective is deeply connected to the Jewish understanding of *Ruach HaKodesh* (the Holy Spirit) as the divine force guiding prophecy and its perceived cessation during the "Second Temple" period. Modern Rabbinical thought also distinguishes between levels of prophecy, recognizing distinct roles such as Navi (public leader), Ro'eh (seer), and Chozeh (visionary). The distinction underscores a nuanced understanding of how God communicated through individuals, with a strong focus on their alignment with Torah and covenantal fidelity.

While Rabbinical Judaism reveres the prophets for their role in pointing Israel back to God, the traditions have largely shifted focus toward the sages and teachers who interpret the Torah.

This shift reflects a broader theological transition from divine revelation to human study and interpretation.

Understanding this framework helps clarify how Rabbinical traditions interpret the term "prophet" and how this view compares and contrasts with other traditions, such as those rooted in Yeshua's teachings and Pauline theology.

Prophets (Nevi'im, נביאים)

Definition and Role: The *navi* (prophet) is a public spokesperson for God, tasked with calling people to repentance, warning of judgment, and revealing God's will for the future.

The *navi* is often associated with charismatic leadership, moral courage, and the ability to perform miracles.

Examples:

- **Moses**: The archetype of a prophet, Moses delivered the Torah and mediated directly between God and Israel.
- **Isaiah, Jeremiah, Ezekiel**: Represent the classical prophets, combining visions, divine messages, and calls to national repentance.

Traits and Distinctions: Prophets speak on God's behalf to individuals, nations, or both.

Their role is more dynamic and often includes direct confrontation with rulers, priests, and the people.

Sages (Hakhamim, חכמים)

Definition and Role: Sages, or *hakhamim*, are primarily associated with wisdom (*chochmah*) rather than direct divine revelation. They are interpreters of the Torah and apply its teachings to daily life. In post-biblical Judaism, sages are seen as successors to the prophets in guiding Israel, focusing on oral law and the practical application of scripture.

Examples:
- **King Solomon**: Renowned for his wisdom (e.g., resolving disputes like in 1 Kings 3:16–28). Solomon's focus was on governance, understanding human behavior, and building the Temple.
- **Ezra**: Known for his knowledge of the law and his efforts to restore Jewish worship and community identity after the Babylonian exile.

Traits and Distinctions: Sages often functioned as educators, judges, and leaders. They are more focused on interpreting and preserving tradition than on receiving direct revelation or visions.

Seers (Ro'im, רואים)

Definition and Role: The term *ro'eh* (plural: *ro'im*) is often translated as "seer" and is closely related to the term *chozeh* (see below). A *ro'eh* is someone who perceives divine messages through visions. Unlike a *navi* (prophet), whose role often includes public proclamation and leadership, a seer may have a more personal or advisory role.

Examples:
- **Samuel**: Referred to as a *ro'eh* (1 Samuel 9:9), Samuel provided personal guidance to individuals like Saul but also acted as a national leader, blending roles.
- **Gad**: Mentioned as "David's seer" (2 Samuel 24:11), he advised King David and delivered messages from God.

Traits and Distinctions: Seers rely on visions and often act as advisors or counselors rather than public figures. They may be more introspective and focused on interpreting divine will than proclaiming it to the masses.

Visionaries (Chozeh, חוזה)

Definition and Role: The term *chozeh* (plural: *chozim*) is often translated as "visionary" and overlaps with the *ro'eh* and *navi* in meaning. *Chozim* often receive symbolic visions that require interpretation, such as Ezekiel's vision of the dry bones (Ezekiel 37).

Examples:
- **Daniel**: While not traditionally classified as a *navi* in Jewish tradition, Daniel fits the role of a visionary, receiving apocalyptic revelations.
- **Amos**: Identified as a shepherd and a "seer," Amos delivers symbolic and moral messages.

Traits and Distinctions: Visionaries are often more focused on esoteric or apocalyptic imagery than on immediate moral or societal reform. They may not have the public, charismatic leadership role associated with *nevi'im*.

Martyrs (Kedoshim, קדושים)

Definition and Role: While not prophets, martyrs are often associated with sanctifying God's name (*kiddush Hashem*) through their faithfulness in the face of persecution or death.

Examples:
- **Abel**: Considered the first martyr, his sacrifice and death symbolize righteousness and the cost of faithfulness.
- **Zechariah ben Jehoiada**: A priest and prophet, he was killed for rebuking the people's idolatry.

Traits and Distinctions: Martyrs in Jewish tradition are those who bear witness to God's truth by their willingness to die rather than compromise their beliefs.

1.3 Table: Summary of Distinctions

Role	Key Focus	Examples	Traits
Navi (Prophet)	Public proclamation and leadership	Moses, Isaiah, Jeremiah,	Charismatic, dynamic, confrontational
Hakham (Sage)	Wisdom, interpretation, and teaching	Solomon, Ezra	Analytical, practical, grounded
Ro'eh (Seer)	Personal visions, advisory roles	Samuel, Gad	Visionary, introspective, counseling
Chozeh (Visionary)	Esoteric visions and symbolic imagery	Daniel, Amos	Apocalyptic, interpretive
Kadosh (Martyr)	Faithfulness unto death	Abel, Zechariah, Maccabees	Inspirational, sacrificial, exposing injustice

Conclusion:

The Hebraic understanding of roles like prophet, seer, visionary, sage, and martyr demonstrates a nuanced approach to divine calling and leadership.

These distinctions provide a richer framework for interpreting biblical figures and their legacy, revealing a diversity of roles and responsibilities that are often oversimplified in modern theological discourse. This layered understanding can enrich discussions about how different figures fulfilled God's will in their time and context.

1.4 Yeshua and the Jerusalem Church: A Balanced Understanding

Prophecy as a Present Reality

Yeshua and His disciples operated with a comprehensive and dynamic understanding of prophecy that seamlessly integrated the historical and the spiritual. For Yeshua, prophecy wasn't confined to predicting the future or recounting past acts—it was about actively aligning hearts and minds with God's covenant.

Yeshua's View of the Prophets as Covenant Enforcers:

- Yeshua frequently referenced the **"Law and the Prophets"** (Matthew 5:17-19), placing them together as inseparable elements of God's instruction. He affirmed their ongoing relevance, emphasizing that the prophets were not just predictors of future events but enforcers of covenantal fidelity.

In calling people back to obedience, Yeshua highlighted the prophets' enduring purpose: to warn against rebellion, offer hope in restoration, and remind Israel of its responsibility to the nations.

Prophecy in Action During Yeshua's Ministry:
Yeshua Himself embodied prophetic behavior, combining foresight, wisdom, and compassion. He rebuked sin and hypocrisy (e.g., the Pharisees in Matthew 23), but He did so in ways that sought to soften hearts rather than harden them.

His prophetic actions, such as healing on the Sabbath (Mark 3:1-6) or His triumphal entry into Jerusalem (Matthew 21:1-11), demonstrated how prophecy could address both immediate social realities and eternal truths.

The Prophets as Role Models of Righteousness:

Yeshua revered the prophets as examples of faithfulness and sacrifice, often pointing to their stories to emphasize the cost of true obedience.

In passages like Luke 4:24-27, He identified Himself with the pattern of rejection experienced by figures like Elijah and Elisha, showing how prophets were often despised for challenging societal norms.

The Jerusalem Church likely echoed this perspective, viewing the prophets as moral exemplars who stood firm in their allegiance to God, even when it meant enduring suffering.

Critiquing Zealotry and Pride with the Prophets:
Yeshua didn't shy away from critiquing the failings of certain prophets or their followers. In **Luke 11:47-51**, He condemned those who built tombs for the prophets while perpetuating the very sins that led to their deaths. This wasn't a rebuke of the prophets themselves but of those who misused their legacy to justify hypocrisy and zealotry.

By doing so, Yeshua illustrated that the effectiveness of a prophet lay not in their martyrdom or confrontational zeal, but in their ability to turn hearts toward God through wisdom and humility.

The Jerusalem Church's Understanding of Prophecy

Prophecy as a Spirit-Filled Role:
- For the Jerusalem Church, prophecy wasn't a relic of the past but a **living, Spirit-filled role** that continued to guide the community. Figures like James (Yeshua's brother) and Peter were seen as prophetic leaders who balanced the traditions of the Hebrew Bible with the covenant-upholding teachings of Yeshua.

- This balance reflected the Church's commitment to maintaining covenantal obedience while emphasizing the transformative power of YHWH's Holy Spirit (Acts 2:16-18, referencing Joel 2:28-32).

Prophetic Wisdom Over Zealotry:
- The Jerusalem Church's emphasis on wisdom and discernment contrasted sharply with the zealotry that characterized many of their contemporaries, such as the Essenes or Zealots. While these groups sought to overthrow Roman rule through violence or separatism, the Jerusalem Church pursued a strategy of peaceful evangelism and moral influence.

- This approach echoed Yeshua's teachings about the importance of winning over oppressors through love and patience, rather than inciting rebellion (Matthew 5:38-48).

Key Distinction: Yeshua's Prophetic Balance

A Contrast to Pauline Mysticism:
- While Paul emphasized prophecy as a mystical gift of the Holy Spirit, Yeshua placed greater weight on its ethical and relational dimensions. For Yeshua, a prophet's success wasn't measured by their visions or miracles but by their ability to guide people back to God's law and love.
- The Jerusalem Church upheld this balanced view, focusing on prophecy as a means of strengthening communal faith and promoting covenantal obedience.

A Contrast to Rabbinical Historicism:
- Unlike Rabbinical Judaism, which often confined prophecy to the past, Yeshua and the Jerusalem Church saw it as an active and ongoing role. This view recognized the Spirit's continued work in guiding the community, not as a replacement for Torah but as its fulfillment.

Yeshua as a Master Bridge Builder

Yeshua's approach to prophecy revealed His ability to bridge divides between competing interpretations. By rooting His teachings in the Hebrew Bible while challenging both legalism and zealotry, He created a model of prophecy that emphasized:

- **Wisdom and Patience**: Avoiding rashness and fostering long-term change through love and humility.
- **Alignment with God's Will**: Calling people back to the foundational principles of Torah, rather than pursuing power or glory.
- **Inclusivity and Grace**: Welcoming all people into God's covenant, while maintaining fidelity to its core tenets.

Takeaway:

Yeshua and the Jerusalem Church offer a model of prophecy that transcends the limitations of both Pauline mysticism and Rabbinical historicism. By emphasizing wisdom, foresight, and covenantal obedience, they highlight the ultimate purpose of prophecy: to align people with God's will and guide them toward a life of love, righteousness, and reconciliation.

This balanced understanding challenges modern readers to rethink the role of prophets, not as mystical forecasters or relics of the past, but as active participants in God's redemptive plan.

1.5 Conceptual Distinctions: Prophets, Martyrs, and Zealots

In both modern Pauline and Rabbinical traditions, the term *"prophet"* is often used as a catch-all, encompassing figures who played drastically dissimilar roles with widely varying outcomes.

This lack of nuance creates confusion, conflating categories like visionaries, martyrs, and zealots under a single label.

To better understand the figures who shaped both scripture and history, we must explore the distinct traits and actions that separate *prophets*—those who point others toward God's will—from *martyrs* and *zealots*, whose approaches often undermined their missions.

Breaking Down the Categories

Prophets: Long-Game Strategists (Survivable Models)

Traits: Prophets who embody patience, foresight, and tactical wisdom tend to preserve themselves and their mission.

They understand that hearts cannot be coerced into repentance; they must be softened through love, wisdom, and divine insight. These figures act as *navi'im*—spokespeople for God who inspire lasting transformation.

Examples:
- **Joseph**: His ability to interpret dreams and navigate political power softened Pharaoh's heart and saved his family and nation from famine.
- **Daniel**: Through steadfast faith and wisdom, he influenced Babylonian rulers without provoking unnecessary conflict.
- **Nathan**: By skillfully confronting King David with tact and storytelling (2 Samuel 12), he brought repentance without alienating the king.
- **David**: While not a "prophet" in the strictest sense, David's strategic use of prayer, humility, and wisdom preserved his life and legacy despite numerous threats.
- **Early Isaiah**: Before adopting a more confrontational tone, Isaiah used visionary messages to guide Israel toward repentance, building trust and credibility.

Takeaway: Long-game prophets demonstrate that true prophecy is not just about delivering divine messages but about doing so in ways that maximize impact while preserving life and mission.

Martyrs: Righteous Yet Unsustainable Models

Subcategory 1: Slain Innocents
Traits: Innocent martyrs act with righteousness and purity of heart but lack the strategic foresight to avoid exploitation or violence.

Their deaths expose sin and injustice but rarely achieve lasting change in their lifetimes.

Examples:
- **Abel**: Slain by Cain for his righteous offering, Abel exemplifies purity but also the vulnerability of naivety.
- **The Jerusalem Church**: Despite their dedication to Yeshua's teachings, their failure to heed His warnings about false prophets (e.g., Saul) led to their co-optation and dispersion.

Subcategory 2: Zealous Martyrs
Traits: Zealous martyrs, though righteous in intention, often act out of frustration or confrontational zeal. Their actions harden hearts rather than soften them, leading to backlash and martyrdom.

Examples:
- **Zechariah**: Killed for his public rebuke of idolatry, his confrontation hardened his audience instead of inspiring repentance.
- **John the Baptist**: His fiery rebukes of Herod and the Pharisees led to his imprisonment and execution, though his role as a forerunner for Yeshua remains significant.
- **Latter Isaiah**: In his later years, Isaiah's increasingly direct critiques led to his alienation and eventual martyrdom (according to tradition).

Takeaway: Martyrs reveal the cost of righteousness but also the importance of discernment.

Their lives highlight the dangers of naivety or untempered zeal, which can undermine their messages and invite violence.

Zealots: Rebellious or Militant Models

Traits: Zealots often act out of anger, pride, or impatience. They use forceful or coercive methods to achieve their goals, which are frequently more about personal or political agendas than divine will.

While their actions may bring short-term victories, they often lead to long-term destruction.

Examples:

- **The Sicarii**: Known for assassinations and guerrilla tactics, the Sicarii exemplify militant zealotry that ultimately brought ruin to Jerusalem.
- **Zealots of the late "Second Temple" Period**: Their rebellion against Rome, rooted in religious fervor, led to the destruction of the Temple and the diaspora.
- **Jonah (Pre-Transformation)**: Jonah's initial refusal to preach to Nineveh stemmed from nationalistic pride, prioritizing his own sense of justice over God's mercy.

Takeaway: Zealotry, whether violent or ideological, often leads to hardened hearts and societal division. It stands in stark contrast to the wisdom and patience modeled by long-game prophets.

By breaking down the inherited confusion surrounding the term *"prophet,"* we see the importance of refining our understanding.

- A true prophet isn't defined solely by their ability to foresee or proclaim divine truths; they are defined by their capacity to align people with God's will through wisdom, foresight, and strategic action.
- This distinction sets the stage for the next sections, where we analyze the historical and spiritual impact of long-game prophets, martyrs, and zealots.
- In doing so, we'll uncover the traits that define sustainable models of faithfulness and highlight the consequences of zealotry and naivety.

These lessons challenge us to rethink the way we interpret the prophets and their relevance for today.

2. Prophetic Analysis:

Exploring the sustainable long-game prophets

2.1 Joseph: The Strategic Dreamer

Context:
Joseph's story begins with betrayal—sold into slavery by his jealous brothers, who were envious of his favored status and prophetic dreams (Genesis 37). Despite enduring servitude and false accusations that landed him in prison, Joseph's unwavering faith and God-given ability to interpret dreams eventually brought him before Pharaoh. By accurately predicting seven years of plenty followed by seven years of famine, Joseph rose to prominence as Pharaoh's second-in-command.

Traits:

- **Patience and Forgiveness:** Joseph endured years of suffering without bitterness, trusting that God was orchestrating events for a greater purpose (Genesis 50:20). His ability to forgive his brothers demonstrates a profound understanding of divine sovereignty and human fallibility.
- **Wisdom and Foresight:** Joseph's preparation during the years of plenty ensured survival during the famine, saving countless lives. His strategic management of resources reflects his deep understanding of both practical governance and spiritual reliance.
- **Resilience Under Adversity:** Joseph turned each setback—whether slavery, imprisonment, or betrayal—into an opportunity to glorify God, showing that faith and wisdom can coexist with worldly success.

Long-Game Strategy:
Joseph's approach exemplifies the "long game" in prophecy. Rather than confronting his brothers or seeking immediate vindication, Joseph allowed time and circumstances to unfold, trusting that God would fulfill His promises. His strategic planning not only saved Egypt

but also preserved the fledgling nation of Israel. Through his faithfulness and humility, Joseph became a vessel for God's providence, influencing even the most powerful ruler of his time.

2.2 Nathan: The Courageous Counselor

Context:
Nathan served as a prophet during the reign of King David, a time marked by both great triumphs and moral failures. Nathan's defining moment came when he confronted David over his sins of adultery with Bathsheba and the orchestrated murder of her husband, Uriah (2 Samuel 12). Instead of condemning David outright, Nathan employed a parable to expose the king's guilt, leading to heartfelt repentance.

Traits:

- **Tact and Relational Wisdom:** Nathan's use of a parable to confront David (2 Samuel 12:1–7) reveals his deep understanding of human psychology and his respect for David's authority. By appealing to David's sense of justice, Nathan allowed the king to recognize his own sin without feeling attacked.
- **Courage and Truth-Telling:** Despite David's immense power, Nathan did not shy away from holding him accountable. His boldness was tempered by grace, ensuring that his rebuke led to repentance rather than rebellion.
- **Faithful Advocacy:** Nathan's loyalty to God and his role as a counselor ensured that David's spiritual well-being was prioritized. He served as a moral compass for the king, helping him navigate both personal failures and national leadership.

Long-Game Strategy:
Nathan's approach demonstrates the power of relational influence in prophetic ministry. By addressing David's sin with wisdom and grace, Nathan not only secured the king's repentance but also preserved the stability of Israel's leadership. His ability to balance truth and compassion serves as a model for sustainable prophetic influence,

showing that confrontation, when done wisely, can lead to transformation rather than destruction.

2.3 Daniel: The Faithful Exile

Context:
Daniel was taken to Babylon as a young man during the Jewish exile, a traumatic event that forced him to live and serve under foreign rulers. Despite the pressures of assimilation, Daniel remained unwavering in his devotion to God. He rose to prominence in the Babylonian and Persian courts, interpreting dreams and visions for kings such as Nebuchadnezzar, Belshazzar, and Darius. His story is marked by moments of miraculous deliverance, including the fiery furnace (with his companions Shadrach, Meshach, and Abednego) and the lion's den, where his faith in God prevailed over persecution.

Traits:

- **Diplomatic Wisdom:** Daniel excelled in navigating complex political landscapes, offering counsel and interpretation that influenced the decisions of pagan kings while never compromising his own beliefs. His diplomacy made him a trusted advisor across multiple regimes (Daniel 6:3).
- **Unwavering Faith:** Despite the threats of death and societal pressure to conform, Daniel maintained his prayer life and obedience to God's commandments, exemplified by his refusal to eat unclean foods (Daniel 1:8) and his open worship of God despite the edicts against it (Daniel 6:10).
- **Humility and Prayer:** Daniel sought divine guidance through prayer and fasting, acknowledging his dependence on God for wisdom and revelation. His intercessory prayer in Daniel 9 demonstrates his deep concern for the spiritual restoration of Israel.

Long-Game Strategy:
Daniel's ability to combine faithfulness with tact allowed him to survive and thrive in exile. By earning the trust and respect of rulers,

he positioned himself to influence entire empires, bringing God's truth into hostile environments. His story illustrates that steadfast devotion to God can coexist with political acumen, showing that wisdom, humility, and patience are key traits of a sustainable prophet.

2.4 Ezra: The Faithful Rebuilder

Context:
Ezra played a critical role in the return of the Jewish exiles from Babylon and the rebuilding of Jerusalem. As a scribe and priest, he was deeply committed to the Law of Moses and sought to restore Israel's covenantal relationship with God. Ezra led efforts to rebuild the temple and reinstitute proper worship, addressing the spiritual and moral decline of the people after years of exile.

Traits:

- **Humble Leadership:** Ezra approached his mission with deep humility and a reliance on prayer, often seeking God's guidance before making decisions. His leadership was marked by a focus on spiritual renewal rather than political ambition.
- **Teacher and Educator:** Ezra emphasized the importance of understanding and internalizing God's law. He read the Torah aloud to the people and explained its meaning, ensuring that their obedience was rooted in comprehension rather than mere ritual (Nehemiah 8:8).
- **Perseverance in Adversity:** Ezra faced significant opposition from local enemies who sought to undermine the rebuilding efforts. Despite these challenges, he remained steadfast, relying on God's provision and the support of faithful collaborators.

Long-Game Strategy:
Ezra's patient, educational approach to leadership ensured that Israel's faith was not only restored but also solidified for future generations. By emphasizing the importance of understanding God's law, he laid a foundation for lasting spiritual renewal. His work

highlights the power of quiet determination, humility, and a focus on internal transformation over external rebellion.

2.5 Nehemiah: The Pragmatic Protector

Context:
Nehemiah served as the cupbearer to the Persian king Artaxerxes, a position of trust and influence, before returning to Jerusalem to lead the rebuilding of the city's walls.

He recognized that the restoration of Jerusalem required both physical and spiritual renewal. Facing opposition from neighboring enemies and internal division, Nehemiah led the people to rebuild and fortify the city while reestablishing covenantal faithfulness.

Traits:

- **Practical Leadership:** Nehemiah was a hands-on leader who worked alongside the people, uniting them around a common goal. He divided the labor efficiently, assigning families to rebuild sections of the wall near their homes (Nehemiah 3).
- **Defensive Wisdom:** Understanding the threats posed by external adversaries, Nehemiah instituted a dual strategy: building and defending simultaneously. Workers carried tools in one hand and weapons in the other (Nehemiah 4:16-18).
- **Spiritual Conviction:** Nehemiah was deeply committed to God's law and sought to restore spiritual integrity among the people. He confronted issues such as intermarriage, exploitation of the poor, and neglect of temple worship, calling the community back to covenantal obedience.

Long-Game Strategy:
Nehemiah's ability to combine prayer, action, and pragmatic leadership ensured the survival and stability of Jerusalem after the exile. By addressing both physical security and spiritual renewal, he provided a comprehensive model of sustainable leadership. His work emphasized the importance of balancing faith with practical action,

showing that spiritual success often depends on strategic foresight and organizational skill.

2.6 Mordecai and Esther: The Subtle Strategists

Context:
Living in exile under Persian rule, Mordecai and Esther faced a dire threat when Haman, a high-ranking official, plotted to exterminate the Jewish people. Through a combination of patience, courage, and strategic timing, they turned the situation around, exposing Haman's plot and securing the king's favor to protect their people.

Traits:

- **Patience and Discernment:** Mordecai demonstrated remarkable patience, refusing to bow to Haman while also waiting for the right moment to act. His guidance to Esther was measured and strategic, ensuring that her intervention would be effective.
- **Courage and Diplomacy:** Esther risked her life by approaching the king uninvited—a bold move in Persian court culture. She used tact and wisdom, inviting the king and Haman to banquets to build trust and create the right context for revealing Haman's plot (Esther 5-7).
- **Faith and Humility:** Mordecai and Esther trusted God's providence, as evidenced by Mordecai's famous words: "And who knows whether you have not come to the kingdom for such a time as this?" (Esther 4:14). Their actions were rooted in faith, but their approach was subtle and respectful of Persian authority.

Long-Game Strategy:
Mordecai and Esther exemplified the power of quiet influence and timely action. Rather than directly confronting the king or Haman with rebellion or defiance, they worked within the system, leveraging relationships and wisdom to achieve their goal.

This strategic approach not only saved the Jewish people but also preserved peace and stability within the empire. Their story demonstrates that effective leadership often involves subtlety, patience, and the courage to act when the time is right.

2.7 Samuel: The Foundational Prophet

Context:
Samuel stands as one of the most pivotal figures in Israel's history, bridging the gap between the period of the judges and the establishment of the monarchy.

He was dedicated to God from birth, growing up under Eli the priest in Shiloh.

As a prophet, priest, and judge, Samuel anointed Israel's first two kings, Saul and David, while providing spiritual and political guidance to a nation in transition.

Traits:

- **Wisdom and Restraint:** Samuel displayed remarkable wisdom in mediating between God and the people, especially during Israel's demand for a king. While he warned them of the dangers of human kingship (1 Samuel 8), he also obeyed God's directive to anoint Saul, demonstrating submission to divine will even when it conflicted with his personal convictions.
- **Prophetic Integrity:** Samuel maintained an unwavering commitment to God's commands, refusing to compromise his prophetic role. When Saul disobeyed God, Samuel confronted him boldly, emphasizing that "to obey is better than sacrifice" (1 Samuel 15:22).
- **Mediator Between God and Israel:** Samuel's intercessory prayers, such as his plea during the Philistine attack at Mizpah (1 Samuel 7), reveal his dedication to standing in the gap for the people and securing God's favor.

Long-Game Strategy:
Samuel's foresight and obedience helped shape Israel's leadership during a tumultuous time. He guided the nation with wisdom,

balancing the people's demands with God's ultimate authority. His ability to maintain his prophetic integrity while navigating political complexities ensured that Israel remained aligned with God's purposes, even as they transitioned to a monarchy. Samuel's life underscores the importance of patience, discernment, and a deep commitment to God's will in achieving sustainable leadership.

2.8 Deborah: The Prophetess and Judge

Context:
Deborah was a prophetess and judge who led Israel during a time of oppression under the Canaanites (Judges 4-5). Her leadership was marked by spiritual authority and military strategy, making her one of the most unique figures in biblical history.

She is the only woman recorded in the Bible to hold both roles simultaneously, highlighting her extraordinary leadership.

Traits:

- **Patience and Discernment:** Deborah displayed remarkable patience, waiting on God's guidance before taking action. She called Barak to lead Israel's forces but emphasized that victory would come through God's hand rather than human strength.
- **Prophetic Judgment:** Deborah's wisdom as a judge earned her the respect of Israel's tribes, who came to her for decisions and guidance. Her prophetic insight ensured that her judgments were rooted in divine wisdom.
- **Encourager and Rallying Leader:** While Barak hesitated to go into battle without her presence, Deborah inspired confidence and unity among Israel's tribes. Her prophetic assurance, "Has not the Lord gone ahead of you?" (Judges 4:14), exemplifies her ability to motivate others through faith in God.

Long-Game Strategy:
Deborah's leadership reflects a balance of spiritual authority and practical action. She relied on God's guidance rather than impulsive

decisions, ensuring that Israel's victory over the Canaanites was both strategic and divinely ordained. Her ability to inspire others while maintaining a focus on God's will exemplifies the traits of a sustainable leader. Deborah's story highlights the importance of humility, discernment, and reliance on God in achieving lasting success.

2.9 Elisha: The Relational Prophet

Context:
Elisha succeeded Elijah as a prophet during a time of spiritual decline in Israel. While Elijah's ministry was marked by dramatic confrontations,

Elisha's approach was more relational and restorative.

He performed numerous miracles, from healing Naaman's leprosy to raising the Shunammite woman's son, demonstrating God's power in ways that met the practical needs of the people.

Traits:

- **Service-Oriented Ministry:** Elisha's miracles often addressed immediate needs, such as providing food for the hungry (2 Kings 4:42-44) or helping a widow pay her debts (2 Kings 4:1-7). His ministry emphasized God's compassion and provision for individuals and communities.
- **Relational Wisdom:** Elisha worked alongside rulers, offering counsel and guidance without antagonizing them. His advice to the king of Israel during the Aramean siege (2 Kings 6:8-23) demonstrated his ability to influence leaders through wisdom and tact.
- **Demonstration of God's Power:** Elisha's miracles, such as purifying water (2 Kings 2:19-22) and healing Naaman (2 Kings 5), showcased God's ability to restore and renew, drawing people closer to faith.

Long-Game Strategy:
Elisha's relational ministry softened hearts and demonstrated God's power in ways that were both practical and spiritual. By focusing on restoration rather than confrontation, he influenced individuals and communities, leaving a legacy of faith and transformation. Elisha's story underscores the importance of humility, compassion, and relational wisdom in prophetic ministry.

2.10 Isaiah (Early Life): The Visionary Reformer

Context:
Isaiah began his ministry during the reign of King Uzziah (Azariah), a period marked by relative peace and prosperity in Judah.

However, this stability masked underlying spiritual corruption, idolatry, and social injustice.

Isaiah's prophetic mission was to call the people of Judah back to covenantal obedience, emphasizing God's holiness and justice.

Traits:

- **Compassionate Clarity:** Early in his ministry, Isaiah's messages were measured and rooted in hope. He called for repentance not with harsh condemnation but with an invitation to restoration. Passages like Isaiah 1:18 (*"Come now, let us reason together"*) reflect his approach to fostering trust and inspiring change.
- **Emphasis on God's Holiness:** Isaiah's vision of God's throne (Isaiah 6:1-8) established the foundation of his ministry. By emphasizing God's unmatched holiness, he encouraged the people to recognize their need for purification and alignment with divine standards.
- **Visionary Reformer:** Isaiah combined divine revelation with practical insight, addressing social injustices while warning against alliances with foreign nations. His messages often balanced

rebuke with promises of redemption, offering Judah a clear path to spiritual renewal.

Long-Game Strategy:
Isaiah's early ministry exemplifies the qualities of a long-game prophet. By balancing rebuke with encouragement and emphasizing God's holiness and justice, Isaiah sought to inspire genuine repentance. His compassionate yet firm approach earned him credibility and positioned him as a trusted voice during a critical time for Judah. Isaiah's early life demonstrates the power of measured, visionary leadership in turning hearts back to God.

2.11 Jeremiah (Early Life): A Prophet of Persistence

Context:
Jeremiah's prophetic ministry began during the reign of King Josiah, a period of religious reform and optimism in Judah. As a young prophet, Jeremiah supported Josiah's efforts to restore covenantal faithfulness, aligning his early messages with the king's reforms. However, Jeremiah's ministry spanned the subsequent reigns of less faithful kings, requiring him to adapt his approach as Judah descended into moral and political chaos.

Traits:

- **Patience and Foresight:** Jeremiah's early messages were measured, reflecting the hope and reformative spirit of Josiah's reign. He emphasized Judah's need to remain faithful to God's covenant while avoiding alliances with foreign powers (Jeremiah 2:13-19).
- **Support for Reform:** Early in his ministry, Jeremiah aligned with Josiah's efforts to rid Judah of idolatry and restore temple worship. His warnings about Judah's disobedience were tempered with hope for renewal under Josiah's leadership.
- **Relational Wisdom:** Unlike his later, more confrontational years, Jeremiah's early ministry focused on building trust and guiding Judah back to God through gentle admonition and encouragement.

Long-Game Strategy:
In his early years, Jeremiah demonstrated the traits of a long-game prophet, prioritizing relationship-building and incremental reform. His alignment with Josiah's reforms allowed him to foster trust and credibility among the people. While Jeremiah's ministry would later take a more confrontational tone, his early persistence and measured approach highlight the importance of patience and strategic thinking in prophetic leadership.

Transitional Reflection:
Both Isaiah and Jeremiah's early ministries reveal the effectiveness of compassionate clarity and relational wisdom in prophetic leadership.

These traits contrast sharply with the zealous and confrontational approaches they later adopted, which often hardened hearts and led to personal suffering.

By examining their early strategies, we gain insight into the qualities that define sustainable, God-honoring prophecy.

---

3. Zealous Martyrs

The Cost of Unchecked Zeal

Prophets are often remembered for their courage and conviction, standing firm in the face of opposition to deliver God's messages. However, the stories of zealous martyrs—those whose righteous passion led to confrontation and ultimately their deaths—serve as cautionary tales. These figures, though faithful and unwavering, often highlight the dangers of unchecked zeal, which can harden hearts and alienate audiences rather than turning them back to God.

In this section, we explore the lives of prophets and figures who, despite their righteousness, allowed their zeal to overshadow wisdom, leading to tragic ends. These stories reveal the fine line between prophetic courage and confrontational zeal, challenging us to consider the role of patience, tact, and strategic foresight in preserving both the messenger and the message.

The Dual Nature of Zeal

Zeal, when tempered with wisdom, can inspire profound change, as seen in the lives of long-game prophets like Joseph and Daniel. Yet, zeal unbalanced by restraint or foresight can lead to unnecessary conflict, resistance, and even martyrdom. While these figures are revered for their faithfulness, their stories underscore the importance of balancing conviction with strategic engagement.

Themes of Zealous Martyrdom

- **Righteous Intentions, Costly Outcomes**
  Zealous martyrs acted out of devotion to God but often overlooked the psychological and spiritual dynamics of their audience. Their uncompromising rebukes hardened hearts, limiting the effectiveness of their messages.
- **Martyrdom as a Warning**
  While martyrdom is often romanticized, these stories remind us that God's messengers are most effective when they live to continue their mission. Martyrdom may inspire, but it also halts the prophet's ability to shepherd people toward repentance and renewal.
- **The Balance of Courage and Strategy**
  Isaiah and Jeremiah exemplify how zeal, when unchecked, can lead to alienation and isolation, undermining the broader goals of reconciliation and covenantal renewal.

Bridging to Zealous Martyrs

The transition from long-game prophets to zealous martyrs reflects a shift in tone and approach. Figures like Isaiah and Jeremiah, whose early ministries were marked by wisdom and relational engagement, later succumbed to frustration and urgency, amplifying their confrontational styles.

Their stories challenge us to examine the role of zeal in prophetic ministry and to seek a balance that preserves both the messenger and their mission.

As we delve into the lives of Isaiah, Jeremiah, and others, we explore how zeal can transform from a righteous motivator to a dangerous force, illustrating the importance of wisdom, patience, and a heart focused on reconciliation.

3.1 Isaiah (Later Life): The Prophet of Vision and Confrontation

Later Life and Ministry
Isaiah's prophetic ministry evolved over decades, moving from a hopeful and redemptive tone in its early years to one of fiery confrontation as Judah's disobedience deepened.

While his early messages sought to inspire change through divine imagery and encouragement, his later ministry reflected a prophet embattled by the persistent rejection of God's covenant.

From Visionary to Confrontational

- **Early Ministry:** Isaiah's initial role was to call Judah back to covenantal faithfulness through visions of God's holiness, such as his encounter in the temple where he saw God on His throne (Isaiah 6). His early messages emphasized restoration, offering hope for those who would repent.
- **Increasing Confrontation:** Over time, Isaiah's tone shifted. The continued rebellion of Judah's leaders, particularly under King Manasseh, hardened Isaiah's approach. His rebukes became more pointed, his imagery more severe, as he sought to awaken a nation steeped in idolatry and injustice.
- **Uncompromising Boldness:** Isaiah's denunciations of Judah's sins were unflinching. He condemned not only the people but also the leaders, calling out their hypocrisy and misplaced trust in foreign alliances instead of YHWH.

Opposition and Isolation
Isaiah's growing zeal and direct rebukes alienated him from Judah's rulers and the people.

- **Alienation:** His uncompromising tone, particularly in addressing King Manasseh, made him a target of animosity. While earlier prophets like Nathan used parables and tact to confront leaders, Isaiah's later ministry often lacked this measured approach.
- **Hardened Hearts:** Instead of inspiring repentance, Isaiah's harsh warnings provoked defensiveness and rejection, reinforcing the very rebellion he sought to counter.

Martyrdom under King Manasseh
Isaiah's fate is a stark reminder of the cost of untempered zeal.

- **Execution:** According to Jewish tradition, Isaiah was executed during King Manasseh's reign, sawn in half after fleeing and hiding in a tree. This gruesome martyrdom highlights the animosity he faced for his confrontational approach.
- **Reflection on His Death:** While Isaiah's martyrdom testifies to his faithfulness, it also underscores the tragic consequences of a prophetic tone that, in its later years, leaned more on condemnation than persuasion.

Did Zeal Lead to Martyrdom?

Isaiah's shift from visionary reformer to confrontational zealot reveals the dangers of unbalanced prophecy:

- **Direct Rebuke:** His later messages focused heavily on judgment, leaving little room for reconciliation or hope.
- **Loss of Influence:** By alienating those he sought to guide, Isaiah's later ministry limited his ability to effect meaningful change.
- **Martyrdom:** His bold denunciations of King Manasseh and refusal to compromise directly contributed to his execution.

A Legacy of Mixed Outcomes
Isaiah's ministry, while faithful, serves as a cautionary tale about the balance between zeal and wisdom. His later years contrast sharply with

his early approach, illustrating how the tone and method of prophecy can shape its impact.

Key Lessons from Isaiah's Later Life

- **Balance in Prophetic Tone:** Effective prophecy requires adapting the message to the audience, balancing urgency with compassion.
- **The Danger of Zeal Without Tact:** Even righteous zeal can backfire when it hardens hearts instead of softening them.
- **Contrast with Yeshua:** Yeshua's use of parables and relational teaching highlights the importance of engaging hearts and minds without inciting rebellion.

3.2 Jeremiah (Later Life): The Prophet of Passionate Zeal

Later Ministry and Challenges

Jeremiah's ministry mirrored Judah's descent into chaos, shifting from measured warnings to desperate appeals as the nation's rebellion intensified. While his early messages aligned with King Josiah's reforms, his later years were marked by increasing isolation and persecution.

From Measured Warning to Confrontational Zeal

- **Confronting Leadership:** After Josiah's death, Jeremiah's tone became more urgent, targeting kings, priests, and false prophets with direct rebukes.
- **Public Persecution:** Jeremiah's confrontational style led to imprisonment, physical violence, and public humiliation, including being cast into a cistern.
- **Frustration and Desperation:** His increasing zeal likely stemmed from heartbreak and frustration as Judah ignored his warnings. This shift made his audience more resistant to his message.

Final Years and Possible Martyrdom

Jeremiah's life ended in exile, forcibly taken to Egypt by rebellious leaders who dismissed his counsel.

- **Fate in Egypt:** Tradition suggests Jeremiah may have been stoned to death by his own people in Egypt for continuing to rebuke their idolatry and rebellion.
- **Legacy of Suffering:** Jeremiah's unwavering commitment to his calling highlights the cost of prophetic zeal, especially when it is met with persistent rejection.

Did Zeal Lead to Martyrdom?
Jeremiah's later ministry underscores the risks of unchecked zeal:

- **Hardening Hearts:** His increasingly confrontational tone alienated his audience, making them more resistant to his message.
- **Personal Cost:** His suffering and possible martyrdom reflect the dangers of prophetic urgency that lacks measured persuasion.

A Lesson in Prophetic Balance

Jeremiah's story reveals the importance of balancing urgency with tact:

- **Early Wisdom:** Jeremiah's initial approach, aligned with Josiah's reforms, exemplified the long-game prophet model.
- **Later Zeal:** His shift to confrontational zealotry illustrates the dangers of losing patience and temperance in the face of rejection.

Key Lessons from Jeremiah's Later Life

- **Prophetic Patience:** Effective prophecy requires maintaining wisdom and tact, even in the face of persistent disobedience.
- **The Cost of Zeal:** Jeremiah's later ministry demonstrates how unchecked zeal can hinder a prophet's mission, alienating those they seek to guide.
- **Faithful Despite Rejection:** Despite his struggles, Jeremiah remained steadfast in his calling, embodying the persistence of God's love for His people.

3.3 Zechariah son of Jehoiada: The Confrontational Priest

Who He Was:

Zechariah, the son of Jehoiada the priest, served as a prophet during the reign of King Joash.

His lineage as the son of a revered high priest lent him moral authority, but it also placed him in direct conflict with a wayward king and people who had abandoned their covenant with God.

Zealous Actions:

Zechariah stood boldly before the leaders and people of Judah, denouncing their idolatry and covenantal unfaithfulness.

His messages were not subtle; he openly declared their rebellion against YHWH and warned of divine judgment:

- **Blunt Denunciation:** Zechariah's rebukes, though theologically accurate, lacked the tact needed to win over an already rebellious audience.
- **Public Confrontation:** He condemned King Joash and the people in the temple courtyard—a setting that magnified the audacity of his challenge.

Outcome:
Zechariah's direct approach backfired spectacularly:

- **King Joash's Betrayal:** Despite the legacy of Jehoiada, who had saved Joash as a child and restored the temple, Joash conspired with Judah's leaders to silence Zechariah.

- **Martyrdom in the Temple:** In a shocking act of violence, Zechariah was stoned to death within the very temple he sought to protect, symbolizing the depth of Judah's rebellion.

Legacy:
Zechariah's death serves as a sobering reminder of the risks of zeal untempered by wisdom:

- **Yeshua's Rebuke:** Yeshua referenced Zechariah's martyrdom in Matthew 23:35, grouping him with Abel as victims of humanity's rebellion against God's messengers. This highlights Zechariah's role as both a prophet and a martyr, whose death exposed Judah's hardened hearts.
- **Hardened Hearts:** Rather than inspiring repentance, Zechariah's fiery approach further alienated the people and sealed their judgment.

Key Lessons from Zechariah's Martyrdom:

- **Tact vs. Zeal:** While his convictions were righteous, Zechariah's lack of measured persuasion limited his ability to influence his audience.
- **The Danger of Public Confrontation:** Direct rebukes, particularly in public settings, can provoke defensiveness and retaliation rather than reflection and repentance.

3.4 Uriah the Prophet: The Blunt Warning

Who He Was:
Uriah, a lesser-known prophet, ministered during the reign of King Jehoiakim. His ministry paralleled that of Jeremiah, as he delivered stark warnings of Jerusalem's impending destruction due to Judah's persistent idolatry and disobedience.

Zealous Actions:
Uriah's prophetic style mirrored Jeremiah's in tone and content but lacked the relational depth and wisdom that defined Jeremiah's earlier ministry:

- **Unyielding Condemnations:** Uriah's prophecies were direct and uncompromising, targeting Judah's leaders and people with warnings of divine judgment.

- **Lack of Diplomacy:** His messages lacked the nuance or strategic foresight to engage his audience effectively, alienating the very people he sought to warn.

Outcome:
Uriah's zeal ultimately led to his downfall:

- **Flight to Egypt:** After delivering his prophecies, Uriah fled to Egypt, likely recognizing the danger posed by King Jehoiakim's hostility.
- **Capture and Execution:** Despite his escape, Uriah was pursued, captured, and brought back to Jerusalem. Jehoiakim personally oversaw his execution by the sword, demonstrating the king's intolerance for prophetic rebuke.

Legacy:
Uriah's story underscores the peril of confronting powerful leaders without strategic preparation:

- **Parallel to Jeremiah:** While Jeremiah faced similar threats, his measured approach and reliance on God's guidance allowed him to endure. In contrast, Uriah's blunt style left him vulnerable.
- **Martyrdom as a Warning:** Uriah's death serves as a cautionary tale about the importance of balancing zeal with wisdom in prophetic ministry.

Key Lessons from Uriah's Martyrdom:

- **The Cost of Zeal Without Strategy:** Uriah's unyielding approach, though well-intentioned, failed to soften hearts or inspire change.
- **The Danger of Rushing to Confrontation:** His decision to flee rather than seek God's guidance highlights the need for patience and reliance on divine wisdom in the face of opposition.
- **Martyrdom vs. Influence:** Uriah's legacy, while tragic, contrasts with prophets who employed tact and relational wisdom to preserve their mission and inspire repentance.

Both Zechariah and Uriah exemplify the dangers of unchecked zeal in prophetic ministry. While their faithfulness to God's message is admirable, their lack of strategic foresight and relational wisdom limited their ability to effect lasting change. Their stories serve as powerful reminders of the importance of balancing conviction with tact, ensuring that the message of repentance is delivered in a way that softens hearts rather than hardening them.

3.5 John the Baptist: The Fearless Forerunner

Who He Was:
John the Baptist, the prophetic voice crying out in the wilderness, was chosen to prepare the way for Yeshua.

His ministry focused on calling people to repentance and baptizing them in anticipation of the coming Messiah. John's ascetic lifestyle, fiery preaching, and uncompromising stance against sin set him apart as one of the most zealous figures of his time.

Zealous Actions:
John's zeal for righteousness led him to confront even the most powerful figures of his day, including Herod Antipas:

- **Confrontation with Herod Antipas:** John publicly condemned Herod for marrying Herodias, his brother Philip's wife, declaring the union unlawful under Torah law. This bold rebuke directly challenged Herod's authority and moral integrity.
- **Public Preaching:** John's fiery sermons not only targeted the religious elite but also called out the hypocrisy and sins of rulers, making him a polarizing figure.

Outcome:
John's zealous approach, while righteous, provoked the ire of those in power:

- **Imprisonment:** Herodias, humiliated by John's public condemnation, harbored a deep grudge against him and manipulated Herod into imprisoning him.

- **Martyrdom by Beheading:** At Herodias's instigation, her daughter Salome danced for Herod at a banquet, leading him to promise her anything she desired. At her mother's prompting, she requested John's head on a platter. Despite his reluctance, Herod complied to save face before his guests.

Legacy:
John's unwavering conviction cost him his life, but his ministry paved the way for Yeshua's teachings:

- **Foreshadowing Yeshua's Ministry:** John's role as the forerunner prepared hearts for the Messiah, emphasizing repentance and the imminent arrival of God's kingdom.
- **A Model of Boldness and Zeal:** John's fearless rebuke of sin inspires admiration, but his untimely death highlights the risks of direct confrontation with hardened hearts.

Key Lessons from John's Martyrdom:

- **Boldness vs. Strategy:** While John's courage was commendable, his direct approach alienated powerful figures and limited his ability to inspire broader repentance.
- **Zeal Without Preservation:** John's martyrdom demonstrates the need for balance between zeal and strategic wisdom in prophetic ministry.

3.6 Stephen: The First Christian Martyr

Who He Was:
Stephen, a deacon in the early church, was known for his faith, wisdom, and the power of the Holy Spirit working through him. As a servant-leader, Stephen cared for the needs of the community while boldly proclaiming Yeshua as the fulfillment of God's promises to Israel.

Zealous Actions:
Stephen's zeal for proclaiming the truth led him to confront the Sanhedrin, the Jewish ruling council:

- **A Fearless Testimony:** In Acts 7, Stephen recounted Israel's history, highlighting their repeated rejection of God's messengers. His speech culminated in an indictment of the Sanhedrin, accusing them of resisting the Holy Spirit and betraying the Righteous One (Yeshua).
- **Direct Rebuke:** Stephen's tone was unapologetically confrontational, calling out the religious leaders for their hypocrisy and complicity in Yeshua's crucifixion.

Outcome:
Stephen's unyielding conviction led to his violent death:

- **Stoning:** Enraged by Stephen's accusations, the Sanhedrin and the crowd dragged him out of the city and stoned him. Saul of Tarsus (later Paul) was present, approving of Stephen's execution.
- **A Vision of Glory:** As he was being stoned, Stephen had a vision of Yeshua standing at the right hand of God, and he prayed for his persecutors, embodying the grace he preached.

Legacy:
Stephen's martyrdom became a pivotal moment in the early church's history:

- **Inspiration to Believers:** His courage and faithfulness inspired others to stand firm in their convictions, even in the face of persecution.
- **A Catalyst for Persecution:** Stephen's death marked the beginning of widespread persecution against the early church, forcing believers to scatter and spread the gospel beyond Jerusalem.

Key Lessons from Stephen's Martyrdom:

- **The Cost of Confrontation:** Stephen's zealous approach hardened the hearts of his audience, leading to his death and the intensification of persecution against the church.
- **Grace Under Pressure:** Despite his confrontational tone, Stephen's prayer for his persecutors demonstrated the transformative power of God's grace.

- **Martyrdom as a Turning Point:** Stephen's death, while tragic, played a critical role in the expansion of the early church, showing how God can work through even the most dire circumstances.

Transition to Section 4:

John the Baptist and Stephen embody the dangers and complexities of zeal when untethered from strategy and wisdom. Their lives and deaths illustrate the cost of confronting hardened hearts and unrepentant authorities without regard for personal preservation.

Their stories set the stage for examining the broader consequences of militant zealotry. The next section explores the dangers of coercion and force, as seen in the actions of the Sicarii, the zealots of the "Second Temple" period, and other historical examples. These figures, driven by righteous anger and impatience, reveal how zeal without wisdom can lead to destruction rather than restoration.

---

4. Militant Zealots: The Danger of Coercion and Force

This section explores the destructive consequences of zealotry when combined with militancy, emphasizing how such approaches often lead to catastrophic outcomes for both individuals and communities. The militant zealot archetype serves as a stark contrast to sustainable prophetic models that rely on wisdom, patience, and the softening of hearts.

4.1 "Second Temple" Destruction – A Catastrophic Outcome of Militant Zealotry

Historical Context:
The destruction of the "Second Temple" in AD 70 by the Roman army under Titus was not a sudden event but the culmination of decades of rising tensions between Jewish factions and Roman authorities.

These tensions exploded into the First Jewish-Roman War (66–73 AD), fueled by growing resentment against Roman taxation, oppression, and cultural interference.

At the heart of this conflict were militant Jewish groups, including the Zealots, who believed that violent resistance was not only justified but divinely mandated.

Their belief that God would intervene on their behalf led them to pursue an aggressive revolt against Rome, ignoring the disparity in military strength and the consequences of their actions.

The Role of Zealotry:

Religious Zeal Without Strategic Wisdom:

- The zealots' passionate commitment to God's sovereignty drove their rebellion, but their actions lacked the strategic foresight and patience necessary for success. Instead of seeking unity or a sustainable solution, they escalated tensions, believing that God would deliver a miraculous victory: forgetting the Torah Law Yeshua himself used during his second temptation in the wilderness:

  "Thou shall not put the Lord thy God to the test" - Deuteronomy 6:16

Fractured Unity:

- The zealots' militancy did not unify Israel but deepened divisions. Infighting among Jewish factions—including the Zealots, Sicarii, and moderates—weakened their collective resistance. During the siege of Jerusalem, zealot factions burned each other's food supplies, contributing to widespread starvation and desperation within the city.

Political and Military Realities Ignored:

- Despite their fervent faith, the zealots underestimated the sheer power and discipline of the Roman military. Their insistence on open rebellion against an overwhelmingly superior force led to catastrophic consequences for the Jewish people.

The Siege and Aftermath:
The Roman siege of Jerusalem was brutal and unrelenting:

- The city's defenders, already weakened by internal strife, were no match for the Roman legions.
- Starvation, disease, and violence ravaged the population, leaving the city vulnerable to the final assault.
- When the Romans breached the walls, they destroyed the "Second Temple", leaving it in ruins—a devastating blow to Jewish religious and cultural identity.

Spiritual Takeaway:
The destruction of the "Second Temple" serves as a sobering example of the dangers of militant zealotry:

- **Misplaced Faith in Violence:**
  The zealots' belief that divine intervention would vindicate their violence ultimately led to their ruin. Instead of trusting in God's wisdom and timing, they relied on their own strength, disregarding the prophetic warnings of figures like Yeshua.

- **Yeshua's Warning:**
  In Matthew 24:1-2, Yeshua foretold the destruction of the temple, saying, *"Do you see all these things? Truly I tell you, not one stone here will be left on another; every one will be thrown down."* This prophecy can be seen as a rebuke of the zealotry that would bring about the temple's destruction. Yeshua's ministry emphasized softening hearts and aligning with God's will rather than inciting rebellion.

- **Unity Over Division:**
  The zealots' failure to unite the Jewish people underscores the destructive power of division. Their infighting weakened their resistance and accelerated their downfall, serving as a warning against prioritizing personal agendas over communal harmony.

Conclusion:
The destruction of the "Second Temple" highlights the catastrophic consequences of combining zealotry with militancy. Instead of bringing about liberation or divine favor, such actions led to devastation and exile. This tragic episode serves as a reminder of the importance of wisdom, patience, and trust in God's plans over human-driven attempts to force outcomes through violence.

4.2 The Sicarii: Assassins in the Name of God

Origins and Actions:
The Sicarii emerged as a radical faction during the First Jewish–Roman War (66–73 AD), though their activities began earlier in the tumultuous decades leading up to the war.

- Their name derives from the *sica*, a small, curved dagger they used to carry out assassinations.

Their most infamous period of operation coincided with the final decades before the destruction of the "Second Temple" in AD 70, but their roots trace back to the broader resistance movements against Roman occupation following Pompey's conquest of Judea in 63 BC.

The Sicarii were active primarily from **the late 50s AD through 73 AD**, when their last stand occurred at Masada. Their tactics included assassinating Roman officials, Jewish elites perceived as collaborators, and even priests they deemed corrupt or complicit in Roman rule.

- These assassinations were often conducted in crowded public spaces, including marketplaces and synagogues, in order to maximize fear and provoke unrest.

Their most notable involvement in Jewish history was their participation in the Jewish Revolt against Rome, a conflict that culminated in the catastrophic destruction of the "Second Temple."

- The Sicarii also played a significant role in the defense of Masada, where their fanatical commitment to resistance led to the mass suicide of nearly 1,000 men, women, and children in 73 AD.

Chronological Context:
The Sicarii predated the **Hashshashin** (commonly known as the Assassins of the Islamic world) by almost **1,000 years**. The Hashshashin, an offshoot of the Ismaili sect, operated during the late 11th to 13th centuries AD in Persia and Syria. While both groups shared the tactic of assassination to achieve political and religious goals, the Sicarii stand as one of the earliest recorded groups to systematically employ such tactics in the name of their cause.

Key Comparison:

The Sicarii (1st century AD):
- **Goal:** Liberation of Judea from Roman rule and the purification of Jewish society.
- **Method:** Public assassinations to provoke rebellion and terrorize perceived collaborators.
- **Outcome:** Contributed to internal divisions and the eventual destruction of Jerusalem and the "Second Temple".

The Hashshashin (11th–13th centuries AD):
- **Goal:** Political and religious influence within the Islamic world through targeted eliminations.
- **Method:** Stealth assassinations of high-ranking leaders to weaken rival factions.
- **Outcome:** Established a long-lasting reputation for terror but failed to achieve lasting political dominance.

While the Assassins left a cultural and historical legacy as shadowy masters of stealth, the Sicarii's legacy is marked by the devastating consequences of their uncompromising zealotry, which contributed to the suffering of their own people.

Moral and Theological Reflection:

The Sicarii's militant approach underscores the dangers of extremism when zeal is untethered from wisdom and discernment:

- **Misplaced Zeal:** The Sicarii believed their violent methods were justified as acts of divine justice. However, their actions violated the ethical principles of the Torah, particularly the prohibition against murder (*Exodus 20:13*).

- **Provoking Division:** Instead of uniting the Jewish people, the Sicarii's tactics sowed discord, alienating moderates and exacerbating Roman retaliation.

- **Contrast with Yeshua's Teachings:** Yeshua advocated for nonviolent resistance and the transformation of hearts through love, wisdom, and patience (*Matthew 5:44*). The Sicarii's reliance on violence represents a stark departure from these principles.

Lessons from History:

The Sicarii's short-lived movement serves as a cautionary tale for those who seek to achieve righteous goals through unrighteous means.

Their failure to consider the broader consequences of their actions led to the devastation of their own people and the destruction of their sacred Temple.

Their comparison to the Hashshashin highlights a broader theme in human history: the allure of militancy in the name of justice and the inevitable fallout when zeal outpaces wisdom.

Both groups serve as reminders that true liberation cannot be achieved through coercion or violence but must be rooted in faith, patience, and a commitment to God's higher principles.

4.3 Samson's Zeal Turned Personal Vengeance (Judges 13–16)

The Nazirite Call

Samson's life began with a divine calling, marked by his miraculous birth to a barren woman. As a Nazirite, he was set apart for God's purpose: to deliver Israel from the Philistines (*Judges 13:5*).

His incredible strength was a sign of God's blessing, but his life was also meant to exemplify obedience and dedication to the covenant.

However, Samson's actions often reflected personal impulses rather than divine intent.

Impulsive Actions and Personal Vendettas

- **Personal Desires Over Divine Mission:**
  Samson frequently allowed his personal desires to dictate his actions, such as his pursuit of Philistine women (*Judges 14:1-3*) and his ill-advised marriage to a Philistine woman, which led to a series of conflicts.
- **Uncontrolled Anger:**
  Samson's fiery temper and impulsive behavior often escalated conflicts. When his wife was given to another man, he sought revenge by burning the Philistines' fields using foxes with torches tied to their tails (*Judges 15:3-5*).
- **Cycle of Retaliation:**
  Samson's actions provoked further retaliation from the Philistines, creating a cycle of violence. His personal vendettas, while sometimes aligning with God's purpose, were driven more by emotion than by strategic or faithful obedience.

Self-Destruction and Final Redemption

Samson's unchecked zeal ultimately led to his downfall. Betrayed by Delilah, he revealed the secret of his strength—his uncut hair—and was captured by the Philistines (*Judges 16:17-21*). Blinded and humiliated, he was paraded as a trophy of Philistine victory.

In his final act, Samson called upon God to give him strength one last time. By collapsing the Philistine temple, he killed thousands of his enemies, fulfilling his mission to deliver Israel but at the cost of his own life (*Judges 16:28-30*).

Theological Reflection

- **Misplaced Zeal:**
  Samson's story demonstrates the dangers of zeal without wisdom. His actions, though occasionally serving God's purpose, were often driven by personal emotion rather than faithfulness to his divine calling.
- **Missed Potential:**
  Despite his extraordinary strength and calling, Samson's lack of discipline and impulsiveness limited his effectiveness as a leader. He failed to unite Israel or provide a sustainable path to freedom from the Philistines.

- **God's Sovereignty:**
  Even amidst Samson's flaws, God's purposes were ultimately fulfilled. This underscores the truth that God can work through human imperfection but also highlights the cost of disobedience and impulsivity.

Key Takeaway:

Samson's life serves as both a warning and an example. While his strength and zeal were unmatched, his failure to align his actions with God's wisdom and purpose led to unnecessary destruction and personal tragedy.

His story illustrates how zeal, when untamed by wisdom, can lead to self-destruction and limit one's effectiveness as a servant of God.

Samson's legacy invites reflection on the importance of humility, patience, and obedience in fulfilling God's mission.

4.4 The Maccabees: Righteous Resistance and Zeal Gone Too Far.

Historical Context

The Maccabean revolt (167–160 BC) arose in response to the brutal oppression of the Jewish people under the Seleucid Empire, particularly the policies of King Antiochus IV Epiphanes. Antiochus sought to eradicate Jewish religious practices, desecrating the "Second Temple" and imposing Hellenistic customs, including the worship of pagan gods (*1 Maccabees 1:41-64*). This triggered an uprising led by Mattathias, a priest, and later by his sons, most notably Judah Maccabee.

Righteous Resistance

Faith-Driven Courage: The Maccabees' revolt was fueled by their unwavering commitment to preserving the Torah and Jewish identity. Their defiance against overwhelming odds demonstrated a profound reliance on God, as exemplified in Judah's famous exhortation: *"It is not by the size of the army that victory in battle depends, but on the strength that comes from Heaven"* (*1 Maccabees 3:19*).

Reclaiming the Temple: One of the revolt's defining moments was the rededication of the temple after its desecration, an event commemorated through Hanukkah. This act symbolized a restoration of covenantal faithfulness and national pride.

The Dangers of Zeal: While the initial stages of the Maccabean movement reflected righteous resistance, its later years revealed the perils of unchecked zeal and ambition.

Internal Corruption: As the Hasmonean dynasty emerged from the Maccabean revolt, its leaders increasingly sought political power, engaging in corruption, factionalism, and alliances with foreign powers. The very dynasty that began as defenders of faith eventually became a source of oppression and division within Israel.

Tyranny and Compromise: Some later Hasmonean rulers, such as John Hyrcanus and Alexander Jannaeus, abandoned the spiritual ideals of their ancestors, prioritizing military expansion and political dominance over covenantal obedience. This trajectory mirrored the power struggles they initially opposed, tarnishing the movement's legacy.

The Judean Destruction of Temple of the Samaritans (Northern tribe remnant of Israel).

Although not detailed in scripture or apocrypha, the Jewish scholar **Josephus** detailed the Hasmonean destruction of the Second Samaritan Temple to YHWH located on Mount Gerizim sometime around 112–110BC.

According to this chronicling, the Samaritan Temple to YHWH was viewed as a competitor of the Judean "Second Temple" to YHWH on Mount Moriah in Jerusalem by John Hyrcanus, the then Judean ruler and high-priest. This event cementing the schism between Judaism & Samaritanism that persists to this day.

- This reveals how easily righteous militancy can become tribalistic tyranny.

A liberating movement that restored a Temple to YHWH desecrated by non-believers devolved into a tyrannical movement that destroyed a Temple to YHWH dedicated by fellow believers.

Tyrannical power, tribalistic pride, and an idolatry of geography and architecture tragically overwhelmed any recognition of their shared covenantal worship of YHWH alone.

Theological Reflection

The Maccabean story is a poignant illustration of the tension between righteous zeal and the dangers of unrestrained ambition:

Zeal with Purpose:
The Maccabees' initial resistance highlights the power of faith-driven action to confront injustice and restore godliness.

Zeal Without Restraint:
Their later descent into corruption and authoritarianism underscores the need for humility, wisdom, and reliance on God rather than human strength or ambition.

As Proverbs 16:18 warns, *"Pride goes before destruction, and a haughty spirit before a fall."*

Key Takeaway:

The Maccabees' legacy is both inspiring and cautionary. Their early actions demonstrate how zeal for God can lead to righteous resistance and spiritual revival.

However, their later history warns of the perils of allowing zeal to devolve into self-serving ambition.

Their story serves as a reminder that true victory comes not from power or might but from faithfulness to God's law and a commitment to humility and justice.

4.5 Peter's Zealous Misstep in Gethsemane (John 18:10-11)

The Incident in Gethsemane

As soldiers and officials came to arrest Yeshua in the Garden of Gethsemane, Peter, one of His most loyal disciples, reacted with impulsive zeal. Drawing his sword, Peter struck Malchus, the servant of the high priest, cutting off his ear.

While Peter's intent may have been to defend Yeshua or resist what seemed like an unjust betrayal, his actions revealed a misunderstanding of Yeshua's mission.

- **Peter's Zeal:**
  Peter's action was driven by loyalty and a desire to protect Yeshua, yet it also betrayed his inability to grasp the larger spiritual purpose of Yeshua's arrest. His reliance on physical force reflected

a worldly mindset rather than the heavenly wisdom Yeshua had taught.

- **Yeshua's Response:**
  Immediately, Yeshua rebuked Peter, saying, *"Put your sword back in its place, for all who draw the sword will die by the sword"* (Matthew 26:52). He then healed Malchus's ear, demonstrating compassion even toward those who had come to harm Him. This act underscored the stark contrast between Peter's reactive zeal and Yeshua's divine mission of reconciliation and peace.

Theological Reflection

- **Misguided Zeal:**
  Peter's attempt to use violence to prevent Yeshua's arrest highlights the dangers of acting out of zeal without understanding God's will. Yeshua had repeatedly foretold His death and resurrection, yet Peter's impulsive response revealed his failure to fully trust in God's plan.
- **A Warning Against Retaliation:**
  Yeshua's rebuke of Peter reflects a core principle of His teachings: that God's kingdom is not advanced through force or aggression. *"My kingdom is not of this world. If it were, my servants would fight to prevent my arrest"*(John 18:36). This principle sets Yeshua's mission apart from the militant zeal that characterized groups like the Sicarii or the Maccabees.

Key Takeaways:

The Limits of Human Zeal: Peter's actions demonstrate that even well-intentioned zeal can be counterproductive when it operates outside of God's will.

His rash decision not only endangered himself but also risked undermining Yeshua's peaceful surrender, a critical step in fulfilling His redemptive mission.

The Power of Restraint:

Yeshua's response to Peter emphasizes the importance of restraint and trust in God's sovereignty. By healing Malchus, Yeshua provided a powerful witness to the nature of His kingdom—a kingdom of peace and restoration rather than violence and retribution.

Faith Over Force:

Peter's misstep serves as a reminder that faith in God's plan often requires laying down worldly weapons and embracing spiritual trust. Yeshua's path to victory came not through swords but through submission to God's will, even unto death.

Legacy and Redemption:

Peter's failure in Gethsemane was not the end of his story. After Yeshua's resurrection, Peter grew into a bold yet wise leader of the early church, demonstrating a deeper understanding of Yeshua's teachings.

His later writings reflect this transformation, urging believers to endure suffering with patience and to *"seek peace and pursue it"* (1 Peter 3:11).

Final Reflection

Peter's zealous misstep in Gethsemane serves as a cautionary tale about the dangers of reacting impulsively without spiritual discernment.

4.6 Thematic Connections

Militant Zealotry: A Flawed Strategy

Throughout history, militant zeal has repeatedly proven itself a dangerous and often counterproductive strategy for advancing God's purposes.

While zeal itself can be a righteous expression of devotion, when untethered from wisdom, patience, and faith, it becomes a destructive force.

The narratives of the Sicarii, Samson, the Maccabees, and Peter reveal the common consequences of unchecked zeal: division, suffering, and failure.

Patterns of Failure:
- **The Sicarii**: Their militant tactics not only failed to deliver freedom from Rome but also fractured Jewish unity and contributed to the destruction of the "Second Temple".
- **Samson**: Though divinely chosen, his personal vendettas and lack of restraint led to cycles of violence and his own tragic end, limiting his effectiveness as a judge.
- **The Maccabees**: Initially heroic, their later leaders fell prey to the very corruption and power struggles they had fought to oppose.
- **Peter**: His impulsive action in Gethsemane was rebuked by Yeshua, underscoring that God's kingdom cannot be advanced through violence or coercion.

Hardening Hearts: These stories highlight a recurring theme— violence and aggression, even when motivated by righteous intentions, often serve to harden hearts rather than soften them.
Instead of drawing people closer to God, militant zealotry frequently alienates, divides, and incites greater rebellion.

Contrast with Prophetic Wisdom: In earlier sections, we examined sustainable prophetic models that relied on wisdom, patience, and strategic action to achieve lasting impact. Figures like Joseph, Daniel, and Deborah demonstrate that God's purposes are best advanced through faithfulness, tact, and the softening of hearts, not through brute force or impulsive action.

---

5. Naïve Martyrs

The thematic connections drawn in this section naturally transition us to the exploration of **passive martyrs**, those who suffered not because of militant zeal but because of their innocence or naivety. Where militant zealotry often leads to self-destruction, passive martyrdom reveals another dimension of failure: the cost of misplaced trust or unguarded vulnerability.

These stories will deepen our understanding of how wisdom and faith must temper both zeal and innocence to ensure God's purposes are fulfilled.

5.1 Exploring Abel – The Naive Martyr

Righteousness and Trust

Abel stands as the first biblical martyr, a symbol of purity and faithfulness to God's covenant. His offering, described as "the firstborn of his flock and of their fat portions" (Genesis 4:4), reflects a deep understanding of sacrificial law and a genuine devotion to God. His faithfulness earned divine favor, as God regarded Abel's offering with acceptance.

However, Abel's righteousness and trust in his brother Cain reveal a significant flaw—naivety. Abel seems to have underestimated the depths of human jealousy and rebellion. His faithfulness unintentionally exposed Cain's lack of obedience, igniting resentment that festered into murderous intent.

Ignored Warning

Before tragedy struck, God intervened, warning Cain, "Sin is crouching at the door; its desire is contrary to you, but you must rule over it" (Genesis 4:7). This moment emphasizes God's awareness of Cain's internal struggle and His attempt to guide him back to righteousness. However, Abel, perhaps blinded by his own innocence, failed to recognize the threat Cain posed.

Unlike the tactical wisdom displayed by long-game prophets such as Joseph or Daniel, Abel's righteousness lacked strategic discernment. His tragic end—being murdered in the field by his own brother— highlights the vulnerability that comes from assuming others will naturally align with righteousness.

Lessons from Abel's Naivety

- **Righteousness Exposes Sin**: Abel's offering was not inherently provocative, but its acceptance by God laid bare Cain's rebellion, turning his jealousy into violence.
- **The Danger of Blind Trust**: Abel's inability to anticipate his brother's resentment demonstrates the peril of underestimating human frailty and sinfulness.
- **A Cautionary Tale**: While Abel's faith and obedience are exemplary, his story warns us that righteousness alone is not enough to navigate a world corrupted by sin. Discernment and vigilance are equally essential.

Takeaway:

Abel's story resonates as a warning to the righteous: faithfulness to God must be accompanied by wisdom and discernment. His tragic end underscores the importance of recognizing human tendencies toward sin and rebellion, even within one's closest relationships. Abel's innocence made him vulnerable, and his death serves as a call to temper purity of heart with an awareness of the world's brokenness.

5.2 Exploring: The Jerusalem Church – Righteous but Over-trusting.

Purity of Intent

The Jerusalem Church, established by Yeshua's direct disciples, stood as a shining example of faith and devotion. Rooted in Yeshua's teachings, they prioritized communal living, prayer, and service, embodying the selflessness and unity that He modeled. Acts 2:42–47 paints a picture of their early life together: sharing possessions, breaking bread, and praising God with sincere hearts. Their purity of intent and unwavering commitment to the Torah-submissive teachings of Yeshua reflected the essence of God's covenant.

Their collective faith in the transformative power of Yeshua's message was unshakable. Like Abel's righteous offering, the Jerusalem Church's spiritual and communal sacrifices were made with wholehearted devotion, believing their righteousness would serve as a beacon for others to follow.

Ignored Warnings

However, the Jerusalem Church, like Abel, underestimated the capacity for deception and rebellion within the human heart. Despite Yeshua's explicit warnings about false prophets and wolves in sheep's clothing (Matthew 7:15; Matthew 24:4–5), they failed to exercise the discernment needed to protect their nascent community.

One of the most significant threats came in the form of Saul of Tarsus, later known as Paul. Saul, initially a zealous persecutor of Yeshua's followers, claimed a dramatic conversion experience on the road to Damascus (Acts 9:1–9).

His claimed transformation from oppressor to self-declared apostle gained him entry into the Jerusalem Church's inner circle. However, instead of preserving Yeshua's Torah-aligned teachings, Saul gradually reshaped the movement into a Greco-Roman institution that deviated from its Hebraic roots.

The Jerusalem Church's over-trust in Saul allowed him to wield influence unchecked.

His letters, which frequently emphasized grace over Torah observance, became foundational to what would later evolve into Pauline Christianity—a faith increasingly detached from the covenantal framework Yeshua upheld.

The Cost of Naivety

Like Abel, the Jerusalem Church's righteousness and trust became vulnerabilities.

- Their openness to Saul's claims, despite Yeshua's clear admonitions about deception, left them susceptible to manipulation.

- This naivety enabled Saul to redirect the movement, transforming it into something fundamentally different from Yeshua's original vision.

The consequences of this shift were profound:

- **Distortion of Yeshua's Teachings**: Saul's emphasis on salvation through faith alone marginalized the importance of covenantal obedience and Torah observance.

- **Separation from Hebraic Roots**: The Jerusalem Church's failure to safeguard its message allowed it to be appropriated into a Greco-Roman context, alienating it from its Judaic origins.

- **Loss of Influence**: Over time, the Jerusalem Church's authority diminished as Pauline Christianity gained dominance, further erasing the teachings and practices that Yeshua had established.

A Warning for All Believers:

The story of the Jerusalem Church serves as a sobering reminder of the cost of naivety. While their purity of intent was commendable, their failure to exercise vigilance and discernment allowed their community to be co-opted.

Their experience underscores the importance of heeding God's warnings, remaining vigilant against deception, and safeguarding the truth of His Word.

Takeaway: The Jerusalem Church's trust in Saul echoes Abel's trust in Cain—both examples of righteous individuals undone by their inability to anticipate the dangers posed by those with rebellious hearts.

Their stories challenge us to balance faith and purity of heart with the wisdom and discernment necessary to navigate a world rife with sin and deception.

5.3 Contrast: The Abel-Jerusalem Church Analogy

Innocence and Trust

Both Abel and the Jerusalem Church serve as poignant examples of pure-hearted devotion to God, rooted in faith, obedience, and selflessness. Yet, their stories also reveal the vulnerability of righteousness when unguarded by discernment.

- **Abel's Naivety**: Abel, the first martyr, offered the best of his flock to God, an act of sincere worship and reverence (Genesis 4:4). However, his trust in Cain—his brother and presumed ally—blinded him to the danger lurking in Cain's growing jealousy and rebellion.
- **The Jerusalem Church's Over-trust**: Similarly, the Jerusalem Church embodied Yeshua's teachings, living in a state of purity and communal faithfulness (Acts 2:42–47). However, their over-trust in Saul of Tarsus, despite Yeshua's explicit warnings about false prophets and deceivers (Matthew 7:15; Matthew 24:4–5), allowed their movement to be subtly co-opted.

In both cases, innocence and trust became fatal vulnerabilities. Abel's righteousness provoked Cain's rebellion, leading to his murder.

The Jerusalem Church's openness to Saul enabled him to redirect their mission away from Yeshua's covenantal focus, ultimately undermining their authority and legacy.

Warnings Ignored

God provided clear warnings in both stories, emphasizing the necessity of vigilance and discernment:

Abel and God's Warning to Cain: Before Abel's death, God directly warned Cain about the sin "crouching at the door" (Genesis 4:7), urging him to master it. Abel, however, seemed unaware of the growing danger in Cain's heart, failing to take protective action.

Yeshua's Warnings to His Followers: Yeshua cautioned His disciples repeatedly about false prophets, wolves in sheep's clothing, and the need for discernment (Matthew 10:16; Matthew 24:4). Despite these admonitions, the Law-Observant Judeo-Christian Jerusalem Church extended trust to Saul without fully scrutinizing his intentions or the theological shifts he introduced.

In both narratives, the failure to act on divine warnings led to tragedy, underscoring the importance of heeding God's guidance and remaining vigilant.

A Lesson in Vigilance

Abel and the Jerusalem Church remind us that righteousness, while essential, must be paired with wisdom, vigilance, and a clear-eyed understanding of human frailty. Faithfulness to God requires not only purity of heart but also the strategic foresight to protect one's mission from deception and rebellion.

- **Abel's Lesson**: While Abel's sacrifice was accepted by God, his inability to anticipate Cain's jealousy highlights the need for discernment even within close relationships.
- **The Jerusalem Church's Lesson**: Their failure to critically assess Saul's influence led to a gradual dilution of Yeshua's teachings, allowing a Greco-Roman worldview to overshadow the Hebraic covenantal framework.

Takeaway:

The stories of Abel and the Jerusalem Church serve as dual cautionary tales. They highlight the dangers of misplaced trust and the need to pair obedience with practical wisdom.

Just as Cain's rebellion brought death to Abel, Saul's theological shift brought a metaphorical death to the original vision of the Jerusalem Church.

These lessons challenge us to pursue vigilance, discernment, and a deep reliance on God's guidance to safeguard the purity of His mission.

5.4 Naboth – The Righteous Victim of Corruption

Righteousness Under Threat

Naboth, a devout man of faith, refused to sell his vineyard to King Ahab, emphasizing that the land was his ancestral inheritance, given by God (1 Kings 21:3). His steadfastness reflected his unwavering commitment to God's law, which forbade the permanent sale of land outside one's family lineage (Leviticus 25:23-28).

However, Naboth's righteousness made him a target for Ahab and his wife, Jezebel. Frustrated by Naboth's refusal, Jezebel plotted a scheme to falsely accuse Naboth of blasphemy. Using her influence, she orchestrated his unjust trial and execution, enabling Ahab to seize the vineyard (1 Kings 21:7-16).

Lessons from Naboth's Tragedy

- **The Cost of Righteousness**: Naboth's unwavering faith and adherence to God's law were admirable, but his isolation and lack of protection left him vulnerable to Jezebel's schemes.
- **The Power of Corruption**: Jezebel's manipulation of religious and legal systems demonstrates how unchecked power can turn righteousness into a liability.
- **God's Justice**: While Naboth's story ends in tragedy, it also sets the stage for divine judgment against Ahab and Jezebel, as Elijah prophesies their downfall (1 Kings 21:19-23). This underscores that, while human systems may fail, God's justice prevails.

Takeaway:

Naboth's story serves as a cautionary tale about the dangers of righteous isolation in the face of corrupt power. His unwavering faith highlights the importance of standing firm in God's law, but it also reveals the necessity of community, strategy, and vigilance to protect against unjust forces.

5.5 The Prophets Slain by Jezebel

Systematic Persecution

Jezebel, the foreign wife of King Ahab, was a fervent worshiper of Baal and a determined opponent of YHWH's prophets. To establish Baal worship as the dominant religion in Israel, Jezebel systematically sought to eliminate all prophets loyal to YHWH, ordering their massacre (1 Kings 18:4).

Despite their righteousness, many prophets fell victim to Jezebel's ruthless campaign. Only a remnant survived, thanks to the efforts of individuals like Obadiah, who hid 100 prophets in caves and sustained them with food and water (1 Kings 18:4-13).

Lessons from Jezebel's Persecution

- **The Vulnerability of Righteousness**: The prophets' faithfulness to YHWH made them targets for Jezebel's wrath, underscoring the dangers of unguarded righteousness in hostile environments.
- **The Need for Strategic Resistance**: While many prophets were martyred, Obadiah's actions demonstrate the importance of wisdom and strategy in preserving the righteous and ensuring the continuity of God's work.
- **The Role of Divine Intervention**: The showdown on Mount Carmel, where Elijah confronts the prophets of Baal (1 Kings 18:20-40), illustrates that ultimate victory belongs to God, even in the face of overwhelming opposition.

Takeaway:

The prophets slain by Jezebel remind us that righteousness must be accompanied by wisdom and discernment to counter systemic opposition. Their martyrdom contrasts with the survival of those who adopted strategic approaches, highlighting the importance of balancing faith with practical foresight.

The stories of passive martyrs like Abel, Naboth, and the prophets slain by Jezebel reveal a common thread: while their righteousness was undeniable, their lack of discernment, protection, or strategic foresight left them vulnerable to opposition. These narratives emphasize that faith alone is not sufficient; it must be paired with wisdom and vigilance to withstand the challenges of a fallen world.

- **Righteousness and Wisdom**: Faithfulness to God's law must be tempered with an awareness of human corruption and the strategies necessary to navigate it.

- **God's Justice**: Though passive martyrs may fall to human schemes, their stories affirm that God's justice will ultimately prevail, bringing accountability to the wicked.

- **A Call to Discernment**: These stories challenge us to pursue righteousness with eyes wide open, recognizing the need for both faith and strategic understanding in fulfilling God's mission.

---

6. Contrasting Wisdom, Zealotry, and Naivety

This section explores the key traits and behaviors that distinguish sustainable prophets, zealous martyrs, and passive martyrs. By examining how these traits affect outcomes, we aim to show how wisdom, as exemplified by Yeshua's teachings, leads to softened hearts and lasting success, while zealotry and naivety often lead to hardened hearts and failure.

6.1 Practical Subquery: "How Does Wisdom Preserve the Righteous?"

Foundation of Wisdom in Scripture

The Bible consistently emphasizes wisdom as a divine gift essential for navigating life's challenges.

> Proverbs 4:7 declares, *"Wisdom is the principal thing; therefore, get wisdom: and with all thy getting get understanding."*

This verse underscores that wisdom is not only desirable but foundational to righteous living and leadership.

Wisdom equips the righteous with discernment, helping them recognize opportunities and dangers, foresee potential outcomes, and act in ways that align with God's purposes.

Wisdom as Discernment: King Solomon's Story

- When two mothers came before Solomon, each claiming the same child, he asked for a sword and commanded that the infant be divided in two (1 Kings 3:16–28).
- His apparent cruelty was actually a test of love. The true mother would rather yield her claim than see her child slain.
- In this moment, Solomon's wisdom preserved the righteous mother, safeguarded the innocent child, and established justice in Israel.
- The account concludes: *"All Israel heard of the judgment that the king had rendered, and they stood in awe of the king, because they perceived that the wisdom of God was in him to do justice"* (1 Kings 3:28). Solomon's discernment didn't just resolve a private dispute — it preserved trust in righteous leadership for an entire nation.

Wisdom as Mentorship and Counsel: Jethro's Story

Before Moses ever stood before Pharaoh, he was a fugitive, welcomed into the household of Jethro, priest of Midian (Exodus 2:15–21). For forty years Moses lived under Jethro's roof, learning humility, patience, and endurance — qualities Egypt had not taught him.

- Jethro's wisdom preserved the young deliverer. Without those years of obscurity and discipline, Moses would not have been ready to shepherd an entire people through the wilderness.

Later, when Israel had left Egypt, Jethro again preserved righteousness through counsel. Watching Moses exhaust himself by judging every case, Jethro advised him to appoint capable men over thousands, hundreds, fifties, and tens (Exodus 18:13–23). Delegation became the key to Israel's survival.

- Jethro's story, like Melchizedek's before him, shows that reverence for YHWH was not confined to proto-Israelites. Just as Melchizedek blessed Abraham, Jethro mentored Moses. Their wisdom ensured that the covenant could advance, preserved through outsiders who worshiped the same God Most High.

Wisdom in Speech and Action: Nathan's Approach

Nathan's confrontation of King David after his sin with Bathsheba (2 Samuel 12) is a masterclass in wise communication.

By using a parable about a rich man stealing a poor man's lamb, Nathan led David to convict himself before delivering God's rebuke.

- This approach avoided alienating David while compelling him to repent.

Nathan's wisdom in timing, tone, and delivery demonstrates how prophets can speak hard truths without provoking defensiveness or rebellion.

Yeshua's Teachings

Yeshua consistently emphasized wisdom in dealing with opponents. In Matthew 10:16, He advised His disciples to be *"wise as serpents and innocent as doves,"* balancing shrewdness with righteousness.

- His use of parables, such as the story of the Good Samaritan (Luke 10:25-37), engaged his audience's hearts and minds without direct confrontation, softening hearts and planting seeds of change.

The Role of Wisdom in Avoiding Unnecessary Conflict

Wisdom enables the righteous to discern when to act, when to speak, and when to remain silent. It protects them from the pitfalls of impulsive zeal or naive trust, ensuring their efforts align with God's purposes.

- By prioritizing wisdom, the righteous avoid provoking unnecessary hostility, allowing their influence to grow over time. This long-game strategy, exemplified by King Solomon, Jethro, and Nathan, contrasts sharply with the destructive outcomes of zealous or naive approaches.

Wisdom as De-escalation: Abigail's Story (1 Samuel 25):

Nabal, a wealthy man of Carmel, was known for his harshness and folly — his very name means "fool." When David's men, who had protected Nabal's shepherds in the wilderness, came seeking provisions, Nabal insulted David and refused aid.

Enraged, David armed four hundred men and set out to destroy Nabal's entire household. His impulsive zeal risked needless bloodshed and would have stained his rise to kingship with bloodguilt.

Abigail, Nabal's wife, recognized both her husband's folly and the danger at hand. Acting swiftly, she gathered food and gifts, rode out to meet David, and addressed him with humility and wisdom.

She acknowledged David's anointing, reminded him of YHWH's purposes, and urged him not to avenge himself.

David relented. Her wisdom defused the conflict, preserved her household, and protected David's integrity.

David declared: *"Blessed be your discretion, and blessed be you, who have kept me this day from bloodguilt and from avenging myself with my own hand!"* (1 Sam. 25:33).

- After Nabal's sudden death, David honored Abigail by taking her as his wife — a recognition of the righteousness and wisdom she had displayed.
- Nabal's arrogance nearly brought ruin upon his house, but Abigail's wisdom turned wrath aside, preserving both her people and David's path to the throne.

Takeaway:

Wisdom preserves the righteous by combining spiritual discernment, strategic foresight, and thoughtful communication. It empowers them to fulfill their divine mission while navigating complex social, political, and spiritual landscapes.

- Wisdom softens hearts, inspires change, and aligns actions with God's will, ensuring success without unnecessary conflict.

6.2 Wisdom: the key trait of Sustainable Prophets

Sustainable prophets are characterized by the wisdom needed to fulfill God's will while navigating complex social, political, and spiritual landscapes.

The trait of wisdom is itself comprised of characteristics:

- Patience
- Foresight
- Strategic Thinking

Patience: Trusting in God's Timing

Sustainable prophets recognize that lasting change often requires time.

They trust in God's timing and avoid forcing immediate results, understanding that enduring trials and waiting for divine intervention can yield greater outcomes.

Example: Moses

- Moses spent 40 years in Midian as a shepherd before God called him to lead Israel out of Egypt (Exodus 3). During this time, Moses developed the patience, humility, and endurance needed to guide a rebellious people through the wilderness for another 40 years.

- His ability to remain steadfast in the face of constant complaints and challenges exemplifies the patience required to fulfill a divine mission.

Yeshua's Teachings

- Yeshua modeled patience throughout His ministry, enduring opposition and misunderstanding while waiting for the appointed time to fulfill His purpose.

- In parables such as the mustard seed (Matthew 13:31-32), He emphasized how small, patient beginnings can lead to great outcomes over time.

Foresight: Anticipating Challenges

The Role of Foresight: Sustainable prophets possess the ability to foresee obstacles and prepare accordingly. This trait ensures they are not caught off guard by opposition, enabling them to adapt and persevere.

Example: Joseph
- Joseph's interpretation of Pharaoh's dreams (Genesis 41) revealed a famine that would devastate Egypt. His foresight led to the creation of a nationwide food storage program, preserving not only Egypt but also his own family.

- Joseph's ability to anticipate challenges allowed him to turn adversity into opportunity, securing his role as a savior figure in God's plan.

Example: Daniel
- Daniel's foresight enabled him to navigate the complexities of serving in the courts of Babylonian and Persian kings.

- He maintained his commitment to God's law while earning the trust of foreign rulers, ensuring his influence endured through multiple regimes.

- His wisdom in interpreting visions (Daniel 2, 7) demonstrated a profound understanding of God's overarching plan for humanity.

Strategic Thinking: Balancing Boldness and Restraint

The Need for Strategy: Sustainable prophets understand that achieving God's purposes often requires a balance of bold action and careful restraint. They approach challenges with discernment, ensuring their actions align with divine wisdom rather than impulsive zeal.

Example: David
- David's response to King Saul's jealousy showcased his strategic thinking. Rather than confronting Saul directly or retaliating when pursued, David exercised restraint, trusting God to establish him as king in His timing (1 Samuel 24, 26).

- This approach preserved David's life and integrity, ensuring his eventual rise to the throne without unnecessary conflict.

Yeshua's Instructions
- Yeshua's command to His disciples to *"be wise as serpents and harmless as doves"* (Matthew 10:16) encapsulates the balance of strategy and righteousness. He encouraged them to navigate hostility with shrewdness, avoiding unnecessary provocation while remaining faithful to their mission.

- Yeshua's strategic use of parables allowed Him to convey profound truths without directly antagonizing His opponents, softening hearts and planting seeds of transformation.

Takeaway:

Sustainable prophets exemplify wisdom by using patience, foresight, and strategic thinking, enabling them to align with God's will while preserving their mission.

- Their wisdom allows them to endure hardship, navigate opposition, and inspire lasting change without succumbing to martyrdom or zealotry.

- Their example highlights the importance of balancing bold faith with careful planning, ensuring that righteousness prevails in the face of adversity.

6.3 Traits of Zealous Martyrs

Zealous martyrs are defined by their fervent conviction and uncompromising stance for righteousness.

While their courage and passion are admirable, their lack of patience, strategic foresight, and tact often alienates their audience and leads to devastating consequences.

This section explores the traits of zealous martyrs, their actions, and the outcomes of their unbridled zeal.

Defining Characteristics

Unyielding Conviction:

- Zealous martyrs are deeply committed to their cause, often to the point of refusing compromise or nuanced engagement with their opposition. Their intense passion for righteousness can blind them to the need for careful strategy or measured speech.

Direct Confrontation:

- Rather than seeking to win hearts and soften opposition, zealous martyrs often engage in direct rebuke and harsh criticism. Their confrontational approach can provoke hostility and harden the hearts of those they hope to influence.

Lack of Strategic Foresight:
- Zealous martyrs frequently fail to anticipate the consequences of their actions, leading to outcomes that undermine their mission and cause unnecessary suffering for themselves and others.

Key Examples:

Zechariah (2 Chronicles 24:20-21): A Case of Direct Rebuke

Story: Zechariah, the son of Jehoiada the priest, confronted King Joash and the people of Judah for abandoning YHWH's commandments and turning to idolatry.

He boldly declared God's impending judgment,
> *"Because you have forsaken the Lord, he has also forsaken you"*
> (2 Chronicles 24:20).

Outcome:
- Enraged by Zechariah's accusations, King Joash conspired with the people to have him stoned to death in the temple courtyard—a shocking act of betrayal and violence against a righteous prophet.

- Zechariah's direct and uncompromising rebuke, while truthful, hardened hearts and incited deadly resistance.

Takeaway:
Zechariah's story demonstrates how untempered zeal can lead to alienation and martyrdom, particularly when it lacks tact and consideration for the audience's receptivity.

John the Baptist (Matthew 14; Mark 6) The Bold Forerunner

Story: John the Baptist fearlessly condemned Herod Antipas for his unlawful marriage to Herodias, his brother's wife. He declared, *"It is not lawful for you to have her"* (Matthew 14:4), publicly exposing Herod's sin.

Outcome:

- John's rebuke enraged Herodias, who manipulated Herod into imprisoning and ultimately beheading John at her daughter's request.

- While John's boldness was rooted in righteousness, his confrontational approach hardened Herodias's heart and led to his execution.

Takeaway:
John's story highlights the dangers of zeal untempered by prudence. His actions, while courageous, alienated his audience and provoked lethal retaliation.

The Sicarii: The Deadly Consequences of Militant Zealotry

Story: The Sicarii were radical zealots who assassinated Roman officials and Jewish collaborators in an attempt to incite rebellion and liberate Judea from Roman rule. Their militant actions escalated tensions and contributed to the Roman siege and destruction of Jerusalem in AD 70.

Outcome:

- Instead of achieving liberation, their tactics provoked severe Roman crackdowns, leading to widespread suffering, the destruction of the "Second Temple", and the dispersion of the Jewish people.

Takeaway:
The Sicarii's zealotry serves as a cautionary tale about the dangers of using violence and coercion in the name of righteousness. Their actions brought about destruction rather than redemption.

Three Common Consequences of Zealotry

1. Hardened Hearts:
- Zealous martyrs often alienate their audience, provoking hostility rather than repentance. Their confrontational approach can make it difficult for others to see the love and wisdom of God.

2. Escalation of Conflict:
- Zealotry frequently intensifies opposition, as seen with the Sicarii and their role in provoking Rome's destruction of Jerusalem.

3. Short-Term Impact, Long-Term Failure:
- While zealous martyrs may achieve immediate attention or inspire momentary courage, their actions often undermine long-term goals, leaving a legacy of division and loss.

Thematic Takeaway:

Zealous martyrs exemplify the dangers of conviction unbalanced by wisdom. While their passion for righteousness is commendable, their lack of patience, tact, and foresight often leads to failure and unnecessary suffering.

Their stories stand in stark contrast to sustainable prophets who rely on wisdom and strategy to fulfill God's purposes. By understanding the traits and outcomes of zealous martyrs, we can better appreciate the importance of tempering zeal with discernment and grace.

6.4 Traits of Passive Martyrs

Passive martyrs embody faithfulness and righteousness but often lack the strategic awareness, discernment, or preparation necessary to protect themselves or their mission.

Their stories serve as cautionary tales about the dangers of naivety, trust misplaced in dangerous circumstances, and the failure to pair devotion with vigilance.

Defining Characteristics

Righteousness Without Discernment:
- Passive martyrs are deeply committed to God and His commandments, but their lack of strategic foresight leaves them vulnerable to manipulation or violence.

Naivety in Relationships:
- They assume the best in others without considering human frailty, jealousy, or rebellion, which often leads to betrayal.

Lack of Defensive Posture:
- Unlike sustainable prophets who balance righteousness with wisdom, passive martyrs often fail to anticipate threats or protect themselves, becoming easy targets for those opposed to God's will.

Key Examples

Abel (Genesis 4): Trust in the Face of Danger

Story: Abel, the second son of Adam and Eve, offered a righteous sacrifice to God, giving the "firstborn of his flock" (Genesis 4:4).

- His offering was accepted by God, while Cain's was not, leading to jealousy and resentment in Cain's heart.

Despite God warning Cain that sin was "crouching at the door" (Genesis 4:7), Abel appears to have placed trust in his brother. This trust ultimately led to his murder in the field.

Consequences:
- Abel's death, while a testament to his righteousness, also reveals the cost of failing to recognize danger.
- His naivety left him defenseless against Cain's rising anger and rebellion.

Takeaway:
Abel's story illustrates the importance of vigilance alongside faith. While his sacrifice was pleasing to God, his lack of awareness allowed sin's destructive power to manifest through his brother.

The Jerusalem Church: Trusting Too Much in Others' Goodwill

Story: The Jerusalem Church, established by Yeshua's direct disciples, embodied the purity of His teachings, emphasizing upholding Torah Law, Prophets, and instructions from Yeshua.

However, their trust in Saul of Tarsus (Paul), despite Yeshua's repeated warnings about false prophets and wolves in sheep's clothing, left them vulnerable.

Saul infiltrated their ranks and co-opted their movement, steering it toward his writings of faith-alone, relaxing the Torah Law, Prophets, and Gospels: creating a gentile-friendly alternative that became hostile opponents of the direct disciples and original Jewish followers who upheld them as Yeshua instructed.

Yeshua's name, meaning "YHWH Saves" – gradually shifted toward Greco-Roman demigod worship of "Jesus" as part of a triune pagan godhead.

Consequences:
- The Jerusalem Church's failure to heed Yeshua's warnings led to a fundamental transformation of their movement, which became increasingly unrecognizable from Yeshua's original intent.
- Their passivity and over-trust allowed external influences to reshape their mission, ultimately diminishing their authority and legacy.
- This, in the long term, led to their functional theological extinction as Pauline Christianity dominated, labeling them "Judaizers", eventually declaring upholding the Law and Prophets as Yeshua instructed a high-heresy.

Takeaway:
Like Abel, the Jerusalem Church's righteousness and faithfulness were undermined by their lack of vigilance.

Their trust in Saul exemplifies the dangers of failing to guard against deception and manipulation, even within a faith community.

Consequences of Passivity

Loss of Influence:
- Passive martyrs often fail to achieve the transformative impact of sustainable prophets because their lack of strategy leaves them vulnerable to opposition.

Symbolic but Limited Outcomes:
- While their deaths may highlight injustice, they rarely lead to lasting change or inspire repentance in those responsible.

A Warning, Not a Model:
- Passive martyrs serve as cautionary figures, emphasizing the need for spiritual and situational awareness to complement righteousness.

Thematic Takeaway:

Passive martyrs remind us that faith alone is not enough; it must be paired with wisdom, vigilance, and preparation. Abel and the Jerusalem Church serve as poignant examples of how naivety, trust misplaced in dangerous circumstances, and defenselessness can undermine righteousness. Their stories challenge us to approach faith with discernment, ensuring that we are not only righteous but also wise stewards of God's mission.

6.5 Yeshua's Teachings: Softening Hearts, Not Hardening Them

Yeshua's teachings offer a profound blueprint for prophetic engagement, balancing wisdom, love, and humility with a pragmatic understanding of human nature.

His approach stood in stark contrast to the zealotry of the Sicarii or the naivety of passive martyrs, emphasizing a model that sought to transform oppressors and inspire disciples through a combination of compassion, strategic action, and self-defense.

Prioritize Winning Over Oppressors

Love and Humility as Tools of Transformation:
- Yeshua's teachings centered on surprising acts of love that disarmed hostility and shifted perspectives.

Example: In Matthew 5:41, Yeshua instructed His followers, "If anyone forces you to go one mile, go with them two miles." This was a direct reference to Roman law, which allowed soldiers to compel civilians to carry their burdens for a mile.

By voluntarily going further, Yeshua's followers demonstrated humility and generosity, challenging the oppressor's expectations and fostering goodwill.

- Such acts of unexpected kindness created opportunities for dialogue and softened the hearts of even the most hostile audiences.

Turning the Other Cheek—But with Purpose:

- Yeshua's call to "turn the other cheek" (Matthew 5:39) was not a command to invite abuse but a challenge to respond to aggression in a way that exposed its futility.
- By refusing to retaliate in kind, His followers could maintain their dignity while holding oppressors accountable for their actions, fostering conviction without escalation.

Avoiding Rebellion

Rejection of Zealotry:
- Unlike the Sicarii or other militant groups, Yeshua did not advocate violent rebellion against Rome or Jewish authorities. His focus was on transforming individuals from within, creating a ripple effect of change.
- His response to the Pharisees and Sadducees was measured and strategic, using parables to provoke introspection and disarm confrontation. For instance, His parable of the Good Samaritan (Luke 10:25–37) dismantled societal prejudices without direct accusations, inviting listeners to reflect and change.

Engagement Without Confrontation:
- Yeshua often avoided direct, inflammatory confrontations, recognizing that hardened hearts require a softer approach.
- His wisdom in answering traps set by His opponents (e.g., "Render unto Caesar what is Caesar's" in Matthew 22:21) revealed His ability to navigate volatile situations without sacrificing truth.

The Power of Example

Self-Sacrifice as the Ultimate Lesson:
- Yeshua's willingness to forgive those who persecuted Him, even as He suffered on the cross ("Father, forgive them, for they know not what they do" – Luke 23:34), became the ultimate demonstration of the power of love and forgiveness to transform hearts and inspire faith.

Shepherd Leadership—Strength in Defense:

Yeshua was not a pacifist but a protector. His instruction to His disciples to "sell your cloak and buy a sword" (Luke 22:36) reflects a pragmatic approach to self-defense and preparedness.

- This directive was not a call to aggression but a recognition that evil exists and that self-defense is sometimes necessary to protect oneself and others.

- Like David, the shepherd who defended his flock with a sling and later became a warrior-king, Yeshua's followers were to be both defenders and peacemakers, embodying the strength of a good shepherd.

Cunning Without Malice:
In Matthew 10:16, Yeshua instructed His disciples,

> *"Behold, I send you forth as sheep in the midst of wolves: be ye therefore wise as serpents, and harmless as doves."*

This dual command emphasizes the need for strategic thinking and spiritual purity.

- Followers of Yeshua were to navigate hostile environments with discernment, avoiding unnecessary conflict while remaining blameless in their conduct.
- Yeshua's teachings encouraged a posture of peace without weakness, embodying both the shrewdness of a serpent and the innocence of a dove.

This balance allowed His disciples to engage with oppressors and skeptics effectively, maintaining integrity while defusing potential hostility.

Takeaway:
Yeshua's teachings and example model a prophetic approach that prioritizes softening hearts through love, wisdom, and humility.

He rejected the pitfalls of zealotry and naivety, instead emphasizing strategic action, patience, and the transformative power of kindness.

Yet, Yeshua also understood the necessity of preparation and defense, teaching His followers to protect themselves and others when needed.

His balanced approach—strength tempered by love—offers a sustainable model for discipleship that transcends cultural and historical boundaries.

6.6 Section 6 Thematic Takeaway

Zealotry and naivety, while often born of genuine conviction, frequently result in unintended consequences that hinder God's work.

- Zealotry, with its aggressive fervor, hardens hearts, escalates conflict, and provokes backlash.
- Naivety leaves the righteous vulnerable to exploitation and manipulation.

Both approaches, though rooted in passion and sincerity, fail to achieve the lasting impact needed to align humanity with God's will. In contrast, wisdom—grounded in patience, foresight, and strategic thinking—preserves the righteous and fosters reconciliation.

- Sustainable prophets like Joseph, Daniel, and Yeshua demonstrate that true spiritual leadership requires not only conviction but also the discernment to navigate complex social and spiritual landscapes effectively.
- Their success lies in their ability to soften hearts, inspire change, and fulfill their mission without succumbing to the pitfalls of zealotry or the vulnerabilities of naivety.

Yeshua's teachings serve as the ultimate guide, emphasizing humility, love, and a profound understanding of human nature. His approach balances wisdom and strength, demonstrating how to transform oppressors and skeptics alike through acts of kindness, strategic foresight, and unwavering faith. The lesson is clear: winning hearts and minds requires more than righteous intent—it demands the wisdom to act in alignment with God's eternal purposes.

7. The Ultimate Role of a Prophet: Pointing People Back to God

Prophets, in their truest form, serve as spiritual shepherds, guiding humanity back to a life aligned with God's will. Their purpose transcends mere foretelling; it lies in calling people to faithful worship of YHWH and promoting godly treatment of one another. This dual mission—reconciling humanity to God and fostering relational righteousness—defines the ultimate role of a prophet.

7.1 Faithful Worship of God

Prophets function as divine messengers, redirecting individuals and communities toward obedience, repentance, and covenantal alignment. Their teachings and actions emphasize that faithfulness to God is the cornerstone of a righteous life.

- **Moses:** Moses interceded on behalf of Israel after their rebellion with the golden calf, pleading with God to forgive their sin. He not only secured God's continued presence but also reestablished the covenant by delivering the second set of tablets (Exodus 32-34). Moses' leadership exemplifies how a prophet redirects rebellion into repentance, ultimately restoring the people's relationship with God.
- **Elijah:** Elijah's dramatic confrontation with the prophets of Baal on Mount Carmel (1 Kings 18:20-40) was more than a spectacle—it was a call to national repentance. After demonstrating God's power, Elijah urged the people to abandon Baal worship and return to YHWH, affirming the role of a prophet as a spiritual signpost.
- **Yeshua:** Yeshua's teachings consistently pointed people back to the heart of the Torah. His Sermon on the Mount (Matthew 5-7) emphasized inward transformation and deeper obedience, reminding His followers that He came not to abolish the law but to fulfill it (Matthew 5:17-19). His life and message embody the ultimate prophetic mission of aligning humanity with God's original intent.

Godly Treatment of Each Other

Beyond calling people to worship God, prophets emphasize relational righteousness, rooted in justice, mercy, and humility.

Their guidance highlights that loving one's neighbor is inseparable from loving God.

Micah:
Micah distilled God's requirements into three fundamental principles:

"to do justice, and to love kindness, and to walk humbly with your God" (Micah 6:8).

This prophetic insight underscores the relational aspect of righteousness, reminding us that faithfulness to God is reflected in how we treat others.

Amos:
Amos denounces empty ritual, highlighting justice and righteousness as the true measure of covenant faithfulness.

"I hate, I despise your feasts... But let justice roll down like waters, and righteousness like an ever-flowing stream." (**Amos 5:21–24**).

This verse reveals the importance of mercy, justice, and humility in daily life — not just temple ritual.

Isaiah:
Isaiah begins his book with a striking call to ethical living:

"Wash yourselves; make yourselves clean... cease to do evil, learn to do good; seek justice, correct oppression; bring justice to the fatherless, plead the widow's cause." (**Isaiah 1:16–17**)

This verse shows that worship of God is inseparable from upholding justice in society.

Takeaway: The Prophet's Mission

The ultimate role of a prophet is to inspire covenantal obedience and relational harmony, not to incite fear, rebellion, or division.

Their success depends on their ability to balance truth with grace, wisdom with humility, and justice with compassion.

By pointing people back to God and fostering godly relationships, prophets fulfill their divine calling and pave the way for transformation.

7.2 Winning Hearts and Minds Through Mirror-Neuron Effects

Prophets and leaders, both ancient and modern, have often succeeded in influencing others through their demeanor and actions rather than just their words.

This phenomenon is rooted in the concept of mirror neurons—brain cells that allow individuals to empathize and align their behaviors with those they observe.

By understanding and leveraging this inherent human trait, prophets and believers alike can inspire godly behavior and promote harmony.

The Science of Mirror Neurons

Mirror neurons were discovered in the early 1990s during experiments with primates and later identified in humans.

These neurons fire not only when an individual performs an action but also when they observe someone else performing the same action, creating an empathetic connection.

Empathetic Resonance:

- When people observe behaviors of others, their mirror neurons activate, stimulating them to replicate those emotions or actions. This biological mechanism can foster trust, cooperation, and shared understanding, or it can foster distrust, division and mutual disdain. The stimulated response depends strongly on the behavior observed, be it positive or negative.

Leadership and Influence:

- Public figures who project confidence, calmness, and compassion naturally inspire similar responses in their audiences. Leaders who model desirable behaviors often see their followers adopt those behaviors in return, making mirror neurons a powerful tool for positive influence.

Biblical Examples of Positive Mirror-Neuron Effects

The Bible provides numerous instances where the actions and demeanor of key figures influenced those around them, often leading to repentance, reconciliation, or transformation.

- **Yeshua's Compassion and Truthfulness:**
  Yeshua's interactions with individuals like the Samaritan woman at the well (John 4) illustrate the power of empathy and gentleness. Initially skeptical and defensive, the woman's heart was softened by Yeshua's nonjudgmental yet truthful approach. His demeanor not only transformed her but also inspired her to evangelize to her community.
- **Joseph's Forgiveness and Grace:**
  Joseph's decision to forgive his brothers rather than seek revenge (Genesis 45:4-15) created an atmosphere of reconciliation. His actions softened the hardened hearts of his brothers, leading them to acknowledge their wrongdoing and restore familial bonds.
- **David's Mercy Toward Saul:**
  On multiple occasions, David had the opportunity to kill King Saul, who sought his life. Instead, David chose restraint, sparing Saul and demonstrating respect for God's anointed (1 Samuel 24, 26). These acts of mercy and integrity momentarily softened Saul's heart, prompting him to acknowledge David's righteousness.

Biblical Examples of Negative Mirror-Neuron-Effects

- Zealous martyrs, faces twisted in indignation, speech dripping with negative emotion, body language displaying micro-expression after micro-expression of hostility bordering on hatred.

- To those being addressed, their already wandering hearts are hardened as their mirror-neurons fire, and their faces twist, their speech begins dripping with disdain, a flood of hostility conveyed in every motion, every expression until violence with murderous intent ensues.

When this happens, that opportunity for repentance, reconciliation, or transformation is lost.

Practical Applications for Believers

The principles demonstrated by Yeshua, Joseph, and David are as relevant today as they were in biblical times. Modern believers can use these lessons to foster understanding and reconciliation in their personal and spiritual lives.

Approach with Love and Humility:

- Confrontations are more likely to yield positive outcomes when approached with gentleness and respect rather than aggression. Proverbs 15:1 affirms, "A gentle answer turns away wrath, but a harsh word stirs up anger."

Model Godly Behavior:

- By embodying patience, forgiveness, and compassion, believers can inspire others to reflect those same values. Leading by example creates an environment where hearts are softened and minds are open to God's truth.

Build Bridges, Not Walls:

- Even in the face of opposition, choosing to build relationships through empathy and understanding can break down barriers of hostility. As Yeshua said, "Blessed are the peacemakers, for they shall be called children of God" (Matthew 5:9).

Takeaway:

Mirror-neuron effects demonstrate the profound influence of modeled behavior. Prophets and believers who exhibit peace, love, and humility inspire others to follow suit, fostering harmony and alignment with God's will. By prioritizing godly actions and attitudes, we can reflect the light of God to a world in need of transformation.

7.3 Modern Behavioral Science Supports the Long-Game Prophet Model

While the wisdom of long-game prophets finds its origins in scripture, modern behavioral psychology and sociology reveal why their strategies are so effective.

These concepts affirm the timeless relevance of traits like patience, empathy, and positive reinforcement, offering insights into how believers today can adopt a similar approach.

The Role of Positive Reinforcement

Behavioral psychology demonstrates that encouragement and affirmation shape behavior far more effectively than punishment or condemnation.

The Bible's recurring theme: God's Loving Reinforcement

- **God's Parental Imagery in Hosea:** YHWH describes Himself as one who taught Ephraim to walk, who led His people "with cords of human kindness, with ties of love" (Hosea 11:3–4). Instead of harshness, He portrays Himself as a nurturing parent—gently guiding Israel through encouragement and care.
- **The Invitation of Isaiah:** Even after deep rebellion, God holds out hope: *"Though your sins are like scarlet, they shall be as white as snow"* (Isaiah 1:18). This promise of cleansing doesn't shame—it draws the heart back with the assurance of forgiveness.
- **Nineveh's Moment of Mercy:** When the people of Nineveh repented, God relented from sending disaster (Jonah 3:10). The unexpected gift of mercy softened them far more than judgment would have, showing that withheld punishment itself can be a form of positive reinforcement.
- **The Father of the Prodigal Son:** Yeshua's parable (Luke 15:11–32) reflects this same divine pattern. The father runs to embrace the wayward son, no punishment ensues. This parable echoes YHWH's promise of open-armed welcome throughout the Hebrew Bible.

In God's story, reconciliation begins not with condemnation, but with open-arms, forgiveness, and loving mercy that restores the human soul.

Together, these examples reveal that God's preferred method of shaping His people has always leaned toward mercy, forgiveness, affirmation, and restoration.

Modern Implications:
Positive reinforcement builds trust and encourages long-term transformation.

Leaders and believers who inspire rather than criticize create an environment where hearts and minds are more receptive to spiritual truths.

Social Conditioning Through Loving Relationships

Yeshua emphasized the transformative power of love, both for individuals and communities.

His command to "love your neighbor as yourself" (Mark 12:31) highlights the relational foundation of spiritual growth.

- **Yeshua's Relational Ministry:**
  Yeshua's interactions with people were deeply personal and marked by compassion. The Samaritan woman at the well (John 4) experienced a transformation not through judgment but through a loving and honest conversation. His relational approach opened her heart and inspired her to spread His message.

- **Trust and Openness:**
  Relationships based on love and humility foster trust, making individuals more willing to consider spiritual truths. Modern psychology affirms that genuine connection builds the foundation for lasting change.

Implications for Believers:
By embodying godly principles in their daily lives, modern believers can serve as "early adopters," spreading God's message through their example.

Conflict De-Escalation Techniques

Modern conflict resolution emphasizes empathy, active listening, and non-aggressive communication—traits consistently modeled by sustainable prophets.

- **Nathan's Tact:**
  Nathan's carefully worded rebuke of David avoided confrontation, focusing instead on restoration. His approach serves as a biblical example of de-escalating conflict while upholding truth.

- **Yeshua's Parables:**
  When challenged by the Pharisees, Yeshua often responded with parables that invited reflection rather than direct condemnation. This technique softened hearts and provoked thought rather than rebellion.

Examples of Positive Behavior

Sustainable prophets demonstrated behaviors that fostered trust, softened hearts, and aligned people with God's will.

- **Patience and Preparation:**
  Daniel's consistent prayer life and refusal to compromise became a model for those around him, showing how quiet faithfulness inspires others.

- **Subtle Influence:**
  Joseph's rise to power was marked by humility and wisdom. By leveraging his position for the good of others, he fulfilled God's promises without unnecessary confrontation.

Takeaway:

Modern behavioral science validates the long-game prophet model, affirming that patience, relational engagement, and positive reinforcement yield greater success than coercion or condemnation. By aligning with these principles, believers can effectively point others to God while fostering genuine transformation in hearts and minds.

7.4 Section 7 Thematic Takeaway:

Prophets who embody wisdom, humility, and love align themselves with God's ultimate purpose: to draw people back into covenantal relationship and godly living.

This section has shown that sustainable prophets are not defined merely by their messages but by their method—one rooted in understanding human nature and working within it to bring about transformation.

Behavioral Psychology Affirms Biblical Wisdom:
Modern studies of human behavior validate the effectiveness of Yeshua's long-game approach. Softening hearts through love and humility, rather than hardening them with aggression or zealotry, creates the environment necessary for lasting spiritual change.

The Role of Prophets in Social Transformation:
Prophets act as divine mediators, calling people to align their lives with God's will while demonstrating godly behavior themselves.
- Their ability to influence comes not from force but from modeling trust, integrity, and wisdom.

Yeshua's Example:
Yeshua demonstrated the ultimate balance of grace and truth.
- His parables, actions, and sacrifice exemplify how wisdom and love can lead even the most hardened hearts toward repentance and reconciliation with God.

A Timeless Lesson:
Whether through the actions of Joseph, the wisdom of Daniel, or the compassion of Yeshua, the message is clear:

- Transformation begins with how we treat others.
- Prophets who reflect God's love through their behavior inspire trust, soften hearts, and pave the way for spiritual renewal.

8. God's Law of Liberty and Marks of the Spirit

This section expands the exploration of prophetic wisdom under the theological framework of God's Law of Liberty and introduces **the biblical marks** people bind to their souls. By examining how prophets, martyrs, and zealots interact with the divine order, we reveal the necessity of wisdom, obedience, and love in preserving individual and civil liberty under God's covenant.

8.1 Prophets, Martyrs, and the Divine Arc of Liberty

The Role of Prophets in Liberty

Agents of Freedom: Prophets are not just messengers; they are instruments of liberation. They call people back to covenantal obedience, freeing them from sin and false worship while guiding them toward godly living.

Examples of Long-Game Prophets:
- **Daniel:** His faith under Babylonian rule demonstrated true liberty—freedom from fear and compromise—even in captivity. Daniel showed that liberty is rooted in steadfastness to God's law, not rebellion against earthly authority.
- **Yeshua:** His teachings emphasized inward transformation over outward rebellion, redefining liberty as alignment with God's will rather than unrestrained autonomy.

Martyrs and the Cost of Freedom

Naivety's Price:
Martyrs like Abel highlight the vulnerability of righteousness when paired with innocence or blind trust.

While their faithfulness remains exemplary, their lack of discernment often left them exposed to exploitation or violence.

Example: Abel: His sincere offering pleased God, but his failure to perceive Cain's jealousy led to his death. Abel's story underscores the need for vigilance and wisdom alongside righteousness.

Freedom Through Sacrifice:
Martyrs often pay the ultimate price for their convictions, but their stories also serve as cautionary tales about the importance of protecting liberty through strategic action.

The Destructive Power of Zeal:
Zealots often confuse passion with purpose, mistaking rebellion or extremism for divine liberty. Their actions frequently lead to division, suffering, and destruction.

Example: The Sicarii: Their violent tactics against Roman rule alienated their own people and hastened the destruction of the "Second Temple". By conflating personal ambition with divine purpose, they eroded rather than preserved liberty.

Theological Reflection:
True liberty under God cannot be achieved through coercion or violence. Instead, it requires wisdom, humility, and alignment with divine principles.

8.2 Wisdom as the Key to God's Law of Liberty

Defining God's Law of Liberty

Not the Absence of Restraint:
Liberty, as outlined in scripture, is not freedom from all constraints but freedom within the boundaries of righteousness. It aligns human behavior with God's will, bringing true peace and fulfillment.

- **James 1:25:** "Whoever looks intently into the perfect law that gives freedom... will be blessed in what they do."

- **Yeshua's Example:** He demonstrated liberty through obedience to God, teaching that true freedom comes from aligning with divine truth rather than resisting it (John 8:32).

The Prophetic Model of Liberty:
Prophets like Joseph and Nathan illustrate how wisdom and patience uphold liberty by fostering trust, unity, and covenantal faithfulness.

Wisdom Preserves Freedom

Softening Hearts Through Tact:
Wisdom ensures that the prophetic message is received rather than rejected, preserving both the messenger's life and their mission.

- **Example: Nathan:** By using a parable to confront David, Nathan inspired repentance without alienation, preserving David's kingship and Israel's stability.
- **Contrast: Zechariah:** His direct rebukes led to his martyrdom, hardening hearts and losing the opportunity for meaningful change.

Preparation and Strategic Thinking:
Prophets like Joseph succeeded by combining faith with preparation, showing how foresight ensures survival and continuity.

- **Joseph:** His preparation for Egypt's famine not only preserved lives but also reinforced God's promise to Israel. His wisdom demonstrated how liberty is preserved through strategic stewardship.

8.3 The Intersection of Prophecy and Covenant

Prophets as Covenant Stewards:
Prophets serve as guides to God's covenant, calling people to align their lives with divine law and principles. Their role is central to preserving liberty by encouraging obedience and relational harmony with God and others.

Yeshua's Teachings and Actions:

Yeshua embodied this role perfectly, focusing not on force but on teaching others to choose covenantal faithfulness.

His parables, such as the Prodigal Son, demonstrate the beauty of voluntary return to God rather than coerced obedience.

Binding God's Law to Thought and Action

How To Be Marked by God: Yeshua exemplified the integration of God's Law into his every thought and every action.

- His teachings instructed living in God's Law.
- His every action upheld and fulfilled it.
- His obedience to the will of our Heavenly Father was total and complete.

Liberty and Choice in God's Covenant

Prophetic Responsibility:

A Prophet's job is welcoming God's Law into every aspect of their lives, and teaching others how to do the same.

Accepting Alignment:

Prophets teach that belief in God should inspire a heartfelt desire to put forth the mental and physical effort needed to master upholding His Law.

- A Prophet's mission is using scripture, wisdom, and patience to show people how much God loves them and wants to bless their lives.

- A Prophet's goal is inspiring people to love God back, voluntarily, and showing their love through relational worship and covenantal obedience.

Looking Ahead:
As we transition to exploring God's law of liberty in greater depth, we will explore the interplay between free will, divine law, marks on the soul, and the preservation of spiritual freedom.

---

9. The Gift and Responsibility of Free Will

Key Insight: *Free will is agency balanced with accountability.*

Free will is often framed as an abstract philosophical concept or a theological puzzle, but at its core, it represents something deeply personal and immediate: self-ownership.

- Self-ownership is not just the freedom *to make choices*, but the sacred weight of knowing that *every choice we make is ours, and has consequences.*

Like a master craftsman handing over delicate tools to an apprentice, God placed free will into humanity's hands—not as a burden, not as a test, but as a gift with a purpose.

- Every choice we make bends reality slightly—toward the light of obedience or into the shadows of rebellion.

Free will isn't passive; it's active, and every chosen action pulls a soul in one direction or the other.

It isn't abstract, it's a mirror placed squarely in front of the soul, reflecting the choices made and what fingerprints those choices leave on the world.

9.1 The Divine Gift of Choice

"I have set before you life and death, blessings and curses. Now choose life." – **Deuteronomy 30:19**

In a moment captured forever in ink and spirit, God spoke through Moses, presenting humanity with the starkest of crossroads: *life or death.* These weren't vague metaphors; they were outcomes, tangible and sharp-edged.

- Choose life and you align yourself with the current of creation, with laws that are not arbitrary but foundational, carved into the architecture of existence itself.
- Choose rebellion, and you swim against the current—straining, breaking, unraveling.

Free will wasn't laid on humanity as a burden; it was given as a gift.

God could have shaped you as a perfect automaton, incapable of error, always aligned with divine will. But love without choice isn't love. Obedience without the possibility of rebellion isn't obedience—it's programming.

God gave you choice—*real choice.* With that choice comes risk, and with that risk comes meaning. Free will is proof of God's divine love, without it there can be no truly reciprocal human response to it.

- Free will is the reason your worship carries weight. Free will is the reason your love brings God joy. However, it is also the reason willful disobedience carries consequences.
- Free will is the gift of agency, self-ownership. However, free will is a tool of varying value that depends more on **how it is used** than **what it is**.

Just as a hammer, depending on the intent and actions of its user, can build a temple or shatter its walls.

Takeaway: *Free will grants liberty with responsibility.* A precious tool God placed lightly in humanity's trembling hands.

9.2 The Misunderstanding of Free Will

Modern culture loves the word *freedom*. It's stamped on flags, etched into statues, and shouted from stages. But the freedom often celebrated isn't the freedom God gave—it's a counterfeit, a hollow echo of something far richer.

Freedom, in its modern interpretation, is often defined by *the absence of restraint. Do what feels good. Follow your truth. No one can tell you otherwise.*

- These are the slogans of a freedom that looks appealing but decays into chaos when applied long enough.
- This version of freedom isn't about alignment with anything greater than the self—it's about feeding the self endlessly.

But the biblical view of freedom is different. It isn't about endless options or limitless autonomy. It's about being *free to align yourself with God's design.* Imagine a river, its banks guiding the water into a clear, purposeful current. Without those banks, the river becomes a swamp—stagnant, lifeless, chaotic.

- God's laws aren't chains; they're riverbanks. They guide the flow of humanity into something beautiful, purposeful, and thriving. True freedom isn't the ability to do anything—it's the ability to do what is *right.*

Yeshua echoed this when He said, *"Take my yoke upon you... for my yoke is easy and my burden is light."* (Matthew 11:29-30) A yoke sounds restrictive, but it's what aligns two oxen to pull in the same direction, to work in tandem toward a goal.

- In rejecting God's yoke, humanity often mistakes chaos for liberty. And in doing so, we chain ourselves with invisible ropes—fear, addiction, pride, self-justification. The world calls these chains *freedom.* God calls them *bondage.*

Takeaway: *True liberty is found in obedience, not lawlessness.* The yoke is easy, the burden light, but only if we're willing to stop fighting against it.

9.3 The Crossroads of Choice

At every moment, at every intersection, there's a choice. It's rarely dramatic—no booming voices from the sky, no flashes of lightning. It's a simple question whispered quietly in the corner of the soul: *Who will you serve?*

Free will isn't a distant theological construct; it's immediate, alive, and relentless.

- It's in the pause before speaking a sharp word.
- It's in the hesitation before clicking that link.
- It's in the heartbeat before zeal outpaces wisdom.
- It's in every choice to align or rebel.

Every decision is a crossroad—every action bends reality toward covenant or rebellion.

There is no neutral ground. The illusion of neutrality is one of the greatest lies humanity tells itself. *I'm not choosing rebellion, I'm just choosing myself.*

But rebellion doesn't always roar; sometimes it whispers.

- Sometimes it's polite.
- Sometimes it's wrapped in good intentions.
- Sometimes it's painted with bright colors.

Every decision, whether obedient or rebellious, sews seeds.

Seeds grow roots and become plants. And eventually, those plants bear fruit—either good or rotten.

- Cain stood at a crossroads when God said, *"Sin is crouching at your door; it desires to have you, but you must rule over it."* (Genesis 4:7) Cain had free will.

He had a choice, and he made it.

Free will isn't just an abstract concept—it's a spiritual tool. And like any tool, it can build or destroy.

Takeaway: *Free will isn't neutral—it's a tool for worship or rebellion.* And it's always in use, whether we recognize it or not.

Conclusion of Section 9:

Free will is not just a philosophical curiosity—it's a mirror. It reflects every decision, every hesitation, every step forward or backward.

It's not something that happens *to* us; it's something we *use*.

It's the sharp edge of responsibility placed into trembling hands. A tool. A gift. A covenant. And every moment—every breath—is an opportunity to ask: *What am I building with it?*

---

10. A Tale of Two Bindings

Key Insight:

There are two spiritual bindings spoken of in scripture—one ancient, one prophetic. Each is anchored to the same places: the **head** and the **hand**.

Both act as symbols, seals of allegiance.

- One binds a soul to God's divine covenant, the other chains it to rebellion.

- One brings alignment and freedom, the other distortion and enslavement.

These two symbols represent the ultimate spiritual choice.

Neither binding is casual. Neither binding is merely ornamental. They are *choices*—decisions sealed into thought and action, signaling loyalty to one kingdom or another.

Every day, every thought, every action carries the potential to tighten one of these bindings. The head shapes intention. The hand carries it out.

10.1 Introducing the Tefillin Principle: The Mark of God

The Symbolism of Tefillin

> *"These commandments that I give you today are to be on your hearts... Tie them as symbols on your hands and bind them on your foreheads." –* **Deuteronomy 6:6-8**

Tefillin, or phylacteries, in Orthodox Rabbinical Judaism, are small black boxes containing scrolls of Torah verses strapped tightly to the forehead and the arm. At first glance, they seem simple—an ancient ritual preserved through millennia.

However, the spiritual declaration is anything but simple.

The *head* represents thoughts, intentions, and the internal world. The *hand* represents actions, works, and the external world. Together, they form a bridge between what is *conceived* in the mind and what is *manifested* in the world.

- Binding God's commandments to these two places isn't just a ritual—it's an alignment. It's a reminder that every thought should be shaped by divine wisdom, and every action should reflect divine instruction.

Beyond physical accessories, **Spiritual Tefillin** are best understood as marks on the soul of those who carry God's word in thought and deed, in head and hand, in internal alignment and external obedience.

Tefillin bound in spirit are marks of spiritual declaration.

- A declaration of love and loyalty for our Father in Heaven, with all of your heart and soul.
- A declaration of desire to live obediently, with God's Law guiding your every thought and action.

Takeaway: Spiritual *Tefillin aren't just ritual accessories—they are spiritual marks of covenant loyalty.* By binding God's Law in our thoughts and actions, believers uphold covenant obedience and resist being bound by forces of deception and rebellion.

10.2 The Mark of the Beast

"It also forced all people, great and small, rich and poor, free and slave, to receive a mark on their right hands or on their foreheads, so that they could not buy or sell unless they had the mark..." – Revelation 13:16-17

Where Spiritual Tefillin symbolize alignment, the *Mark of the Beast* represents distortion.

It's not an accidental parallel; it's an intentional counterfeit. Just as Tefillin bind thought and action to divine obedience, the Mark of the Beast binds them to rebellion.

- The *head* becomes the throne of twisted intention—ambition without restraint, justification without humility. The *hand* becomes the instrument of rebellion—action without reflection, desire without discipline.

But the Mark isn't just about thought and action—it's about *allegiance.* It's a declaration, stamped in spiritual ink: *I belong to this world. I serve its systems. I trust its promises.*

- The Mark is a transaction—a spiritual exchange where loyalty is traded for temporary power, comfort, or survival. It's not always as literal as branding or a barcode. Sometimes, it's simply a life shaped by greed, pride, or fear.

- If Tefillin say, *"My allegiance is to God,"* the Mark of the Beast says, *"My allegiance is to everything that stands against Him."*
- It's a counterfeit covenant—a twisted binding that mimics holiness while dripping with rebellion.

Takeaway: *The Mark of the Beast mirrors Tefillin but in opposition—it's rebellion codified.* The same head and hand, the same gates, but locked to opposing kingdoms.

10.3 Choosing Life or Bondage

There's no neutral ground between these two bindings. There's no third strap, no middle box, no compromise knot. Every thought pulls toward one binding, every action tightens one strap.

It doesn't always feel that way. Some choices seem small, harmless, inconsequential. But every thought plants a seed, and every action waters it.

Over time, those seeds grow into roots—one vine reaching upward into alignment, the other twisting downward into rebellion.

The choice between these two bindings isn't always made in grand, theatrical moments. More often, it happens quietly—in the silence before a spoken word, in the pause before clicking a link, in the stillness of an unchecked impulse.

Over time, the bindings become visible. Thoughts take form in habits. Actions become patterns. And patterns become allegiances.

The question isn't whether you'll be bound—it's which binding you'll wear.

Takeaway: *Our choices reveal our spiritual allegiance—whether to obedience or rebellion.* Every thought is a step. Every action is a signature.

Section 10 Conclusion: A Tale of Two Bindings

The head and the hand—intention and action—are battlegrounds. They are gates where allegiances are declared and choices are cemented.

Spiritual Tefillin and the Mark of the Beast are not just historical symbols or future prophecies—they are *living principles.*

- Every moment binds the head and the hand to one kingdom or the other.

There is no third strap, no middle box, no neutral mark, no opting out.

It's not about avoiding one mark; it's about intentionally choosing the other.

11. James's Law of Liberty: Obedience Brings Freedom

Key Insight: *God's Law isn't a prison—it's the blueprint for true liberty.*

Freedom is one of humanity's most celebrated ideals—sung about in anthems, etched into monuments, and promised by every ideology that wants followers.

But in scripture, freedom isn't presented as limitless autonomy; it's shown as alignment—alignment with a design, a rhythm, a purpose.

James called it the *"Law of Liberty"* (James 2:12), and it might sound contradictory at first. *How can a law produce liberty? Aren't laws about restrictions and boundaries?*

But this paradox is the heart of God's covenantal design. The Torah doesn't chain humanity—it *frees* humanity. Not by releasing us from responsibility, but by aligning us with reality.

11.1 The Paradox of Liberty Through Law

> *"Speak and act as those who will be judged by the law that gives freedom."* – **James 2:12**

The idea of freedom through obedience feels backward to modern ears. Laws, rules, commandments—they're seen as limits, obstacles, or cages. But the Law of Liberty doesn't operate like human laws; it operates like the laws of physics.

- You can't *break* the law of gravity—you can only break yourself against it. God's Law is the same. It isn't arbitrary or oppressive— it's foundational. It describes *how reality works.*

When James wrote about the *Law of Liberty*, he wasn't inventing something new. He was echoing a truth embedded in the Torah: *obedience to God isn't about avoiding punishment; it's about accessing abundance.*

The commands given weren't designed to crush humanity under legalism—they were given to protect humanity from self-destruction.

- A fish out of water isn't free—it's dying. A tree pulled up from its roots isn't free—it's withering. Freedom isn't about the absence of constraints; it's about living within the right ones.
- God's commands are the riverbanks that guide the water into life-giving flow. Without them, the water becomes stagnant or floods into chaos.

The Law isn't a prison—it's a *path.* And walking that path isn't about appeasing a demanding overseer; it's about moving in harmony with the Architect of existence.

Takeaway: *True freedom flows from obedience, not from casting off God's commands.* The Law isn't a cage; it's a bridge.

11.2 Freedom From Sin's Bondage

"Very truly I tell you, everyone who sins is a slave to sin... If the Son sets you free, you will be free indeed." – **John 8:34-36**

Sin has an unfair marketing advantage—it rarely looks like bondage. It's dressed in bright colors, wrapped in easy promises, and framed as empowerment. But behind the curtain, every act of rebellion ties another knot, tightens another chain.

- **Sin doesn't just wound—it enslaves.**

- **Sin doesn't just hurt—it *owns*.**

Every indulgence that seems harmless—every moment of pride, every unchecked anger, every little compromise—lays down a thread. And before long, those threads become a web.

But the Torah isn't a web—it's a *map*. It doesn't just say, *"Don't do this."* It says, *"Here's how to avoid the snare altogether."*

- Yeshua's words in John 8 cut through every illusion: *"Everyone who sins is a slave to sin."* Not *might become*. Not *could be*. *Is*.

Freedom from sin isn't about willpower—it's about alignment.

- It's about stepping into the path that was designed to lead out of bondage.
- It's about accepting the *Law of Liberty* not as a burden but as a lifeline.

Because sin isn't freedom—it's slavery.

Takeaway: *God's Law protects us from sin's chaos and enslavement.* The commands aren't chains—they're keys.

11.3 Mercy and Justice in the Law of Liberty

"Speak and act as those who will be judged by the law that gives freedom, because judgment without mercy will be shown to anyone who has not been merciful. Mercy triumphs over judgment." – **James 2:12-13**

There's a fragile beauty in the balance of justice and mercy. Too much justice without mercy becomes cruelty. Too much mercy without justice becomes indulgence.

But the *Law of Liberty* holds these two in perfect tension. God's commands aren't cold legalities—they're relational blueprints. They aren't distant rules carved into stone—they're a Father's voice, calling His children to live well.

- When James speaks about mercy triumphing over judgment, he isn't dismissing justice. He's showing its fulfillment. Mercy doesn't erase justice; it completes it.

A father doesn't stop being just when he shows mercy to a wayward child. He doesn't stop caring about right and wrong when he offers forgiveness. Justice and mercy are not opposites—they're two halves of the same whole.

- Obedience under the *Law of Liberty* isn't mechanical. It isn't about ticking boxes or avoiding penalties. It's about *alignment with God's heart.*
- When we follow the Law, we don't just carry out commands—we reflect God's character. Justice is upheld. Mercy is offered. And love sits at the center of it all.

Takeaway: *The Law of Liberty balances justice and mercy in perfect harmony.* Obedience isn't cold legalism—it's a relational dance.

Reflection: The Law of Liberty

The Law of Liberty isn't a cage.

- It's a set of riverbanks guiding life into abundance.

- It's a lifeline pulling us out of sin's illusion of freedom.

- It's a mirror showing us our hearts, a bridge leading us back to the Father, and a map pointing toward true liberty.

Freedom isn't about escaping laws—it's about living within the right ones.

- Every step toward obedience is a step into alignment.
- Every act of rebellion is a step into bondage.

The Law doesn't oppress—it protects. It doesn't bind—it frees. But the choice remains.
- Alignment or rebellion.
- River or swamp.
- thriving or withering.

The Law of Liberty isn't about avoiding chains—it's about wearing the yoke of the Shepherd. And His yoke is easy. His burden is light.

11.4 Liberty vs. Libertine: A Road Diverged

Key Insight: *There's a world of difference between liberty and libertine. One mindset leads to freedom: the other to bondage.*

There are two roads.

- One is wide, glittering with promises of unrestrained indulgence, painted in the colors of self-fulfillment, with no rules, no consequences—only endless autonomy.
- The other is narrow, disciplined, and often quiet. It doesn't promise indulgence; it promises alignment. It doesn't boast of lawlessness; it speaks of covenant.

The two roads are not distant from one another—they intersect at every choice. They diverge not in geography but in intention. Every decision, every impulse, every pause at the crossroads asks a question: *Will you choose liberty or libertinism?*

- One road leads upward, though the steps are steep and deliberate.
- The other spirals downward, though the descent feels effortless.

The paths aren't neutral. Neither are the outcomes.

11.5 Liberty: Freedom with Ethical Restraint

- Liberty isn't the absence of rules—it's the presence of the *right ones.* True liberty is not chaotic; it's disciplined. It doesn't reject boundaries—it flourishes within them.
- God's commands aren't a series of arbitrary restrictions—they're markers on a map, showing where the ground is solid and where it gives way to quicksand. Liberty operates within those markers, not to restrict joy, but to protect it.
- The world offers a cheap version of liberty—do what you want, when you want, however you want. But true liberty asks a deeper question: *What do you want most?*

Do you want fleeting pleasure, or do you want enduring peace? Do you want shallow indulgence, or do you want deep purpose? Do you want chaos, or do you want order?

- Liberty aligns wants with wisdom. It aligns desires with design. It aligns the will of the created with the will of the Creator.

It doesn't eliminate choice—it *elevates* it. It doesn't strip away freedom—it *purifies* it.

Takeaway: *Liberty is doing what you want in a way that honors YHWH's commands.* It isn't lawless; it's luminous.

11.6 Libertine: Freedom Without Restraint

Where liberty-minded person submits to alignment, a libertine rejects it. Where a liberty-minded asks, *"What is right?"* a libertine person shrugs and says, *"Who cares?"*

- Libertinism wears a mask—it looks like freedom, but it's just rebellion with good marketing. It promises empowerment but delivers exhaustion. It whispers, *"You're free!"* but the chains are tightening the whole time.

The irony of libertinism is that the pursuit of total autonomy doesn't make someone free—it makes them a prisoner. A prisoner to their appetites. A prisoner to their pride. A prisoner to their own broken compass.

Libertinism isn't new

- The Tower of Babel was libertinism on a grand scale—humanity grasping at godhood without submitting to God's design.
- The golden calf at Sinai was libertinism—a moment of indulgence, framed as celebration, but rotting with rebellion underneath.

Every age has its golden calves. Every culture builds its towers.

And every individual stands at the same crossroads:

- *Will I live as if I am my own god, or will I submit to the One who made me?*

Libertinism isn't freedom—it's *bondage disguised as choice.*

Takeaway: *Libertinism takes slaves while pretending to offer freedom.* It doesn't lead upward; it sinks downward.

11.7 The Spiritual Crossroads

Every moment is a crossroads. Every choice is a binding. Every action bends the arc of allegiance toward one road or the other.

- James doesn't leave room for neutrality. He doesn't give space for indifference. The *Law of Liberty* isn't just a suggestion—it's a warning flare, a lighthouse on a stormy sea.

The narrow road isn't an easy one, but it's the only one that leads to anywhere worth arriving at.

- Liberty and libertinism are not just philosophical concepts— they're lived realities. One mindset *builds altars*. The other *tears them down*. One mindset *protects the flock*. The other *feeds on it*.
- And the difference between them isn't found in dramatic moments—it's found in the quiet ones. In the small decisions. In the unguarded thoughts.

You don't stumble onto the path of liberty by accident.

You deliberately *choose* it, and choose to be disciplined in it, again and again.

Alternatively, you don't drift into libertinism by design—you drift there because you made a spiraling set of choices.

Choices that became habits, habits that become behaviors, and behaviors that became a lifestyle: a libertine lifestyle of godlessness.

The road diverges every day, in every thought, in every action.

Takeaway: *Liberty frees slaves; libertinism makes slaves.* The difference is a single step in one direction or the other.

Section 11 Conclusion: The Road Diverged

There's nothing neutral about the crossroads. No safe middle path. No gray zone where intentions aren't counted and actions don't matter.

- One road leads upward—aligned with God's design, protected by His commands, and leading toward true freedom.
- The other spirals downward—masked as autonomy, driven by rebellion, and ending in bondage.

Both roads make promises, but only one delivers.

James isn't subtle about the choice. He doesn't leave space for vagueness. The *Law of Liberty* isn't a suggestion; it's a foundation.

- The world will keep calling the wide road freedom. It will keep mocking the narrow road as restrictive.
- But the results will always tell the truth.
- One binding leads to peace. The other to chaos. One gate leads to life. The other to destruction.

And every moment—every choice—tightens the straps.
- There's no third gate.
- No third strap.
- No neutral choice.

Life and Liberty, or Rebellion and Death.

Choose life- Choose YHWH.

---

12. Free Will and God's Justice: Consequences and Mercy

Key Insight: *God's justice honors our choices, but His mercy always provides a way back.*

Free will is a double-edged sword. It offers both the dignity of choice and the weight of consequence. Every decision carries ripples—some small, others tidal. But no choice is insignificant.

- God is not a puppet master pulling strings behind the curtain. He doesn't coerce obedience, nor does He block rebellion. Instead, He honors our choices. But honoring choice doesn't mean erasing consequences.

Justice and mercy dance together in God's kingdom. Justice says, *"Your choices matter."* Mercy says, *"But I will always leave the door open for you to return."*

- One without the other is incomplete. Justice without mercy is crushing. Mercy without justice is indulgent. But in God's hands, they form a perfect balance.

This section is about seeing both sides of that balance—the weight of consequence and the depth of mercy.

12.1 Consequences of Rebellion

Every choice builds something—a bridge or a wall, a temple or a ruin. And rebellion doesn't always start with a loud proclamation. Often, it begins with a whisper: *"Did God really say...?"*

- Sin carries consequences, not because God is vengeful, but because sin is corrosive. It doesn't just offend God—it erodes the soul. It fractures relationships. It creates chaos.

Adam and Eve's rebellion wasn't just about a piece of fruit; it was about trust. Cain's rebellion wasn't just about murder; it was about envy and resentment unchecked. Israel's rebellion in the wilderness wasn't just about complaining; it was about rejecting the path God had laid before them.

Every act of rebellion carries its own fallout. Sometimes the consequences are immediate—broken relationships, squandered opportunities, spiritual numbness. Other times, they ripple forward in ways unseen, like cracks spreading through glass.

- But God doesn't intervene to erase consequences. He honors them because He honors *free will*.

There's a haunting clarity in that. If He didn't honor our choices, free will wouldn't be real.

And yet, even when rebellion carries us far from Him—even when the consequences feel unbearable—He doesn't slam the door shut. He doesn't leave the ruin untouched.

The consequences remain, but so does the way back.

Takeaway: *God honors our choices, even when they lead to destruction.* Free will carries responsibility, and rebellion always leaves fingerprints.

12.2 God's Patience and Mercy

"The Lord is not slow in keeping His promise... He is patient with you, not wanting anyone to perish, but everyone to come to repentance."
— 2 Peter 3:9

Patience is often misunderstood as passivity. People mistake God's patience for distance, His silence for indifference. But patience isn't weakness—it's *restraint*. It's the act of holding back judgment long enough for redemption to step in.

- If justice is the blade, mercy is the hand holding it back.

Scripture is filled with moments of divine patience. God didn't strike Adam and Eve dead in the garden. He gave Cain a chance to turn away before striking Abel. He sent prophet after prophet to warn Israel before exile.

- And even today, patience remains His posture.
- God isn't slow. He isn't asleep at the wheel. His delay isn't a failure to act—it's an *invitation* to return.
- Mercy isn't indulgence. It's not a loophole. It's a space—a pause— a holy silence where repentance can grow.

But mercy has a shelf life. The door doesn't stay open forever. God's patience isn't eternal, and at some point, justice will roll down like a mighty river.

- That's not a threat—it's a truth. And it's spoken not from anger but from love.
- Because God doesn't want anyone to perish.

- Not the rebellious son. Not the bitter father. Not the wandering child.

But mercy can only be received if it's accepted. The door can only be walked through if one chooses to step forward.

Takeaway: *God's patience isn't weakness—it's love in action.* Mercy creates space, but repentance must step into it.

12.3 The Exodus Parallel

The Exodus isn't just history—it's a blueprint. It's a mirror held up to every human soul wrestling with bondage and freedom.

- Israel was enslaved, but the chains weren't just physical—they were spiritual. The Exodus wasn't just about leaving Egypt; it was about learning how to live *outside* of Egypt.

Freedom didn't end at the Red Sea. The wilderness stretched ahead, and every day, Israel had to make choices:

Will we trust God, or will we grumble? Will we follow His commands, or will we turn back to familiar chains?

Exodus isn't just *a* story—it's *our* story.

- Every person is born in some version of Egypt—a place of spiritual bondage, unhealthy patterns, inherited brokenness. And every person is given a path out—a narrow road paved with God's instructions, illuminated by His presence.

But freedom isn't passive. It's not a one-time event. It's a *daily choice.*

Israel had manna from heaven, water from rocks, and a pillar of fire to guide them. Yet they still rebelled.

They still turned to idols. They still longed for Egypt. The same tension exists today.

- Freedom requires trust. It requires walking forward even when the road is unfamiliar. It requires obedience even when rebellion feels easier.
- The Exodus isn't about escaping—it's about *becoming*.

Takeaway: *Freedom isn't passive—it's a choice made daily.* The path out of bondage isn't automatic. It's walked one step at a time.

Section 12 Conclusion: Consequences and Mercy

- Free will is honored.
- Choices are honored.
- Consequences are honored.
- But so is mercy.

God doesn't erase rebellion's fallout, but He does offer a way back. His patience isn't passivity—it's an open door. His justice isn't cruelty—it's integrity.

- Sin carries weight, but grace carries power. Rebellion builds walls, but mercy builds bridges.

The Exodus happened once, but its rhythm echoes through every generation. Every person stands at the edge of their own Red Sea, with Egypt behind and the wilderness ahead.

- The choice isn't made once—it's made every day, in every thought, in every step.
- Justice and mercy aren't opposites—they're two halves of the same story.

---

13. Conclusion: Shackles or Wings?

Key Insight: *Free will isn't an abstract gift—it's the daily choice between covenant obedience and spiritual rebellion.*

Free will isn't a trophy displayed on a shelf or a philosophical curiosity debated in dusty rooms. It's not theoretical—it's *operational*. It's a tool, a mirror, a weapon, and a key.

It's the quiet weight resting in every breath, every thought, every hesitation before an action.

And it's sharp. It cuts both ways.

In one hand, it can build altars. In the other, it can tear them down. It can lift chains, or it can forge them tighter.

But the power of free will isn't in the tool itself—it's in how it's *used*.

This conclusion isn't an ending—it's an opening. A final moment to stand at the crossroads and make a choice: *Shackles or wings? Chains or freedom? Covenant or rebellion?*

The choice was always yours.

13.1 The Crossroads of Choice

Every moment—every heartbeat, every thought, every action—is a crossroads.

- It doesn't feel that way most of the time. Decisions slip by unnoticed, like leaves drifting downstream. But each one carries weight. Each one bends the arc of a life toward light or shadow, obedience or rebellion.

- You are always wearing *something*. On your head, on your hand— there is always a mark. Tefillin or the Mark of the Beast. Alignment or distortion. Covenant or counterfeit.

- One symbolizes a head bowed in reverence and hands lifted in obedience. The other marks a mind enslaved to rebellion and hands bound to self-destruction.

- These aren't just future symbols—they are *living realities.*

- They are present-tense choices written into every interaction, every relationship, every sacrifice made—or avoided.

James didn't talk about neutrality. Yeshua didn't leave space for apathy. The Law of Liberty doesn't allow for passive drift.

- Every choice is a declaration. Every thought plants a flag.

The question isn't *if* you're aligned—it's *who* you're aligned with.

Takeaway: *Every thought and action is a declaration of allegiance.* Choose Tefillin or the Mark of the Beast.

13.2 Living the Law of Liberty

The Law of Liberty isn't a set of dusty commandments locked in a stone box—it's alive. It breathes. It stretches across time, echoing in every moment of obedience and rebellion.

- It's not about avoiding punishment.

- It's not about checking boxes.

- It's about *alignment.*

Obedience isn't legalism—it's worship.

Every act of obedience—every choice to follow God's instruction, every moment of submission to His design—is an act of worship. It's not about fear of consequence; it's about love of alignment.

The Law of Liberty isn't heavy. The chains of rebellion are heavy. The Law of Liberty isn't oppressive. The weight of sin is oppressive.

Yeshua said, *"Take my yoke upon you... for my yoke is easy and my burden is light."* (Matthew 11:29-30)

- The Law isn't a cage—it's a compass.

- It's not about earning love—it's about responding to it.

And yet, the world will always sell rebellion as freedom. It will always whisper: *"This is too restrictive. You deserve more. You deserve better."*

But rebellion doesn't lead upward—it spirals downward.
- Obedience doesn't lead to less—it leads to *more*.
- More peace. More clarity. More alignment.

The Law of Liberty isn't about avoiding chains—it's about spreading wings.

Takeaway: *Obedience isn't legalism—it's worship.* And worship isn't passive—it's lived.

13.3 The Final Invitation

The road diverges here. It always has.
- One path is wide, smooth, and easy to follow. It's lit with neon promises and decorated with glittering distractions. But it ends in chains.
- The other is narrow. It winds upward, often steep and rocky. But it ends in light.

YHWH doesn't force anyone onto the narrow road. He doesn't shove, drag, or manipulate. He simply *invites*.

> *"I have set before you life and death, blessings and curses. Now choose life, so that you and your children may live."* – **Deuteronomy 30:19**

It was never about rules for rules' sake. It was never about blind obedience or fearful compliance. It was always about *love*.

Free will isn't a test, it's a gift that you get to decide how to use.

Wandering through the wilderness, being made ready for delivery into the covenantal promised land, is what YHWH's children have always done.

It is a pattern repeated both personally and generationally across time, and will remain so as long as Heaven and earth exist.

Every day, every choice, every thought led Gods people closer to sanctification or farther from it.

Choices made and actions taken always define where YHWH's children are on the cyclical sinusoid of delivery or diaspora, **yourself included**.

Choose covenant, or rebellion. Choose liberty, or chains. The invitation isn't vague. It's not hidden. It's not complicated. Choose life. Choose liberty. Choose covenant.

Takeaway: *Free will is God's greatest gift, it gives us agency, the option of rebellion is what gives our love for Him the value He holds in it.*

Choice is not accidental, nor can it be avoided.

Every day, every choice, every action binds us either to the covenant of life or the chains of rebellion.

Reflection: Shackles or Wings?

There's no third option. No middle gate. No neutral ground.

- Free will wasn't handed to humanity as a burden—it was handed as a *gift*. But like all gifts, it carries responsibility.

Every choice bends the head. Every action marks the hand. You've seen the path laid out before you—the stories, the symbols, the shadows, and the light.

It's not a mystery. It's not hidden in riddles. It's there, in black and white.

- The wide road is easy. The narrow road is steep.
- The chains are real. So are the wings.

And when the world screams rebellion, when pride whispers seduction, when comfort promises an easier way—remember this:

Every step is a choice. Every choice is a binding. And every binding declares allegiance.

The decision was never God's. It was never Yeshua's.

It was, and always will be, *yours.*

Epilogue: A Book of Secrets – The Arc of Volume 1

We began with a modern Christianity at a crossroads, awaiting its fifth great awakening. We moved on to a crash course on modern Christianity, marred by schism - divided, conflicted, drifting farther afield from the Judeo-Christianity defined by Yeshua, and his direct disciples. We were confronted by the words of messiah himself in two key scriptures that, if read properly, demand profound reflection on what Yeshua expected of His followers.

Matthew 5:17-19

Christ Came to Fulfill the Law

"Do not think that I have come to abolish the Law or the Prophets; I have not come to abolish them but to fulfill them.

For truly, I say to you, until heaven and earth pass away, not an iota, not a dot, will pass from the Law until all is accomplished.

Therefore whoever relaxes one of the least of these commandments and teaches others to do the same will be called least in the kingdom of heaven, but whoever does them and teaches them will be called great in the kingdom of heaven."

Matthew 7:21-23

I Never Knew You

"Not everyone who says to me, 'Lord, Lord,' will enter the kingdom of heaven, but the one who does the will of my Father who is in heaven.

On that day many will say to me, 'Lord, Lord, did we not prophesy in your name, and cast out demons in your name, and do many mighty works in your name?' And then will I declare to them, 'I never knew you; depart from me, you workers of lawlessness.'".

These scriptures of Jesus's expectations demanded immediate inquiry- especially in light of Jesus's warning to his followers:

"See to it that nobody deceives you." (Matthew 24:4)

In light of Jesus's instruction and warnings, Inquiry 1 asked How did Jesus understand and teach scripture?

The question, seeking to align with messiah's scriptural lens, revealing the Bible as A Book of Secrets, with long held knowledge hidden in plain text. Using the two lenses of scripture and history we discover what the two have to say for themselves, we seek God's will with Jesus's view of scripture.

We learned Jesus saw scripture Hierarchically – Torah Law was supreme – the Prophets turned humanity back to covenantal relationship with God through the Law, and the Writings chronicled the lived experiences of those striving toward, and living in, God's covenant through His Law.

We learned about how sequence of books was secondary to how they fit in the structural tapestry of God's Covenant. We learned about the translations of scripture as they evolved over time through translation, interpretation, and the interests and intent of those translating them.

We learned how linguistic differences between Hebrew, Greek, and Latin, shaped the scriptures that we now hold in our hands today – their cultural and political influences often subtly altering how readers understood God. Far from a distant sovereign, God is present, relational, a closely watching Father.

We learned Jesus understood, and taught, that every last stoke of the pen in the Law & Prophets was binding so long as Heaven and earth exist.

We learned that this structure carried over to the New Testament, whereby Law & Prophet submissive Gospels carry the most weight, the Judaic Epistles upheld the Law as Jesus did, and Saul's letters should always be closely scrutinized. Understanding how Jesus taught and understood scripture helps us do as he instructed, and worship as he worshipped.

In Inquiry 2, Jesus's scriptural lens then turned to the scriptures about Jesus himself. We asked "Who was Jesus, and who Wasn't he?".

This inquiry taught us Jesus was really Yeshua, his name means "YHWH Saves". We learned that the name we learned was a product of translative drift and phonic incompatibilities between Hebrew, Greek, Latin, and English.

Messiah: God's Anointed Servants – an archetype not a monolith. We examined the difference between Biblical Messiah, and modern reimagining's. We looked at foundational scripture to learn that while Greek and Roman traditions extolled demigods, Hebraic biblical understanding stands in stark opposition to celestial/human hybrids – understanding them as Nephilim – an abomination forcing God to cleanse the earth with the flood to destroy them and all they had corrupted.

We examined Yeshua's own prayers, teachings, rebukes, behavior to see a completely submissive servant: not a co-deity. We read upward directed, third party worship. We read how Yeshua consistently deflected worship or praise upward to God, testifying to YHWH being greater, and more-knowing than himself.

We learned the difference between God's Throne in Heaven and the Seat of Glory at the right hand of God. We read how every biblical account of the exalted messiah did not "merge" with God on the Throne, he didn't replace God on the Throne, we saw that he sat at **the Right Hand of YHWH – where he intercedes** for humanity: as foretold in the Old Testament.

We saw repeatedly, Yeshua was Fully Obedient, from this faith in God he was able to do as he did, not of his own accord. We confronted trinitarianism with scripture in the Law and Prophets, and in Yeshua's Gospels, and came to the only conclusion possible. **God is one: and we are to only serve Him.**

We learned Yeshua did not come to abolish the Law, he came to show that it was an easy yoke and light burden, and told us to take up our cross and follow his example. As he lived so should we. Upholding God's Law & Prophets as Yeshua upheld.

We saw a messiah who viewed God's Law as life-giving, nurturing, fulfilling – a Law of Liberty & Prosperity. The Torah Law he expects us to uphold as well.

This led us to Inquiry 3: As Yeshua upheld the Prophets, How Do We Best Interpret the Prophets?

Long Game Prophets, Tefillin & the Law of Liberty

The narrative of Inquiry 3 has revealed that a prophet is not merely a messenger but a steward of God's intentions—one who must act with wisdom, foresight, and alignment to God's Law to ensure their words resonate and bear fruit. The contrast between long-game prophets, zealous martyrs, and passive victims serves as a critical framework for understanding how God's servants can either soften hearts and turn others toward covenantal obedience or unintentionally harden hearts through missteps of zealotry or naivety.

The Lessons of Long-Game Prophets

The stories of Joseph, Nathan, Daniel, and David illustrate that sustainable prophets are marked by patience, restraint, and strategic thinking. These traits allowed them to endure opposition and persecution, influencing kings, nations, and even empires without compromising their loyalty to God. They understood that their role was not to coerce or confront in anger but to guide others to God through wisdom, love, and tempered action.

In contrast, the tragic fates of figures like Zechariah and John the Baptist reveal the dangers of zeal unchecked by wisdom. While their convictions were righteous, their confrontational approaches often led to hardened hearts and violent ends, limiting their ability to effect lasting change. Similarly, the passivity of figures like Abel and the Jerusalem Church demonstrates that trust without vigilance can invite exploitation and subversion.

The Call to Tefillin: Godly Liberty, Not Coercion

The thread tying these narratives together is the Tefillin principle: God's desire for voluntary covenantal obedience, rooted in love and free will. This principle underpins the Law of Liberty, emphasizing that true worship cannot be coerced or manipulated. Prophets who succeeded in God's mission operated within this framework, recognizing that their role was to inspire hearts to choose God, not to force compliance or antagonize rebellion.

Yeshua, the ultimate long-game prophet, exemplified this balance perfectly. His teachings, rooted in love and wisdom, emphasized softening hearts and transforming oppressors into allies. His actions and words pointed not to coercion or zealotry but to a path of enduring influence and reconciliation, fulfilling the Law and the Prophets by embodying both their spirit and their letter.

The lessons of Inquiry 3 resonate far beyond the prophets of old. In a world rife with division and zealotry, the call to emulate long-game prophets is more urgent than ever. True prophecy is not about shouting louder or wielding greater force—it is about understanding, wisdom, and the humility to lead others gently back to God. Whether as individuals or as a community, the path of covenantal obedience must be chosen freely, rooted in the liberty God has always intended for His children.

The Arc of Volume 1 showed The Bible is a book of secrets – but - only if we use Yeshua's scriptural lens and ask it the right questions.

We will continue, in Volume 2, by asking scripture and history three more questions in the hope of answering one:

What are God's Holy Terms & Hidden Times?

Published by Foundationalist Press
in consultation with the **Judeo Christian Church™**

The stylized **Yodh** emblem is the mark of the Judeo Christian Church.
"Judeo Christian Church" and "Judeo Christians" are trademarks of the Judeo
Christian Church.

"Foundationalist Press" is a trademark of Foundationalist Press.

www.ingramcontent.com/pod-product-compliance
Lightning Source LLC
Chambersburg PA
CBHW021659120626
46545CB00004B/1307